A GUIDE TO

Customer Service Skills for the Help Desk Professional

Donna Knapp

COURSE
TECHNOLOGY

Thomson Learning™

ONE MAIN STREET, CAMBRIDGE, MA 02142

Australia • Canada • Denmark • Japan • Mexico • New Zealand • Philippines
Puerto Rico • Singapore • South Africa • Spain • United Kingdom • United States

A Guide to Customer Service Skills for the Help Desk Professional is published by Course Technology.

Associate Publisher:	Kristen Duerr
Product Manager:	Margarita Donovan
Production Editor:	Christine Spillett
Development Editor/Project Manager:	Robin Romer
Associate Product Manager:	Tricia Coia
Composition House:	GEX, Inc.
Text Designer:	GEX, Inc.
Cover Designer:	Efrat Riess
Marketing Manager:	Susan Ogar

Photo Credits: Chapter 1 CloseUp: Donna Yeager-Hengel photo courtesy of Joan Hare; Chapter 3, CloseUp: Speakerphone image Digital Imagery ©copyright 1999 PhotoDisc, Inc.; Fig. 4-7: Screenshot courtesy of Applix, Inc.; Chapter 8 CloseUp: Chair and footrest photos courtesy of 3M Stationery & Office Supplies Division., Keyboard photo courtesy of Logitech, Inc., Headset image Digital Imagery © copyright 1999 PhotoDisc, Inc.

Disclaimer

ISBN 0-7600-7262-0

Printed in Canada

1 2 3 4 5 WC 02 01 00 99

PREFACE

Simply put, customer service is my passion. Whether I am traveling, shopping, or calling a software publisher or hardware manufacturer for help with a problem, I demand excellent service. I acknowledge excellent service when I get it and, when possible, reward the service provider. When I don't get it… well, let's just say I can be *very* demanding. I'm sure you're thinking, "Oh great, just what we need, a demanding customer writing a book." The reality is, though, that I understand how hard it is to deliver excellent service and support—particularly technical customer support. For the past eighteen years I have worked in the Information Technology industry. Twelve of those years have been devoted to providing help desk-related consulting and training services. I understand how difficult it can be for an individual and for an organization to deliver high-quality technical customer support. I understand that customers can be demanding and company policies sometimes make it difficult for you to satisfy customers. I also understand that you are often asked to support complex technologies with inadequate training, tools, and information. This book is designed to give you the skills and insight you need to enjoy and excel in the challenging and dynamic environment that a help desk offers. You will also find that the soft and self-management skills described in this book are excellent life skills that will serve you well regardless of your chosen profession.

THE INTENDED AUDIENCE

This book is intended primarily for three kinds of readers.

- Those who are considering career opportunities at a help desk, and who want to understand how to provide high-quality technical customer support in any situation. They can use this book to develop the skills they need to interact effectively and appropriately with customers, whether face-to-face, on the telephone, or in written documents.

- Those who are working at a help desk and want a better understanding of how to communicate effectively, handle difficult customer situations, solve and prevent problems, and minimize stress. They can use this book to learn proven techniques for working with customers in any situation, being a team player, and maintaining a positive attitude and sense of well-being while providing support.

- Those who are taking a course in help desks and technical customer support or a related degree program. They can use this book to obtain additional knowledge and depth about the ins and outs of providing winning customer support as well as clear definitions and explanations of key concepts. These readers will especially benefit from the end-of-chapter activities that provide practical experience with the concepts and skills they will use on the job.

THE HELP DESK CURRICULUM

This book is designed for a customer service course in any Help Desk Curriculum. It is intended for use in community and technical college courses, such as Customer Service Skills, Customer Service and the Help Desk, and Problem Solving for the Help Desk. These courses are part of rapidly emerging programs in schools that aim to prepare students for the following degrees or certificates: IT Support Professional; Computer Help Desk Specialist; Computer Technical Support; Help Desk Support Specialist; Computer User Support; and Computer Support Technician. As the need for help desks grows, companies are turning to community and technical colleges to prepare their graduates to fill existing entry-level positions in the technical support industry.

No longer are technical skills the only requirement for the field of technical support. Companies now want to attract individuals who have the appropriate balance of business, technical, "soft," and self-management skills that contribute to making their help desks successful. Increasingly, organizations that are committed to providing high-quality technical customer support view their help desks as a strategic asset. Whether the help desk provides support to the customers who use their companies' products or the help desk provides technical support to the companies' employees, the need for qualified help desk professionals is on the rise.

THE APPROACH

The text is designed to provide an in-depth look at the soft skills and self-management skills people need to provide effective customer service and support in a technical environment. The first chapter is devoted to a discussion about the role of the help desk and the dynamic nature of customer expectations. Chapters Two through Six explore in detail the soft skills needed for a successful career in customer support. The author's goal was to provide readers with proven techniques they could implement immediately. These techniques are introduced in chapters dedicated to subjects such as listening and communicating, interacting by telephone, disseminating knowledge through the written word, handling difficult customer situations, and solving and preventing problems. Chapters Seven and Eight are devoted to self-management skills, including being part of a team, minimizing stress, and avoiding burnout.

Although this book is very "how to" oriented, the author has tried to describe the "bigger picture" benefits of acquiring and demonstrating soft and self-management skills. For example, this book will help you understand that soft and self-management skills will enable you not only to find a good job and achieve success in the help desk industry, but also to feel considerable job satisfaction while avoiding the frustration and burnout that is inherent in the customer support industry.

To derive maximum benefit from this book, the reader must be an active participant in the learning process. The end-of-chapter activities are specifically designed to develop the reader's knowledge and help the reader assimilate the chapter concepts. They encourage the reader to expand his or her knowledge through self-study, as well as help prepare the reader for the team-oriented technical support environment by having the reader work with classmates in project groups or teams. Many of the end-of-chapter activities encourage readers to utilize information resources and solve problems—skills that are essential in the dynamic help desk industry.

ASSUMED KNOWLEDGE

This book assumes that readers have experience in the following areas, either through course work, work experience, or life experience:

- Basic help desk and customer service concepts
- Basic computer concepts or computer literacy
- Internet and World Wide Web concepts

OVERVIEW OF THIS BOOK

The outline of this book takes a detailed look at the characteristics of excellent technical customer support and at soft and self-management skills needed to deliver it. Each chapter explores in detail a particular skill required to provide effective customer support and includes proven techniques for implementing the concepts.

Chapter 1, Achieving High Customer Satisfaction, explores what's involved in delivering excellent customer support, the role of the help desk and all of the technical support providers within a support organization, and how that role is changing. It also discusses the mix of business, technical, soft, and self-management skills required in today's dynamic technical support setting.

Chapter 2, Developing Strong Listening and Communication Skills, focuses on how support providers can become better listeners and communicate effectively with customers and co-workers. These skills are considered the two most basic and important skills that support providers must possess.

Chapter 3, Winning Telephone Skills, discusses the skills support providers need to interact with customers over the telephone as well as how to avoid the most common call handling mistakes. This chapter helps support providers develop excellent telephone skills that will send a positive, professional message to customers.

Chapter 4, Technical Writing Skills for Support Professionals, discusses the dramatic changes in the support industry and the consequent change in how services are delivered. Web-based service, e-mail, remote control technology, and knowledge bases are becoming increasingly important and all require written communication. This chapter provides tips and techniques to help support providers improve their writing skills.

Chapter 5, Handling Difficult Customer Situations, focuses on the leading cause of stress in customer support—calming irate customers, handling extremely demanding customers, saying no to customers while maintaining their goodwill. This chapter includes specific techniques for handling difficult situations and minimizing the anger and stress support providers may feel afterward.

Chapter 6, Solving and Preventing Problems, presents a methodical approach support providers can use to navigate the problem-solving process. It also discusses how the information support providers capture can be used to prevent problems and minimize their impact.

Chapter 7, Teams and Team Players in a Help Desk Setting, discusses the fact that customer support is an ideal environment for working in teams due to the complexity of the work and the diversity of skills required. This chapter will help support providers understand their role in the help desk and the support organization, and how to respect and value their team members' contributions.

Chapter 8, Minimizing Stress and Avoiding Burnout, deals with the fact that customer support is one of the ten most stressful professions. It helps support providers determine the factors that may be causing them stress and provides specific techniques they can use to manage their stress, time, and workload as well as avoid the physical and emotional exhaustion—burnout—caused by long-term stress.

FEATURES

To aid you in fully understanding customer service and technical support concepts, there are several features in this book designed to improve its pedagogical value.

- **Chapter Objectives.** Each chapter in this book begins with a list of the important concepts to be mastered within the chapter. This list provides you with a quick reference to the contents of the chapter as well as a useful study aid.

- **Illustrations and Tables.** Illustrations help you visualize common components and relationships. Tables list conceptual items and examples in a visual and readable format.

- **Notes.** Chapters contain Notes designed to expand on the section topic, including resource references, additional examples, and ancillary information.

- **Tips.** Chapters contain Tips designed to provide you with practical advice and proven strategies related to the concept being discussed.

- **Examples.** Sample dialog, writing, and phrasing demonstrate the communication styles and methods being discussed. These examples provide you with concrete reinforcement of concepts.

- **Quotations.** Quotations from business leaders and authors provide interesting and inspirational summaries of key concepts.

- **Bulleted figures.** Selected figures contain bullets that summarize important points to give you an overview of upcoming discussion topics and to help you review material as you skim through the chapter.

- **CloseUps.** CloseUps provide more in-depth looks at particular topics or present detailed real-life examples. Taken from actual experiences, CloseUps confirm the importance of the topic and often contribute related information to give you additional insight into real-world applications of the topics.

- **Chapter Summaries.** Each chapter's text is followed by a summary of chapter concepts. These summaries provide a helpful way to recap and revisit the ideas covered in each chapter.

- **Key Terms.** Each chapter contains a listing of the boldfaced terms introduced in the chapter and their concise definitions. This listing provides a convenient way to review the vocabulary you have learned.

- **Review Questions.** End-of-chapter assessment begins with a set of approximately 25 to 30 review questions that reinforce the main ideas introduced in each chapter. These questions ensure that you have mastered the concepts and have understood the information you have learned.

Hands-on Projects. Although it is important to understand the concepts behind help desk topics, no amount of theory can improve on real-world experience. To this end, along with conceptual explanations, each chapter provides eight Hands-on Projects aimed at providing you with practical experience. Some of these include applying customer service skills to your personal life and researching information from people who work in or have experience with the support industry, printed resources, and the Internet. Because the Hands-on Projects ask you to go beyond the boundaries of the text itself, they provide you with practice implementing customer service skills in real-world and help desk situations.

Case Projects. There are three Case Projects at the end of each chapter. These cases are designed to help you apply what you have learned to business situations much like those you can expect to encounter in a technical support position. They give you the opportunity to independently synthesize and evaluate information, examine potential solutions, and make recommendations, much as you would in an actual business situation.

TEACHING TOOLS

The following supplemental materials are available when this book is used in a classroom setting. All of the teaching tools available with this book are provided to the instructor on a single CD-ROM.

Electronic Instructor's Manual. The Instructor's Manual that accompanies this textbook includes:

- Additional instructional material to assist in class preparation, including suggestions for lecture topics.

- Solutions to all end-of-chapter materials, including the Review Questions, and when applicable, Hands-on Projects, and Case Projects.

Course Test Manager 1.2. Accompanying this book is a powerful assessment tool known as the Course Test Manager. Designed by Course Technology, this cutting-edge Windows-based testing software helps instructors design and administer tests and pre-tests. In addition to being able to generate tests that can be printed and administered, this full-featured program also has an online testing component that allows students to take tests at the computer and have their exams graded automatically.

PowerPoint presentations. This book comes with Microsoft PowerPoint slides for each chapter. These are included as a teaching aid for classroom presentation, to make available to students on the network for chapter review, or to be printed for classroom distribution. Instructors can feel free to add their own slides for additional topics they introduce to the class.

ACKNOWLEDGMENTS

Publishing a book is a team effort and each and every person's contribution is valued and appreciated. I wish to thank the team members at Course Technology who contributed their talents to the creation of this book, including, Kristen Duerr, Associate Publisher; Margarita Donovan, Product Manager; and Christine Spillett, Production Editor. Also, thanks to Abby Reip, AR Photo Research, for locating many of the images used in this book.

I greatly appreciate the efforts of the industry professionals and educators who reviewed the draft manuscript and made suggestions that significantly enhanced the quality and completeness of this book, including, Margaret Leary, Virginia Community College; Brenda Nielsen, Mesa Community College; Joyce Parker, Independent Help Desk Consultant; and John Ross, Fox Valley Technical College. Thanks also to Joe Leggiero for serving as a sounding board and for contributing his knowledge, experience, and support.

I am very grateful to the following people for taking time out of their busy scheduled to contribute to the CloseUp sections that offer a "real-world" view of the subject matter presented in each chapter: Ann Cook, American Accent Training; Ron Muns, Help Desk Institute; Bill Rose, Software Support Professionals Association; Bo Wandell, SafeHarbor.com; and Donna Yeager-Hengel, Hewlett-Packard Company.

Special thanks to my partner in crime Robin Romer, who agreed to edit this book even after enduring the pain of editing my first book. I think—hope—this one was easier. Thanks also to Brian who lived with this project as much as Robin and I did. Till next time, Cheers!

Love and thanks to my family and friends who are, I am sure, glad this book is done, as they are tired of hearing about it. I promise, no more books... [for a while].

I also tip my hat to the thousands of help desk professionals who are out there doing a great job day in and day out. You have a tough job and you rarely receive the support and respect that you deserve for doing it. I hope through this book that you see that you certainly have mine.

Donna Knapp
Tampa, Florida

TABLE OF CONTENTS

CHAPTER ONE

ACHIEVING HIGH CUSTOMER SATISFACTION

After reading this chapter and completing the exercises you will be able to:

➤ Describe the role the help desk plays in delivering quality technical customer support

➤ Explain how to manage, meet, and exceed customer expectations

➤ Describe the mix of skills needed to have a career in technical customer support

Technology pervades our lives. People of all ages, backgrounds, and skill levels use computers at work, at school, and increasingly at home. This growing use of computing technology results in an enormous need for technical support. More and more companies are meeting this need by setting up help desks. A **help desk** is a single point of contact within a company for managing customer problems and requests and for providing solution-oriented support services. Companies worldwide know that they must provide high-quality customer service and support if they want to survive in today's fiercely competitive business environment. The help desk plays an extremely important role in delivering that service and support. An integral component of the help desk is people. Having the right people on a help desk helps ensure high customer satisfaction. Finding and keeping people who like working with technology and enjoy helping customers is a great challenge facing companies.

Historically, the help desk was considered a stepping stone to other professions within the computer industry. Today, the help desk has been elevated to a profession in and of itself and provides a tremendous opportunity for people who want to pursue an exciting career in the technology field. The growing recognition that the help desk is a critical part of any customer-oriented business has led to the recognition that people who possess the skills needed to deliver quality customer service and technical support are extremely valuable and somewhat rare.

To work in a help desk, you must possess a mix of skills, including business skills, technical skills, soft skills, and self-management skills. You must understand the characteristics of quality customer service and technical support. Finally, you must understand that how you interact with each and every customer influences that customer's perception of your company and its products.

DELIVERING QUALITY TECHNICAL CUSTOMER SUPPORT

The information age is upon us, and the technology we employ to obtain and use information has found its way into every aspect of our lives. For the average person, keeping that technology up and running and getting it to do what he or she wants and needs it to do can be a challenge. A person may turn to any number of help desks for support. For example, when at home, a person may contact the particular company that manufactured her computer or the company that publishes a software package she uses. When at work, this person may contact her company's help desk for aid using programs that are unique to her company. A person working as a help desk analyst may even contact other help desks, such as a vendor's help desk for assistance in diagnosing a hardware, software, or network problem. How a help desk treats people influences their level of satisfaction and perception of the entire company and its products.

Customer Support and the Help Desk Role

The term "help desk" was originally coined in the late 1970s; however, the technical support industry has changed dramatically since that time as has the role of the help desk. Originally established simply to screen calls, today's help desk serves as a key part of any technical support organization. **Technical support** refers to the wide range of services that enable people and companies to continuously use the computing technology they acquired or developed. Technical support services include installing the hardware, software, network, and application components that enable technology users to do their work; keeping the system in good repair; upgrading hardware and software when needed; and providing customer support. **Customer support** includes services that help a customer understand and benefit from a product's capabilities by answering questions, solving problems, and providing training. A **customer** is a person who buys products or services.

Historically, the help desk delivers customer support services, while other groups, such as a field services group or a network support group, handle technical support services. This division of responsibilities is changing, however, as the support industry transitions to the support center model. A **support center** is a help desk with a broader scope of responsibility and with the goals of providing faster service and improving customer satisfaction. New technologies, such as remote control systems and software distribution systems, have enabled this enhanced help desk to absorb many of the customer-related activities from other support groups, such as field services and network support. By expanding its responsibilities to include activities such as network monitoring and network and system administration, the help desk can be more proactive and timely because it doesn't have to engage other groups to perform these tasks. **Network monitoring** involves using tools to observe and control network performance in an effort to prevent and minimize the impact of problems. **Network and system administration** involves activities such as setting up and maintaining user accounts, ensuring the data that the company collects is secure, and performing e-mail and database management.

The help desk and these other support groups are often structured in a series of levels, an approach commonly known as a multi-level support model. In a **multi-level support model**, shown in Figure 1-1, the help desk refers problems it cannot resolve to the appropriate internal group, external vendor, or subject matter expert. A **subject matter expert (SME)** is a person who has a high level of experience or knowledge about a particular subject. The goal of this multi-level support model is to have the help desk resolve as many problems as possible at level one. This approach ensures the most efficient use of level two and three resources.

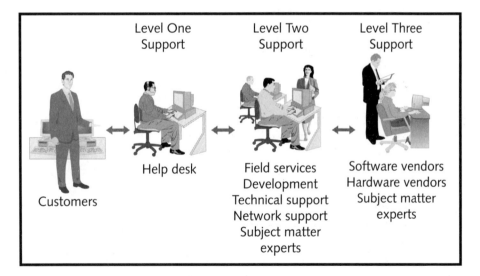

Level One Support

Level Two Support

Level Three Support

Help desk

Customers

Field services
Development
Technical support
Network support
Subject matter
experts

Software vendors
Hardware vendors
Subject matter
experts

Figure 1-1   Multi-level support model

The successful help desk plays an important role in providing quality technical customer support. A successful help desk is made up of many tightly integrated components. Each component relates to the others in some way and all of these components together enable the help desk to satisfy customers. The components of a successful help desk include:

➤ **People** — The staff and structure put in place within a company or department to support its customers by performing business processes. The principle roles that people who work in a help desk play include the **front-line service providers** who interact directly with customers and help desk management personnel. Although titles and job descriptions will vary from one help desk to the next, the most common types of help desk positions include dispatcher or call screener, level one analyst, level one specialist, help desk supervisor or team leader, help desk manager, and senior help desk manager.

➤ **Processes** — Interrelated work activities that take a set of specific *inputs* and produce a set of specific *outputs* that are of value to a customer. **Value** is the perceived worth, usefulness, or importance of a product or service to the customer. The consistent use of processes leads to customer confidence and employee satisfaction as both customers and help desk employees know what and how something needs to be done. Some common processes found in a help desk include problem management, request management, and service level management.

➤ **Technology** — The tools and technologies people use to do their work. Help desk employees and managers use technology to perform processes. They also use technology to capture and use information about their customers and their work. Some tools found in a typical help desk include call tracking and problem management systems, expert (knowledge management) systems, telephone systems, and Web-based systems.

➤ **Information** — Data that are organized in a meaningful way. People need information to do their work. For example, help desk analysts need information about customers and the details of their problems to provide support. Management needs information to evaluate team and individual performance and identify improvement opportunities. For example, help desk managers need information that tells them how quickly, completely, and accurately services are delivered. Without data, help desks have trouble creating the information required to understand customer needs and expectations and measure customer satisfaction. Consequently, successful companies consider information a resource in the same way that well-trained employees, well-defined processes, and well-implement technology are resources. Types of data captured by help desks include customer data, incident data, status data, and resolution data.

People are by far the most important and expensive component of a help desk. Finding qualified people to deliver quality customer support is a great challenge being faced throughout the support industry. People are the most important component because customers are people who have feelings and expectations that only other people can understand. In fact, customers do not buy products or services so much as they buy expectations. Customer **expectations**, results that customers consider reasonable or due to them, are a moving target and it is this movement that makes it so difficult for companies to get and stay ahead. Customer expectations are a moving target for a number of reasons. As customers become more comfortable using technology, they become more demanding of the support they require. Also, as companies improve the quality of the services they deliver, the standard of what great service is gets redefined. When companies consistently deliver a high level of service, that high level becomes the standard, making it extremely difficult, and sometimes quite costly, for companies to go beyond what customers have come to expect. Companies must go beyond customers' expectations in order to compete in today's business world. If a company's service is worse than or only as good as that of a competitor, customers may be tempted to do business with the competitor.

Customers have expectations not only about what a product can do, but also about what the company can do to enable them to fully use that product. This is particularly true in the world of high technology where customers increasingly use customer service and technical support to differentiate between companies and their products. Vendors are constantly striving to duplicate the features offered by their competitors. Companies that do gain a competitive edge through product innovation can quickly lose that edge when their competitor publishes its next release. In other words, the products themselves can be very similar at any point in time. Companies that deliver excellent service—that is, they meet and exceed their customers' expectations—can use that excellent service, as well as a great product, to maintain their competitive edge. Also, the more complex and pervasive technology becomes, the more people crave personalized service and support. This notion is summed up in the phrase "high tech, high touch"; that is, the more technological (high tech) the world becomes, the more people desire one-on-one personalized (high touch) service and support. Companies that deliver excellent customer service work hard to treat every customer as an individual. They pay attention and attend to the details of each customer's need.

Delivering high touch service can be very costly, so most companies also strive to deliver "low touch" services that meet and exceed their customers' expectations. Self-services offered via the Web, such as Frequently Asked Questions (FAQs) and online forms, are excellent examples of low touch ways that companies use technology to support customers, twenty-four hours a day, seven days a week.

Benefits of Quality Customer Support

Delivering excellent customer support brings many substantial benefits to the companies that do so and the employees who work for them. Some benefits that companies derive are very tangible, such as return business and the positive word-of-mouth that leads to new business. These then lead to higher sales and profits. Industry recognition is another benefit, and many companies are striving to be recognized as "world class." A **world class** company has achieved, and is able to sustain, high levels of customer satisfaction. World class companies often reap the benefit of customer loyalty. Loyal customers are willing to pay slightly more for products and suffer minor inconveniences, such as temporarily living without a feature that a competitor's product has, in exchange for excellent service.

Other benefits that companies derive are somewhat less tangible, such as customer feedback. Companies that deliver great service often receive feedback from their customers about how they can make their service even better: "This is great, but you know what would be even better…." Companies that deliver poor service don't receive that kind of feedback because less than 5 percent of dissatisfied customers complain. Most dissatisfied customers just walk away and don't come back. Service providers need to understand that customer complaints are a good thing and they need to be responsive to and even encourage complaints. Companies that are receptive to customer feedback often are given an opportunity to further improve or a second chance when they fall down. Companies that deliver poor service or fail to listen to their customers do not typically receive that second chance; customers just take their business elsewhere.

Another benefit of quality customer support is the very real phenomenon that happy customers result in happy employees who in turn create more happy customers. Some companies believe that if they treat their employees well, their employees in turn will treat their customers well. Regardless of who came first, the happy customer or the happy employee, companies that are committed to delivering high-quality service and support derive many benefits, and those benefits are often passed on to their employees.

The most obvious benefits that companies pass on to their employees are reward and opportunity. For example, companies are increasingly offering their employees "pay for performance" plans that are tied to customer satisfaction. Some companies offer profit-sharing plans that enable employees to directly benefit when the company is doing well. Some companies offer bonuses to employees who consistently go the extra mile for their customers. Job security is another benefit, and while few companies guarantee jobs in this day and age, people with the right mix of skills are highly employable and can more easily find work.

> *One of the most important principles of success is developing the habit of going the extra mile.* Napoleon Hill

Employees also derive intrinsic benefits from supporting customers, such as the pride and satisfaction that comes from helping other people. People who

1

enjoy the technical customer support field also tend to demonstrate a strong sense of purpose. They know the role they play is important to their customers and their company and they take it very seriously.

Trends Influencing the Help Desk

The support industry has changed considerably in recent years and will continue to change due to a number of trends. Many of these trends have resulted in elevating the help desk to a more strategic role within companies and help desk professionals to a position that is valued and rewarded.

Some trends are creating many new and flexible job opportunities. For example, companies are increasingly being challenged to provide **24 × 7 support**, which means that help desk services are provided twenty-four hours a day, seven days a week. In addition, many companies need to support a global customer community. This brings opportunities to people who can read, write, and speak multiple languages and who understand the cultural differences that must be considered when providing global support.

The fact that technology is increasingly complex, highly integrated, and ever more pervasive is also having a considerable impact on the support industry. Finding people who possess the needed technical skills and the "softer" skills (such as listening and communicating) is a challenge. This is good news for people who possess and want to grow and maintain both of those sets of skills. Although it was once acceptable for highly technical people to lack interpersonal skills, companies are now looking for and rewarding people who have a more balanced skill set.

This emphasis on communication skills is particularly important in light of the fact that computing technology is beginning to converge with communications technology. For example, people are using computers to make telephone calls and they are using Web TV devices to access the Internet. WebTV devices are bringing a whole new set of customers to the computer industry, and with those customers come the need for technical support. This trend highlights one of the challenges particular to technical customer support—varying customer skill levels. Some customers have been using computing technology for years and are highly skilled and capable. When they have a problem, it is a big, ugly problem that may be extremely difficult to resolve. Other customers are just getting started and ask what technicians often consider "simple" questions that they have answered many times before. Being able to communicate with customers at all of these varying skill levels is a skill in and of itself that must be nurtured and maintained.

Not everyone wants to be in a position where they interact with customers who have varying skills levels. If you prefer to be highly technical at all times, you may prefer to work in a level two or level three support group.

Two other trends that are influencing the role of the help desk and that are changing the face of the technical support industry are outsourcing and fee-based support. **Outsourcing** is when companies have help desk services provided by an outside supplier (service agency or outsourcer), instead of providing them in-house. Typically, companies partner with external service agencies in an effort to deliver high-quality support services at a reduced cost. How companies pay service agencies can vary greatly. Under some agreements, service agencies are paid to provide support for certain products or equipment, regardless of how often customers call for support. Under other agreements, service agencies are paid each time a customer calls. How customers interact with service agencies can also vary greatly. For example, upon purchasing a particular product or piece of equipment, customers may be given a telephone number that they can use to reach a service agency. In this case, the customer knows they are calling a service agency. In other cases, customers may call the help desk where they work or they may contact a vendor and they are not even aware that they are in fact reaching a service agency. People can also purchase service contracts that enable them to obtain support as needed.

Outsourcing is not the only time customers are charged a fee for support services. Increasingly companies, such as software publishers and hardware manufacturers, are offering **fee-based support** services on a per-use basis. These companies typically provide some free services, such as Web-based support services, and charge a fee for other services, such as telephone support and onsite support. They also may charge a higher rate for premium services, such as support provided outside of normal business hours or support for non-standard products.

This trend toward offering fee-based support services is a response to the high cost of delivering those services. Front-line service providers often "bear the burden" of these programs because they are required to capture more detailed information about each service transaction then they normally would for accounting purposes. For example, they may have to capture the exact amount of time that they spend on the telephone with a customer or the amount of effort they devote to solving a problem so the Accounting department can determine how much to charge a customer.

All of these trends influence the availability and the quality of opportunities within the support industry. Companies are striving to attract and retain people who possess and want to use both technical and interpersonal skills. Companies are also seeking people who work well with others, whether they are customers or members of other support groups within the company.

The Help Desk Analyst's Role in the Service Delivery Chain

1

There are two principal types of help desks: internal help desks and external help desks. An **internal help desk** responds to questions, distributes information, and handles problems and service requests for its company's employees. Each employee is considered an **internal customer**, a person who works at a company and at times relies on other employees at that company to perform his or her job. A company can have any number of internal help desks that employees contact for support. For example, employees may contact the Human Resources (HR) department when they have questions about their medical insurance or other employee benefits. They may contact the Facilities department to have office fixtures installed or repaired. And, they may contact the company's Information Technology (IT) department when they need help with the hardware and software they use to accomplish their work.

An **external help desk** supports customers who buy its company's products and services. An **external customer** is a person or company that buys another company's products and services. For example, most companies that manufacture hardware and publish software packages have external help desks to support their customers. Many computer stores offer help desk services to customers who purchase products or equipment at the store. And, as discussed earlier, some service agencies offer fee-based help desk services to external customers. External help desks provide a number of services on behalf of their companies. For example, some external help desks provide **pre-sales support**, meaning that they answer questions for people who have not yet purchased the company's products or service, and may take orders and respond to billing inquiries. Most external help desks provide post-sales support as well. **Post-sales support** involves helping people who have purchased a company's product or service. Post-sales support activities include answering questions, helping the customer learn to use the product, explaining the advanced features that the product offers, and resolving problems.

If you are not supporting the external customers of your company, you are supporting someone who is. In other words, by delivering great service to an internal customer, you enable that person to—ultimately—deliver great service to the company's external customers.

The relationship between internal and external customers is tightly linked. For example, every interaction the internal help desk has with an internal customer affects that person's ability to provide excellent service to his customers, who may be the external customers of the company. Conversely, the support an external help desk receives from other people or groups within the company (such as the internal help desk or the Sales, Marketing, Field Services, and Research & Development departments) greatly affects its ability to support the company's external customers. This concept, shown in Figure 1-2, is known as a customer service delivery chain.

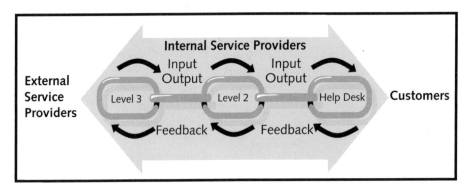

Figure 1-2 Customer service delivery chain

The customer service delivery chain shows the relationship that exists between customers, internal service providers, and external service providers. Feedback is used to communicate customer expectations through the service delivery chain. Using the feedback as a guide, internal service providers receive input from other service providers, and deliver output to other service providers, until the expected service is delivered to the customer. Sometimes, external service providers are engaged by internal service providers in an effort to meet the customer's expectations. A help desk analyst, a level two service provider, or a level three service provider may contact a vendor for help resolving a particularly difficult problem. The internal service provider at that point becomes the vendor's customer. The vendor will have its own customer service delivery chain that must now work together to meet *its* customer's expectations.

The customer service delivery chain illustrates that all of the departments within a company—all of its internal service providers—are interdependent and must work together to deliver services to external customers. Even departments that do not interface directly with customers do work that results in the delivery of services to external customers. Because of this, each and every role in a company's service delivery chain adds value and must be respected and supported.

Day in and day out everyone can be considered at times a customer and at other times a service provider. For example, a co-worker may ask you to provide information needed to complete a project. In this case, you are the service provider and your co-worker is the customer. Later in the day, you may ask this same co-worker to help you solve a problem; now you are the customer and your co-worker is the service provider. Whether a customer or a service provider, you must respect the fact that each person you interact with has a role to play—a job to do—and you must strive to understand the other's needs and expectations. Ultimately, the job each of you does leads—via the customer service delivery chain—to the delivery of service to the company's external customers. As a result, you must also strive to understand your external customers' expectations. Typically, how your efforts contribute to meeting those expectations will be communicated in the form of your job description and feedback relative to your job performance.

One of the best ways to become an excellent service provider is to pay attention when you are the customer.

Customer-oriented companies understand and nurture each of the customer–service provider relationships that make up their customer service delivery chain. They understand that every link is important and that the chain is only as good as its weakest link. These companies also realize that productivity and profit gains are possible only when the help desk, whether it is an internal help desk or an external help desk, is seen as a strategic corporate resource. How customers perceive the entire company, the entire service delivery chain, is influenced every single time they interact with the help desk—meaning, each and every time they interact with you!

INFLUENCING CUSTOMER PERCEPTION

Customer satisfaction reflects the difference between how a customer perceives he or she was treated and how the customer expects to be treated. This reality is one of the things that makes supporting customers a challenge. It is common knowledge that two people who experience the same event will *perceive* the event differently. For this reason, help desks must work hard to manage their customers' expectations by clearly defining their mission, spelling out their services and policies, and continuously assessing their mission, services, and policies in light of their customer's needs. To do this, some companies have established Service Level Agreements with their customers. A **Service Level Agreement (SLA)** is a written document that spells out the services the help desk will provide the customer, the customer's responsibilities, and how service performance is measured. These agreements are an excellent way to manage customer expectations because they spell out exactly what services can and cannot be delivered. As illustrated in Figure 1-3, SLAs must take into consideration every group in the company's customer service delivery chain or customer expectations will not be met. For example, if the company guarantees a customer that certain types of problems will be resolved in two hours, and one of the groups in the service delivery chain cannot respond within two hours, the customer's expectations will not be met.

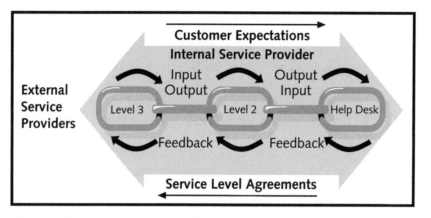

Figure 1-3 Impact of SLAs on the customer service delivery chain

Understanding Customer Needs and Managing Expectations

Managing expectations in today's rapidly and radically changing business world is indeed a challenge. It is not hard to understand why. Expectations are influenced by many factors and vary from one person to another, one situation to another, and even one day to another. Although the varying nature of customer expectations may make it seem that satisfying customers is an impossible task, Figure 1-4 lists three things you can count on customers wanting.

> • Responsiveness
>
> • A caring attitude
>
> • Skill

Figure 1-4 Customer needs

Each of these characteristics of excellent customer support addresses a particular customer need and ignoring any one of these characteristics can cause customer dissatisfaction.

➤ **Responsiveness** — Responsiveness refers to the help desk's ability to: (1) be available when customers need help and (2) make it easy for customers to contact the help desk. Responsiveness involves answering the telephone promptly or responding to voicemail and e-mail inquiries within the timeframe promised. For example, some companies guarantee that all voicemails will be returned within thirty minutes and all e-mail inquiries will be answered within twenty-four hours. Given these options, customers can decide whether they want to wait on the telephone line for an analyst or send an e-mail for a less immediate response. Unfortunately, some help desks do not seem very responsive. They are not available when they say they will be or their hours of operation do not match the needs of their customers. They implement complex telephone systems that have long menus with numerous confusing options and no easy way to reach a "live" person or, they offer a telephone number that more often than not connects customers to a voice mail box where they can leave a message. Customers often perceive that these messages go unanswered because they have left a message or messages in the past and those messages have gone unanswered. Optimally, responsive help desks have hours of operation that are comparable to the business hours during which their customers are most likely to need support. They also set up technology in a way that is easy for customers to navigate and that actually adds value to the interaction. For example, some telephone systems capture information about the customer and use that information to transfer the customer to the help desk analyst best suited to handle the customer's problem or request. Simply put, responsiveness refers to the help desk's ability to *be there* for customers.

➤ **A caring attitude** — A caring, positive, and helpful attitude goes a long way to keeping customers satisfied. One of the biggest reasons that customers choose to stop doing business with a company is that they feel an attitude of indifference. In other words, no one made the customers feel that the company wanted to satisfy their needs. Although the help desk may not always be able to give customers exactly what they want, when they want it, there is always something the help desk *can* do. It can take the customer's request and log it in its problem tracking system so the request is not lost or forgotten. It can take ownership of the customer's request and ensure the request is forwarded to the person or group that can satisfy it. If nothing else, it can let the customer know where to obtain help. Customers occasionally contact the help desk with questions about a product or system that the help desk does not support. What the help desk can do in those situations is give the customer the name and telephone number of the person or group that does support the product. In other words, the help desk must *be willing* to assist customers in any way it can.

> *Your customers don't care how much you know until they know how much you care.* Gerhard Gschwandtner

➤ **Skill** — Skill refers to the help desk's ability to quickly and correctly resolve customer problems and requests. Given today's complex technology and sophisticated, demandin g customers, it is not enough for help desk analysts to be polite, perky, and caring. Help desk analysts must also be efficient and knowledgeable. They must have the ability and authority to solve problems or know exactly how to get problems solved. If customers perceive the help desk cannot help, they will simply go around. They may turn to **peer-to-peer support,** a practice where users bypass the formal support structure and seek assistance from their co-workers or someone in another department whom they believe can help. They may find out who in their company or department can help and contact that person directly. Other times, they may simply give up and take their business elsewhere. The help desk must convince customers that contacting the help desk is the fastest, cheapest, and best way to obtain a solution. They must *be able* to handle any request that comes their way.

 To satisfy customers, the help desk must be there, be willing, and be able.

While these characteristics may seem very nice and "fluffy," they are actually very measurable. Companies are increasingly using performance measures, or **metrics**, to evaluate the performance of their help desk in these areas. Figure 1-5 shows some of the metrics that help desks use to ensure they are meeting the needs of their customers.

BE THERE

✔ Answer the telephone within 20 seconds

✔ Respond to voicemail messages within 30 minutes

✔ Respond to all e-mail messages within 4 hours

✔ Maintain a monthly average abandon rate of less than 5 percent

BE WILLING

✔ Answer the telephone with a smile on your face

✔ Gather the facts and approach each problem in a methodical fashion

✔ Speak clearly and use terms your customer can understand

✔ Accurately assess the severity of problems you must escalate

✔ Take ownership and track 100 percent of problems to closure

✔ Maintain a high customer satisfaction rating

BE ABLE

✔ Use all available resources in an effort to resolve problems and requests

✔ Resolve 75 percent of reported problems and requests

✔ Resolve or escalate 100 percent of problems and requests within the time required for the stated severity

✔ Assign 100 percent of escalated problems and requests to the correct level two group

---

Figure 1-5   Sample help desk customer satisfaction metrics

Metrics are used to measure the help desk's responsiveness and its ability to demonstrate a caring attitude and skill. In other words, metrics enable each and every member of the help desk team to know how well they are meeting their customer's needs and managing their expectations. Additionally, metrics provide help desk analysts the information needed to determine what else they can do to satisfy their customers.

Help desks use data captured by tools and technology to produce these metrics. They also use techniques such as customer satisfaction surveys and monitoring. **Customer satisfaction surveys** are a series of questions that ask customers to provide their perception of the support services being offered. **Monitoring** is when a supervisor or team leader listens to a live or recorded call in order to measure the quality of an analyst's performance during the call.

Demonstrating a Positive CAN DO Attitude

Delivering high-quality customer support is incredibly challenging for a number of reasons. One, customers are people whose feelings and expectations can change from minute-to-minute. Two, customers today are more sophisticated and are demanding cheaper, faster, and better service. Three, technology is increasingly complex and changes so rapidly that it can be difficult for help desk analysts to keep up. Although these factors may tempt you to consider the possibility of satisfying customers a hopeless scenario, remember, there is always something you CAN DO.

A **CAN DO attitude** means that rather than telling a customer what you cannot do, you tell them what you *can do*. A subtle distinction, for sure, but it will go a long way in satisfying customers. That is, enabling customers to *perceive* that they have been helped.

> *There is little difference in people but that little difference makes a big difference. The little difference is attitude. The big difference is whether it is positive or negative.* Author Unknown

To be successful, help desk analysts must learn to strike all negative phrases from their vocabulary. For example, rather than telling a customer "We don't support that product," an analyst can say, "What I can do is give you the telephone number of the company that supports that product." If you were the customer, wouldn't being pointed in the right direction satisfy you more than simply hearing "We can't help?"

Saying no is one of the most difficult things for help desk analysts to do. This is because many of us grew up hearing phrases such as "The Customer Is King" and "The Customer Is #1." Although the spirit of these phrases lives on, the execution is often much more difficult and costly than companies expect. In today's competitive marketplace, few companies have the resources to give customers everything they want, when they want it. Rather, companies are trying to maximize their resources and provide a high-level of service, even if it means limiting the scope of their services. For example, many companies are establishing standards in terms of the products they support, rather than supporting all of the possible products their employees may want to use. In doing so, the help desk can acquire the training, tools, and talent needed to support that limited set of products. If the help desk tried to be "all things to all people," its resources would quickly be stretched too thin and its level of service would decline across the board.

Another adage is "The Customer Is Always Right." Unfortunately, companies have found that customers are not always right. For example, a customer may install a product that conflicts with your company's product and then ask, "What are you going to do about it?" Or, a customer may download a document from the Web that contains a virus and corrupts the system. Again, they turn to the help desk for support. Should the help desk support customers in these situations? Absolutely, because, remember, the customer may not always be right, but they are always the customer. The policies of your company will spell out what you *can do* in these situations.

When facing these challenging situations, a CAN DO attitude will always serve you well. Sometimes it is necessary to say "no" to customers. Sometimes it is impossible to respond as quickly as customers would like when they have a problem. A CAN DO attitude enables you to give customers this information without offending or alienating them. Throughout this book, you will learn how to maintain a CAN DO attitude day in and day out and how it will positively influence not only your interactions with customers, but each and every person you come into contact with each day.

Going the Extra Mile

Are satisfied customers loyal? Not necessarily. Satisfying a customer simply means that the company has fulfilled the customer's need. The customer contacted the help desk with a problem and that problem was resolved. If the help desk does that consistently, will customers contact the help desk when they have a need in the future? Yes. Will they, however, rave about the service they received, thus attracting new customers?

CLOSE UP

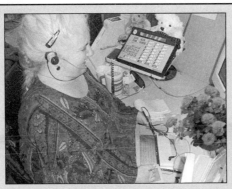

DONNA YEAGER-HENGEL
HEWLETT-PACKARD COMPANY
CUSTOMER SERVICE REPRESENTATIVE
MOUNTAIN VIEW, CALIFORNIA

Saying that Donna Yeager-Hengel has a CAN DO attitude would be an understatement.

For the past 15 years, Donna has worked at Hewlett-Packard Company (HP) as a Customer Service Representative. HP is one of the world's largest computer companies with more than 29,000 products, including computers that range in size from palmtops to supercomputers. HP is also the world's leading supplier of printers. Donna works in the Response Center of the Americas, which is one of five Response Centers situated throughout the world. She supports the company's internal Engineers, who are typically in the field supporting customers. She also handles calls directly from the company's external customers, many of whom work for their company's help desk.

The fact that Donna has worked in the support industry for 15 years makes her special, but it is not the only thing that makes her special. Donna is a congenital (from birth) quadruple amputee with short legs. She uses a headset to talk on the phone with customers and is able to type — using a small laptop-like keyboard — 55 words per minute *with her toes*. Her primary responsibilities are to log and diagnose technical problems, dispatch Engineers when necessary, and track problems until they are resolved to the customer's satisfaction. Her responsibilities also include ensuring problems are resolved in a timely manner. HP service representatives use an in-house developed system to log and track calls and obtain needed information. It is not uncommon for service representatives to have 17 to 20 different Windows open that they can use to quickly access the latest customer and product information.

Years of experience have taught Donna that what most customers want is for you to 1) listen, and 2) solve their problems as quickly as you can. Some customers also want to know that you empathize with what they are experiencing. For example, some of the customers that contact HP's Response Center are calling from their company's help desk. When their mainframe is down, these help desks are receiving numerous calls from *their* customers trying to determine why they cannot access the system. These help desk analysts want to know what HP is going to do so that they can pass that information on to their customers. Some callers are computer operators who are not only trying to work with HP in an effort to resolve the problem, but are also trying to field calls from their customers and managers who are asking for status updates. They want to know that you understand that this problem is difficult for them and that you are going to help them as quickly as you can. In some cases, solving the problem involves working through the problem with the customer on the phone. In other cases, customers with premium service contracts want an Engineer to be sent onsite right away; they don't want to walk through a lot of steps over the phone.

Donna feels that listening skills are extremely important because they enable her to understand what the customer is saying and what they need in each situation. She has also learned that you cannot assume that the answer that worked with one customer last week will work for another customer this week. She tries to treat each customer as an individual and each problem as unique. Donna has taken classes to improve her listening skills and learn how to calm people down when they are upset. Additionally, HP offers training classes to help service representatives improve their telephone skills, time management skills, and diffuse anger. As new products are constantly being introduced, service representatives also receive training to update their technical skills. HP service representatives typically receive 5 to 6 weeks of technical training per year and they can opt to take additional training, such as the "soft" skills training discussed above, for their personal growth. HP also monitors calls, and conducts customer satisfaction surveys on a monthly basis. Response Center managers use the customer feedback these techniques provide to give analysts one-on-one training. Donna also provides informal training by serving as a mentor to her teammates. Her teammates seek her out when they are facing a difficult situation, and they occasionally ask her to conference in on calls. By conferencing in on calls, Donna is able to help her teammates develop the skills needed to handle calls themselves in the future. Donna also serves on the Procedures Committee and helps to continuously streamline and maintain the Response Center's 900-page procedures manual.

So what keeps Donna going after all these years? Donna tries to keep an upbeat, positive attitude and counts on her friends and family to help her maintain her sense of humor. She has also learned that it is important to have a comfortable workspace. She has tried numerous headsets through the years and has finally found one that is light and comfortable. Her headset covers only one ear so that she can hear what is going on in the Response Center, along with any announcements that are made (such as orders to evacuate the building in anticipation of one of California's infamous earthquakes.) After a bout with carpal tunnel syndrome in her toes, she found a smaller keyboard, lowered the keyboard, and is now pain free.

Donna genuinely enjoys working with customers who appreciate the fact that she is going to help as quickly as she can. Donna has also learned not to take it personally when a customer is upset or angry. She reminds herself that they are not angry with her, they are upset about a situation. After a difficult call Donna takes a deep breath, glances at the picture of her husband

and the Hawaii calendar she keeps on her desk, gives herself a quick pep talk, and gets ready for her next call. She always answers the phone with a smile and believes that customers can hear it in her voice. "Hewlett-Packard Response Center, This is Donna, How may I help you?"

Not necessarily. Figure 1-6 shows the reasons why companies lose customers.

1% Die

3% Move away

14% Form new relationships

14% Dissatisfied with product

68% Felt an attitude of indifference

Figure 1-6   Common reasons companies lose customers

As shown in the figure, feeling an attitude of indifference is the number one reason that customers choose to do business with another company. The scary part is that customers don't always tell *you* how you're doing, but they will tell *others* when they are dissatisfied. According to some estimates, 96 percent of unhappy customers never speak up. However, 13 percent of dissatisfied customers will tell their story to twenty other people. Furthermore, one in four unhappy customers will just take away their business. Although it is sometimes hard to listen to complaints day in and day out, these statistics illustrate why it is so important to thank customers who provide feedback.

Complaining customers are giving you and your company an opportunity to improve. Listen carefully!

How, then, do companies generate customer loyalty? How do companies go beyond customer satisfaction, to customer delight? Companies must go the extra mile—give a little something extra. Most help desks define boundaries of what analysts can do to delight their customers. For example, some help desks authorize analysts to make exceptions to company policies in certain situations. Other help desks authorize analysts to waive product shipping charges or offer a free product upgrade in certain situations. Those situations are typically clearly spelled out. These boundaries are important. Without boundaries, the cost of going the extra mile would quickly deplete the company's profits.

In technical support, just as in customer service, it is often the little things that delight customers—the unexpected. Two key ways to delight customers are to (1) save them time, and (2) enhance their self-sufficiency. For example, you can save customers time by teaching them a faster or easier way to use their computer, such as clicking the right mouse button or setting up shortcuts on their desktop. You can enhance customer self-sufficiency by teaching them how to maintain their system and prevent problems by performing mainte-nance tasks, such as backing up their data and using utilities such as scandisk and defrag. Taking an extra moment to teach customers a simple trick or a way that they can diagnose and perhaps fix problems on their own will come back to you tenfold in customer goodwill.

> *Goodwill is the one and only asset the competition cannot undersell or destroy.* Marshall Field

DEVELOPING THE RIGHT MIX OF SKILLS

The support industry is evolving and companies are continuously changing the ways they do business in an effort to gain customer loyalty. This dynamic busi-ness climate represents a tremendous opportunity for people that possess the mix of skills needed to take on the help desk's expanding responsibilities. Figure 1-7 shows the principle skills needed to work successfully at a help desk.

- Business skills

- Technical skills

- Soft skills

- Self-management skills

Figure 1-7 Principle help desk skills

Each of the help desk roles, such as dispatcher, level one analyst, level one special-ist, and help desk manager, requires a specific set of skills. The level of skill and experience required will vary from company to company, but most companies will explore a job candidate's qualifications in each of the following categories:

➤ **Business skills** — The skills people need that are unique to the profession they support, such as accounting skills or banking skills. Business skills also include skills that are unique to the service industry, such as understanding the importance of meeting customer's needs and managing their expectations.

➤ **Technical skills** — The skills people need to use and support the specific products and technologies the help desk supports. Technical skills also include basic computer and software literacy.

➤ **Soft skills** — The skills and personality traits that people need to deliver great service, such as listening skills, verbal communication skills, customer service skills, problem-solving skills, writing skills, and the ability to be a team player.

➤ **Self-management skills** — The skills, such as stress and time management, that people need to complete their work effectively, feel job satisfaction, and avoid frustration or burnout. Self-management skills also include the ability to get and stay organized and to continuously and quickly learn new skills.

Chapters 2 through 6 explore in detail the soft skills needed to have a successful career in customer support. Chapters 7 and 8 explore in detail the self-management skills needed to enjoy that career.

Finding people for front-line positions that have the right mix of skills is one of the most difficult challenges facing help desk managers today. People who have very strong interpersonal skills—that is, soft and self-management skills—may lack the technical skills required to support today's increasingly complex technology. People with strong technical skills may lack the skills such as patience and empathy that are needed to support customers with varying skill levels. Some people prefer a more hands-on approach to technical support and may be more comfortable working in a field service role away from the front-line. The employee and the company benefit when the right skills are matched with the right position.

When hiring people for front-line positions, companies look for people who genuinely enjoy helping other people and enjoy solving problems. Companies also look for individuals who are team-oriented and enjoy working with other people. This is because it is generally thought that technical skills can be developed more easily than interpersonal skills. Companies are willing to provide technical training to individuals with good interpersonal skills and a customer service orientation. Also, technology is constantly changing and the technical skills must be continuously updated. This is not to say that technical skills are unimportant. At times, companies may hire people with very strong technical skills and then provide extensive customer service training. Or, companies may need people who have a very specific business skill or technical skill that would take an extensive amount of training to develop and so they hire people who already possess that skill. Smart companies let their customers' needs and expectations drive their hiring decisions. For this reason, people who understand that all of these skill sets, business, technical, soft, and self-management, are important will create for themselves the greatest opportunity.

Contrary to popular belief, interpersonal skills can be developed. You must be willing to work at them.

Companies worldwide know they must deliver high-quality customer support, or lose to their competition. These companies are seeking people who have the mix of skills and the desire needed to not just satisfy but also delight customers day in and day out. The rapidly growing support industry represents a tremendous opportunity for people who want to use all of their skills: business, technical, soft, and self-management. To seize this opportunity, you must understand the characteristics of excellent technical customer support and remember at all times that you are supporting people using technology, not just technology. People who have needs and expectations that will take all of your skills to meet and exceed.

This book focuses on the soft skills and self-management skills needed to pursue a successful career in technical customer support. Although the business skills and the technical skills you may choose to develop are wide-ranging and diverse, soft skills and self-management skills are somewhat universal. It is possible to build a solid foundation of these latter skills upon which you will always be able to draw.

Skills such as listening, communication, and stress-management skills are excellent "life" skills that will serve you well regardless of your chosen profession.

CHAPTER SUMMARY

- The pervasive nature of increasingly complex computing technology has created a tremendous demand for technical support. The help desk is the first point of contact for this support. How people are treated by the help desk influences their level of satisfaction and how they perceive the entire company and its products. To be successful, a help desk must effectively utilize all of its assets: people, processes, technology, and information. People are by far the most important component because customers are people who have needs and expectations that only other people can understand.

■ Managing customer expectations is a challenge, but you can count on customers wanting the help desk to be there, be willing, and be able. Even when it seems customer expectations cannot be met, you can avoid offending or alienating customers by demonstrating a CAN DO attitude and by going the extra mile. A CAN DO attitude means that rather than telling a customer what you can't do, you tell them what you *can do*.

■ The support industry is evolving and the dynamic nature of this industry represents a tremendous opportunity for people who possess the right mix of skills. Skills needed include business, technical, soft, and self-management. This book focuses on the soft and self-management skills, which are somewhat universal and will serve you well throughout your life and career.

KEY TERMS

24 × 7 support — Help desk services that are provided twenty-four hours a day, seven days a week.

a caring attitude — A help desk's ability to communicate the fact that it wants to satisfy its customer's needs.

business skills — The skills people need that are unique to the profession they support, such as accounting skills or banking skills. Business skills also include skills that are unique to the service industry, such as understanding the importance of meeting customer's needs and managing their expectations.

CAN DO attitude — Telling a customer what you *can do* rather than what you cannot do.

customer — A person who buys products or services.

customer satisfaction — The difference between how a customer perceives he or she was treated and how the customer expects to be treated.

customer satisfaction surveys — a series of questions that ask customers to provide their perception of the support services being offered.

customer support — Services that help a customer understand and benefit from a product's capabilities by answering questions, solving problems, and providing training.

expectations — Results that customers consider reasonable or due to them.

external customers — A person or company that buys another company's products and services.

external help desk — A help desk that supports customers who buy their company's products and services.

fee-based support — Customers pay for support of certain services on a per-use basis.

front-line service providers — People who work in a help desk who interact directly with customers and help desk management personnel.

help desk — A single point of contact within a company for managing customer problems and requests and for providing solution-oriented support services.

information — Data that are organized in a meaningful way.

internal customer — A person who works at a company and at times relies on other employees at that company in some way to perform his or her job.

internal help desk — A help desk that responds to questions, distributes information, and handles problems and service requests for its company's employees.

metrics — performance measures.

monitoring — when a supervisor or team leader listens to a live or recorded call in order to measure the quality of an analyst's performance during the call.

multi-level support model — A common structure of help desks, where the help desk refers problems it cannot resolve to the appropriate internal group, external vendor, or subject matter expert.

network monitoring — the use of tools to observe and control network performance in an effort to prevent and minimize the impact of problems.

network and system administration — Activities such as setting up and maintaining user accounts, ensuring the data that the company collects is secure, and performing e-mail and database management.

outsourcing — When companies have help desk services provided by an outside supplier (service agency or outsourcer), instead of providing them in-house.

peer-to-peer support — A practice where users bypass the formal support structure and seek assistance from their co-workers or someone in another department whom they believe can help.

people — The component of a help desk that consists of the staff and structure put in place within a company or department to support its customers by performing business processes.

post-sales support — Helping people who have purchased a company's product or service.

pre-sales support — Answering questions for people who have not yet purchased the company's products or service.

1

processes — Interrelated work activities that take a set of specific inputs and produce a set of specific outputs that are of value to a customer.

responsiveness — The help desk's ability to (1) be available when customers need help and (2) make it easy for customers to contact the help desk.

self-management skills — The skills, such as stress and time management, that people need to complete their work effectively, feel job satisfaction, and avoid frustration or burnout. Self-management skills also include the ability to get and stay organized and to continuously and quickly learn new skills.

Service Level Agreement (SLA) — A written document that spells out the services the help desk will provide the customer, the customer's responsibilities, and how service performance is measured.

skill — The help desk's ability to quickly and correctly resolve customer problems and requests.

soft skills — The skills and personality traits that people need to deliver great service, such as listening skills, verbal communication skills, customer service skills, problem-solving skills, writing skills, and the ability to be a team player.

subject matter expert (SME) — A person who has a high level of experience or knowledge about a particular subject.

support center — A help desk with a broader scope of responsibility and with the goals of providing faster service and improving customer satisfaction.

technical skills — The skills people need to use and support the specific products and technologies the help desk supports.

technical support — A wide range of services that enable people and companies to continuously use the computing technology they acquired or developed.

technology — The tools and technologies people use to do their work.

world class — A company that has achieved, and is able to sustain, high levels of customer satisfaction.

value — The perceived worth, usefulness, or importance of a product or service to the customer.

REVIEW QUESTIONS

1. Why is there a tremendous need for technical support?

2. What is a help desk?

3. What influences customers' level of satisfaction and how they perceive a company and its products?

4. How is technical support different than customer support?

5. How is a support center different than a help desk?

6. What are the goals of a multi-level support model?

7. What are the components of a successful help desk?

8. Why do companies have a hard time meeting and exceeding customer expectations?

9. What is "high touch" service and what is "low touch" service?

10. List three benefits that companies derive when they deliver excellent customer support.

11. List three benefits that employees derive when they work for a company that delivers excellent customer support.

12. List two intrinsic benefits that employees of a help desk derive from supporting customers.

13. List three trends that are currently influencing the support industry.

14. How are the three trends you listed in response to question 13 influencing the industry?

15. What are the two principal types of help desks?

16. What is the most important link in a customer service delivery chain?

17. A customer service delivery chain is only as good as its _____.

18. What is customer satisfaction?

19. Name one way that companies are managing customer expectations.

20. What three things can the help desk count on customers wanting?

21. Name three ways that companies produce the metrics needed to measure their performance.

22. Is a customer always right?

23. What turns a satisfied customer into a loyal customer?

24. What are two things that help desk analysts can do to delight customers?

25. What are the four principle skills needed to work successfully at a help desk?

26. Which of the four principle skills sets are universal or life skills?

HANDS-ON PROJECTS

Project 1.1

Evaluating technical support needs. The average person may contact any number of help desks for support. Talk to at least three friends or classmates who use computers about their experiences with technical support. Ask each person the following questions:

- Have they ever contacted a help desk for support?

- What were their expectations when they contacted the help desk?

- Were their expectations met?

- Did they receive "high touch" service?

- Did they use any "low touch" services?

Write a one-page report that summarizes each experience and presents your conclusions about each experience.

Project 1.2

Exploring team benefits. Working on a help desk involves working in a team setting. Just as the company and individuals benefit when customer service excellence is the norm, teams benefit. List five ways that the help desk team will benefit if each and every one of its members are committed to delivering excellent customer service and support.

Project 1.3

Understanding the service delivery chain. Day in and day out we are all sometimes a customer and other times a service provider. Think about your experiences as a customer and as a service provider during the past twenty-four hours. Write a paragraph describing your experiences as a customer. For example, contacting a company for technical support or going to a store to purchase needed equipment. Were your expectations for service and support met? What did the service provider do well? How could the service provider have done better? Write a paragraph describing your experiences as a service provider. For example, assisting customers at the company where you work or helping a friend or family member with a project. Do you feel you met your customer's expectations? How do you know?

Project 1.4

Understanding perceptions vs. expectations. Describe in a paragraph or two a situation where your perception of an event was different than what you expected. Include, if possible, a description of how a person with you had a different perception and different expectations. For example, you go to Mardi Gras in New Orleans expecting it to be fun and exciting and find that you are actually overwhelmed by what you perceive is the unruly nature of the crowd. On the other hand, your friend has a great time and can't wait to go back next year.

Project 1.5

Understanding customer needs and expectations. Assemble a team of at least three of your classmates. Discuss each of the three things you can count on customers wanting: responsiveness, a caring attitude, and skill. Discuss the ramifications if any one of these customer needs is not consistently met. Write a brief summary of your findings and discuss them with the class.

Project 1.6

Demonstrating a CAN DO attitude. Sometimes we forget that in life, there is always something you CAN DO. For the next twenty-four hours, write down any negative phrases you catch yourself using such as "I can't," "It's not my job," and "There's nothing I can do." For each situation, how can you restate the negative phrase in a positive way? Place your list and your restated phrases somewhere easy to locate. You'll revisit these phrases again in Chapter 8.

Project 1.7

Hitching a ride on the extra mile. When was the last time you received service that absolutely delighted you? What was it about the service that made you feel the service provider was really going the extra mile? What characteristic can you take from that experience and use when providing technical customer support? Write a one-page report that describes your experience and what you learned from that experience.

Project 1.8

Assessing your skills. Customer support requires a special person with the right mix of skills. Ask yourself the following questions:

- Do I enjoy helping other people?

- Do I enjoy solving problems?

- Do I consider myself a team-oriented person?

- Do I enjoy working with other people?

You will consider your answers in Chapter 8.

Case Projects

1. **Way Cool, Inc.**

   Way Cool, Inc. has hired you to determine how they can minimize their costs in terms of customer service and support. Their focus is on their product, a state-of-the-art virtual reality game that is extremely popular and attracting new users each day. They would like to invest as much as possible in developing their game and as little as possible in terms of providing support. In fact, they believe the game is so easy to use that support is not needed and as such they are thinking of eliminating customer support services all together. Prepare a brief report that outlines the pros and cons of minimizing the company's investment in support. Suggest ways the company can minimize their costs without eliminating support services altogether.

2. **Bill's Cyber Cycle Shop**

   Bill, of Bill's Cyber Cycle Shop, has hired you to help him survey his customers and determine whether his business is meeting its customer's needs. Bill wants his customers to perceive that his staff is there, willing, and able to support customers when they need help ordering bicycles and associated accessories from his Web site. Draft a customer satisfaction survey that Bill can use to measure his customer's satisfaction. Remember, he wants to know if customers perceive his staff is responsive, if they demonstrate a caring attitude, and if they have the skill needed to answer customer inquiries.

3. **Bayside Unlimited**

   You work for a help desk that supports the internal employees of Bayside Unlimited. Your boss has asked you to identify any resources your help desk can use to improve the quality of its support services. Search the Internet and locate any organizations your help desk can join or magazines your help desk can buy to learn more about the help desk industry and how other companies run their help desks. Prepare a report of your findings that includes the name and brief description of each organization and magazine you found along with the URL of its associated Web site.

CHAPTER TWO

DEVELOPING STRONG LISTENING AND COMMUNICATION SKILLS

After reading this chapter and completing the exercises you will be able to:

➤ Describe the characteristics and benefits of active listening

➤ Understand how to avoid the distractions that prevent good listening

➤ Describe how to communicate with customers who have varying communication styles in a manner that builds rapport and trust

Listening and communication skills are two of the most basic and important skills that help desk analysts must possess. Analysts take in information by listening. They exchange information with both verbal and nonverbal communication. These skills are important because analysts must communicate and listen actively when customers provide information about their problems or requests. In return, analysts must respond in ways that give customers a sense of confidence that they are being heard and understood. They must also deliver information in a way that is meaningful to their customers. Good listening and communication skills benefit both of the parties involved in a conversation and can be improved through practice.

When working as a help desk analyst, you must develop strong listening and communication skills so that you can communicate effectively with customers, co-workers, managers, and other service providers, such as internal support groups and vendors. This chapter focuses on how to be an active listener and avoid the distractions that prevent good listening. You will also learn how to be an effective communicator and how to identify and respond to the varying communication styles you may encounter.

THE POWER OF LISTENING

Listening is a skill that is important to many professions. For example, skilled negotiators carefully listen and understand the other party's needs before they make a compromising offer. Top sales people concentrate on listening to avoid talking themselves out of a sale. What does this have to do with customer support? Well, at times in customer support, analysts must be skilled negotiators—remember that CAN DO attitude—and at times analysts must be sales people. You can't always give customers what they want, but if you listen actively you can at least acknowledge and try to address what customers need.

In a survey conducted by the Help Desk Institute, a membership organization for help desk professionals, 99 percent of respondents cited listening as the most important quality for a support person (*Help Desk and Customer Support Practices Report*, 1998, p. 18). Why? Because customers are living, breathing human beings and a basic human need is to be heard and understood.

> *You can convey no greater honor than actually hearing what someone has to say.* Philip Crosby

Listening, like speaking and writing, is hard work; it requires thought and can be improved through practice. You have to *want* to listen. Whether you are interacting with customers, co-workers, friends, or family members, listening enables you to understand the other person's needs. Only then can you concentrate on fulfilling those needs. Furthermore, it is not enough to just listen, you must listen *actively* so the other person knows that you are listening.

Being an Active Listener

Listening means paying attention—making an effort to hear something. Analysts with good listening skills can focus on what the speaker is saying to obtain the information needed to handle problems and requests quickly and correctly. They can convey a caring attitude and build rapport with the speaker by using active listening. **Active listening** involves participating in a conversation and giving the speaker a sense of confidence that he or she is being heard. **Passive listening** involves simply taking in information and shows little regard for the speaker. Table 2-1 compares the characteristics of active and passive listening.

Table 2-1 Active versus passive listening

Active Listeners	Passive Listeners
Ask questions and respond to the speaker	Take in information without questions
Verify understanding	Accept information at face value
Pay attention to *what* is being said and *how* it is being said	Show little regard for the feeling with which the information is being communicated

2

Let's explore each active listening characteristic and discuss ways that you can demonstrate the fact that you are actively listening.

Ask questions and respond to the speaker — Customers do not typically contact the help desk because everything is going well. They are calling because they have a problem or because they need information about a product or service. Sometimes, customers can succinctly articulate their needs. Other times, customers aren't exactly sure why they are experiencing a problem or what it is that they need. They just know they can't get their job done. By asking appropriate and relevant questions and by assimilating and acknowledging the information the customer is providing, you can solve the problem or at least determine the next steps to take.

Successful analysts often develop checklists they can use to diagnose problems and methodically identify solutions. In some companies, level two service providers also develop checklists in an effort to enhance the abilities of level one analysts. These checklists help to ensure that analysts have correctly identified the failing hardware, software, or network component. A methodical approach also enables analysts to avoid making assumptions when diagnosing problems. Remember, just because a customer was using Microsoft Word when a problem occurred does not mean that software package is the failing component. By asking questions and validating the facts given, you can better ensure that you fully understand what the customer needs.

Chapter 6, *Solving and Preventing Problems*, discusses in detail how to develop problem-solving checklists.

Knowing what questions to ask is an important skill for analysts. It is also important to know when to question the answers received. This is because customers occasionally provide information that can be misleading. Customers do not intentionally provide misleading information, they may simply lack the skills needed to provide an accurate diagnosis. Good listening and tactful questions help you assess your customers' skill level, which in turn helps you in determining how to respond or proceed. Tactful questions obtain information without offending customers. For example, asking a customer "Can you describe the steps you took before this problem occurred?" is much better than asking "What did you do?" The latter question has a condemning tone and most likely will make the customer defensive.

Keep in mind, too, that not all customers feel comfortable using technology. Some customers may be just getting started and have not yet mastered the basics. Asking a customer questions such as "Do you have Internet access?" or "Do you know how to download a patch?" is much better than assuming that the customer has Internet access or simply stating that he can download the needed patch from the Internet. On the other hand, some customers may be quite sophisticated and, in fact, may have a better understanding of a product or system than some analysts do. Active listening enables you to avoid asking questions that are unnecessary or too simple. For example, if a customer says, "I looked on your Web site and could not find any information about this problem," you know not to ask the customer if she has Internet access. Asking questions that are too simple will offend a sophisticated customer just as quickly as asking questions that are too complicated will offend a customer who is just getting started.

You can get a good idea of customers' skill level by listening to how they use jargon and describe a problem or request. **Jargon** is the specialized or technical language used by a trade or profession, in this case, the computer industry. For example, a customer who reports in a panicked voice that he has "lost" the report for his boss that he worked on all afternoon will need to hear some assurance that you can help before you begin asking questions in a nontechnical manner. On the other hand, a customer who reports that she is having a chronic, repeatable problem when running a spreadsheet macro but only in a certain spreadsheet will need you to acknowledge the detailed information she has given and then proceed accordingly.

Although it is best to avoid using jargon and slang altogether, it is particularly important when you are supporting a global customer community. Many of the terms used freely in the United States may be unfamiliar or offensive to customers from other countries.

Good listening also enables you to learn the business language customers are using to describe their work. When you better understand how customers are using the technology you support to do their work, you can then provide tips that will help them. Or, you may identify ways your company's product can be enhanced, thus making it more marketable. If nothing else, you can help bridge the gap that can exist between the business needs of your company and the technology used to fill that need. Remember that many customers simply want to *use* technology to do their work. When they have a problem using technology or want to use the technology more efficiently or effectively, they turn to the help desk for support. Good listening enables you to understand and adjust to your customers' needs—no matter what their skill level.

Knowing when *not* to ask questions while still being responsive to customers is one of the nuances of customer service. For example, when customers are angry or in a highly agitated state, it is best to let them vent before asking questions. Customers who are upset have a story to tell. If you interrupt their story with questions they may become more upset. In this situation, it is best to simply listen and respond to what the customer is saying in the least intrusive way possible. For example, when interacting with a customer face-to-face, maintain eye contact and nod your head to let the customer know you are listening. When interacting with an upset or angry customer over the telephone, use a verbal nod of the head to let the customer know you are listening. Verbal nods of the head include phrases such as "Uh-huh," "I see," "Go on," and "I understand" at appropriate points in the conversation. For example, use the phrase "Uh-huh" or "Go on" when you want to encourage the customer to continue. Use phrases such as "I see" and "I understand" when you understand what the customer is telling you or when you can appreciate his or her point of view. Although you may be tempted to just be quiet and listen, that may cause the customer to become more upset. If a customer asks, "Are you listening?" you are not being responsive enough.

When in doubt, keep asking questions until you feel comfortable that you have the information you need to solve the problem.

Verify understanding — One of the most important aspects of active listening is to verify understanding. For help desk analysts, this means verifying that you understand what a customer said and verifying that the customer understands your reply. If you are unsure of the customer's meaning or think they may be unsure of yours, then you may decide to ask a follow-up or clarifying question. For example, when interacting with a customer face-to-face, the customer may furrow his brow or stare vacantly at you, his computer, or something on his desk. In other words, he will *look* confused. When interacting with a customer over the telephone, you may hear silence on the other end of the telephone. In either situation, the customer may question the course of action you are suggesting by inquiring, "Are you sure?" The following questions will enable you to determine the customer's level of understanding in any of these situations.

> "Would you like me to repeat that?"
>
> "Would you like to go through that again?"
>
> "How does that sound?"

These questions enable you to verify that the customer understands the course of action that you are proposing.

Another good technique for verifying that you understand what a customer is telling you is to **paraphrase**, or restate, the information given by the customer using slightly different words. In other words, paraphrasing repeats something using new words. Paraphrasing enables you to verify the meaning of, or clear away any confusion about, the information you have received.

> **Customer:** I printed the page and the words were okay but the pictures didn't print right.

> **Analyst (paraphrase):** Let me make sure I understand. You printed a document and the text printed correctly but the graphics did not?

When you verify understanding, you not only satisfy the customer by ensuring the customer's needs are being met, you also promote a good working relationship with other service providers. Level two service providers commonly complain that they received a problem from the help desk that they perceive the help desk should have been able to solve or that should have been assigned to a different level two group. Very often this occurs because help desk analysts failed to ask a sufficient number of questions or "assumed" they knew the answer to an unasked question. For example, you may be tempted to immediately transfer a customer who is having trouble signing on to the mainframe to the operations group that resets passwords. However, there are actually a number of reasons a customer may have trouble logging on. Asking questions is the only way to determine the actual source of the problem. Again, it never hurts to ask additional questions in an effort to make sure you fully understand your customer's needs. Be sensitive, though to the fact that customers can become impatient or frustrated if you ask too many questions or if you ask the same question over and over again. Choose your questions carefully and actively listen to the responses so that you can quickly determine what your customers need.

Pay attention to *what* is being said and *how* it is being said — Ultimately, your goal as an analyst is to solve a problem a customer is experiencing or to provide the customer with needed information or instructions. This is the "what" component of a conversation you need to listen for. How the customer is delivering that information is also important. Customers are often experiencing emotion as a result of having a problem or not having what they need to use the products or services you support. For example, they may be confused by the instructions shipped with the software. Or they may be frustrated that the hardware they purchased is not functioning properly and they have just spent a considerable amount of time trying to determine why. Or, they may be angry because they have experienced this same problem before and they perceive that a solution offered by another member of the help desk did not work. By listening actively, you hear both the problem and the emotion, and acknowledge both. In other words, you hear *what* is being said and *how* it is being said.

A basic human need is to be understood. When you acknowledge customers' emotions, you address that need. Often, what customers want most is for analysts to say that they understand. When you acknowledge customers' emotions, customers perceive that you care about their well-being and are more willing to work with you to resolve the problem. When you don't acknowledge customers' emotions, the customers may become more upset or angry. Have you

2

ever contacted a company and expressed dissatisfaction with a product or service only to hear, "There's nothing we can do"? Didn't that response make you feel more frustrated or angry than you were to begin with? A much better response would be, "I'm sorry you're frustrated," or "Those instructions can be confusing. Let's walk through them together."

Some help desk analysts have a hard time dealing with emotions and they lack the people skills needed to interact effectively with customers. They are very logical thinkers and just want to solve the problem. Most customers, however, are unable to actively participate in problem solving until the analyst acknowledges their emotion.

Pay attention when you are the customer. Notice how service providers respond when you are upset or angry. Do they acknowledge your emotion? When they do, does it make you feel better? Most likely you will find it does.

Being a good listener requires concentration. Communicating the fact that you are listening requires thought and caring. If a customer does not *perceive* that you are listening, you must take responsibility and determine why that is. Are you ignoring what the customer is saying? Are you failing to acknowledge how he or she feels? Determining how you can be more responsive requires that you listen to what the customer is saying. When a customer says, "That doesn't answer my question" or "Let me say this again," you are being given strong cues that the customer *perceives* you are not listening. Good listeners acknowledge what the customer has said when responding and they respond to both *what* is being said and *how* it is being said.

It is important to control your own emotions when interacting with customers. In other words, it is important to pay attention to *what* you say and *how* you say it. When a customer is angry or upset, it is neither helpful nor appropriate for you to become angry or upset as well. Chapter 5, *Handling Difficult Customer Situations*, provides specific techniques you can use when facing "sticky" customer situations, such as calming an irate or extremely demanding customer or saying "no" to customers while maintaining their good will.

> *Nothing is ever gained by winning an argument and losing a customer.* C. F. Norton

Benefits of Active Listening

The benefits of active listening far exceed the benefits of speaking. Active listening helps you to establish rapport with the customer. The most common way to build rapport is to listen for the customer's name and use it respectfully during the remainder of your conversation.

Listen carefully to how customers provide their name. If a customer uses a title, such as Professor Brown, Dr. Jones, or Ms. Smith, address the customer using that title until the customer gives you permission to use a first name or nickname. When supporting international customers, avoid using first names unless you have been given permission to do so.

Active listening also enables you to determine the customer's emotional state. If a customer is upset or angry, you must acknowledge and address that emotion before you can begin addressing the technical problem. Active listening can help you build trust by enabling you to respond in a way that acknowledges your customer's sense of urgency. For example, helping a customer route a presentation she is scheduled to make in an hour to another nearby printer when her personal printer jams will go a long way in terms of building trust. Quick thinking and a viable workaround may not solve the actual problem, but it can satisfy the customer's immediate need. If you do not at least try to satisfy the customer's immediate need—that is, if you do not respond in a way that acknowledges the customer's sense of urgency—the customer may become demanding and challenge you to do more than is possible. When customers come to understand that you will go the extra mile when they have a critical need, they will not feel the need to be demanding in the future.

In addition to enabling you to establish rapport, address emotions, and build trust, active listening helps you keep the conversation on track so you can quickly determine the nature and likely cause of the customer's problem or request. If you are not listening carefully, you may miss an important detail or you may have to ask the customer to repeat what he or she has said. Either one may instill a lack of confidence if the customer perceives that he or she has to repeat information because you were not listening. Active listening will also enable you to determine situations that require management involvement. For example, if a customer is unhappy with the service that he received from another department in your company, you need to pass that information on to your manager. It is then your manager's responsibility to relay that information to the manager of the other department.

Most importantly, active listening enables you to show customers that they are important and that you want to do all you can to satisfy their needs. This leads to customer confidence, and the customer is left with a positive image of you and your company.

Avoiding Distractions That Prevent Good Listening

Professionals earn between 40 and 80 percent of their pay by listening (*How to Be a Great Communicator*, 1997, p. 97), and yet, we're not good listeners. In fact, studies indicate that we usually listen to about 25 percent of our listening capacity and that we ignore, forget, distort, or misunderstand 75 percent of what we hear. The truth is that while we spend much of our time listening, we are not good listeners. Why aren't we better listeners? Well, in today's society, a lot of things get in the way, including those listed in Figure 2-1.

- Distractions and interruptions
- "Third ear" syndrome
- Jumping ahead
- Emotional filters
- Mental side trips
- Talking

Figure 2-1 Factors that prevent good listening

Let's look more closely at each of these factors that influence your ability to be a good listener.

Distractions and interruptions — Whether you work for a large or small help desk, you work in a high-energy environment. In a typical help desk on a typical day, telephones are ringing, electronic reader boards are flashing information and may be sounding alarms, customers and service providers are wandering about talking and perhaps entering your workspace, and all are demanding your attention. It is easy to lose focus in this dynamic working environment. Good listeners find ways to minimize these distractions by, for example, turning into their workspace when talking on the telephone or working on problems and signaling to visitors when they are already engaged.

"Third ear" syndrome — Many analysts believe they can listen to their customers and keep a "third ear" tuned in to what is happening around them. This concept of being aware of what is happening is valid, but must be used appropriately. Few people can truly listen and still do other things at the same time. For example, if you are speaking with a customer and hear a co-worker discussing a similar problem, you may want to ask the customer if you can put him on hold while you determine if there is a system-wide problem. On the other hand, if you are speaking with a customer and hear several co-workers talking about their lunch plans, you must focus on your customer's needs and avoid the distraction your chatting co-workers represent.

Jumping ahead — The concept of jumping ahead is best explained by the adage, "Listening is not waiting for your turn to talk." Unfortunately, analysts sometimes decide they know the solution to a problem or they have rehearsed a standard response to an inquiry and they are simply waiting for the customer to stop talking so they can begin. Analysts who jump ahead run the risk of missing key information from the customer that changes the nature of the problem. They may waste time diagnosing the wrong problem because they were not listening and missed important information. They also may appear insensitive because they have failed to hear the customer out. As a result, the customer may become defensive or uncooperative. The customer may reject an analyst's solution because she does not feel that she has been heard or understood. Good listeners wait until the speaker has provided all available information before reaching a conclusion.

Emotional filters — We all have prejudices that influence our thinking and, as a result, our ability to listen. You may not like a speaker's appearance, voice, race, religion, or nationality. You may not like a speaker's temperament. For example, some people have a hard time dealing with negative people or people who whine. You may simply disagree with what the customer is saying. It is important to remember, however, that as a help desk analyst it is your job to uphold the policies of your company and assist all customers to the best of your ability.

Mental side trips — As a card-carrying member of the human race it is inevitable that your "life" will at times intervene when you are working. It may occur to you that you need to buy your friend a birthday gift or that you have to take your child to baseball practice after school. As these thoughts race through your mind, they make it hard for you to listen. This ability to manage several conversations in your mind at once is a result of the fact that most people speak about 125 words per minute, while you can think more than 400 words per minute. Good listeners focus on what the speaker is saying and resist thoughts that sidetrack their attention.

Talking — Talking is a necessary part of communication, but it is possible to talk too much. A common mistake in customer service is delivering too much information. For example, a customer asks you for the status of an outstanding problem and you answer by saying that Joe Brown in the programming department is working on it. The customer promptly calls Joe Brown and asks him for a status, thus taking him away from solving the problem. Also, the customer now has Joe Brown's name and telephone number and may call him directly in the future, rather than calling the help desk. A more appropriate response is to let the customer know the problem is being worked on and that you will give the customer a call when the problem has been solved. Or, if the problem is critical in nature, promise the customer you will provide periodic updates. Then, make sure you do!

Knowing when not to talk too much is also an important part of communication. This is because it is sometimes necessary to listen for cues that the customer is following your instructions. For example, if you have asked a customer to restart her computer, you can listen for the Microsoft jingle to know the restart is underway. There is sometimes the tendency to engage in idle chatter during this type of lull in the problem-solving process, but remember you cannot listen if you are talking too much. It is better to stay focused on working with the customer to solve a problem. For example, rather than simply chatting while a customer is restarting her computer, you may want to describe for the customer what steps you will be taking once her computer has restarted. Use the active listening techniques described earlier in this chapter to verify that the customer is following the plan of action.

Knowing What to Listen For

Listening requires concentration and it helps to know what you are listening for and how to record the information you receive. Begin by taking note of the key points the customer is making. If your company has a call tracking or problem management system, record the information directly into that system, so that you do not have to handle the information again when you finish your conversation with the customer. If your company does not have a system, the system does not facilitate real-time logging of information, or you are simply not in a position to log information (for example, you are at a customer site), take notes as neatly and precisely as possible. Be as specific as possible so you can restate, using the customer's words when appropriate, the information the customer provides. A good guideline is to note who, what, when, where, and how. That is, who is experiencing a problem or has a request? What product or service is involved? When is the problem occurring, for example, chronically, intermittently, and so forth? Where is the problem occurring, for example, where is the failing device located or on what server is the failing software installed? How severe or widespread is the problem or how is the problem affecting the customer? *Why* the problem is occurring is determined once a solution is identified.

When taking notes about a problem or request, capture details such as who, what, when, where, and how.

When listening to customers, your ultimate goal is to determine their needs. It is important to remember that customer needs can go beyond obtaining details about a technical problem or request. It is also important to remember that you and your company can learn a lot by listening closely to customers. Challenge yourself to comprehend and retain as much as possible when communicating with customers. Skillful listening will enable you to:

➤ Detect any emotion the customer is experiencing that you need to acknowledge and address

➤ Obtain the details of the customer's problem or request

➤ Gratefully receive any complaints the customer has about your company, its products, or its services

➤ Detect any misconceptions the customer has about your company and products that you or others in your company such as the sales or marketing department need to clarify

➤ Learn ways your products and services can be enhanced and improved

➤ Gain insight about your customers that will enable you to improve the quality of your services

Remember, too, that listening involves keeping your eyes open as well as your ears. When interacting with customers face-to-face, watch their face and body language. Speakers often deliver information through nonverbal cues, such as folded arms, a furrowed brow, or poor eye contact. These cues may indicate that the customer is having a hard time understanding or believing what you are saying. If a customer rubs her eyes or scratches his head, it may be because they are confused and need you to slow down or restate your instructions.

In the Americas and most of Europe, steady eye contact is considered a sign of trust and respect. In Asia, eye contact is considered a personal affront and is kept to a minimum.

When interacting with customers over the telephone, remember that silence can be very telling. If a customer is unresponsive or fails to comment on the information you are delivering, the customer may be confused or may disagree with what you are saying. Although there is nothing wrong with a brief interlude of silence (for example, the customer may be processing what you have said), you want to avoid the temptation to view that silence as acceptance. A tactful clarifying question, such as "Would you like for me to repeat that?" or "Is that acceptable to you?" will enable you to avoid incorrect assumptions.

Good listening requires discipline and begins with a willingness to fully comprehend and retain everything that customers are saying both in terms of *what* they are saying and *how* they are saying it. Also, good listening does not begin and end with the conversations we have with customers. Listening is a skill that you can use and apply on a daily basis in all areas of your life.

COMMUNICATING WITH CUSTOMERS

Communication is the exchange of thoughts, messages, and information. It requires skills such as listening, speaking, and writing. It also requires the desire to convey information in a meaningful and respectful way. Technology is helping us to communicate faster and with a larger audience, but it cannot help us formulate the information we transmit. Knowing what to say and how to say it when communicating with customers takes practice and patience.

Chapter 4, *Technical Writing Skills for Support Professionals*, explores in detail ways that support analysts can improve their writing skills.

2

Establishing Rapport

What you say is a simple matter of knowing and selecting the right words to use for a given situation. The words you choose should also communicate to customers that you appreciate their business and want to assist them in any way you can. *How* you say it is much more complex and requires an understanding of how people communicate. Figure 2-2 illustrates the factors that influence customer perception when people are communicating face-to-face and over the telephone (*Effective Telephone Communication Skills*, 1995, pp. 6, 7).

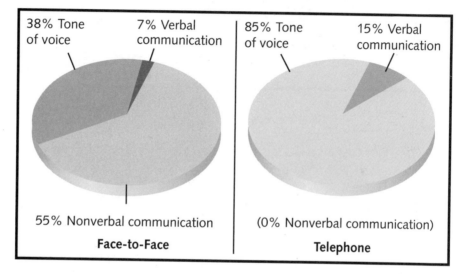

38% Tone of voice	7% Verbal communication	85% Tone of voice	15% Verbal communication
55% Nonverbal communication		(0% Nonverbal communication)	
Face-to-Face		**Telephone**	

Figure 2-2   How people communicate

It is easy to see from this chart that communicating with customers over the telephone requires a very different approach than communicating face-to-face. When communicating over the telephone, "how people say it" makes all the difference.

Verbal Communication

Verbal communication is the exchange of information using words. The words you choose to use can greatly influence the response you receive from customers. If you speak in a straightforward manner using everyday language that customers can understand, then your message will be well received. If you speak in riddles or use technical language that customers cannot understand, you can alienate customers. In addition, some phrases, such as those listed in Figure 2-3, tend to provoke customers and should be considered forbidden phrases.

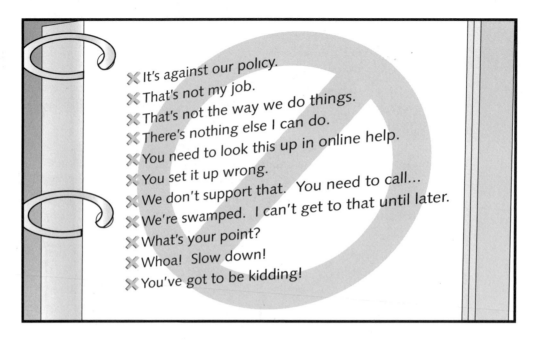

Figure 2-3 Forbidden phrases

These forbidden phrases can quickly turn even a reasonable, calm customer into a charging bull. That is not to say that you won't ever be faced with the need to deliver the message these phrases represent. However, even when you have to deliver bad news to customers, you can present it in a positive, respectful way. Let's look at how these "forbidden phrases" can be replaced with more positive statements.

➤ "It's against our policy." — This is a tough one because what your customer is asking for may very well be against your company's policy. Rather than state the negative, try stating your response as a positive. For example, "Our policy states…." Or, if the policy enables you to offer the customer options, let the customer know what those options are. For example, "According to our policy, what I *can do* is…."

➤ "That's not my job." — It may not be your job, but it *is* your job to determine who *can* assist the customer. Here's where you put your CAN DO attitude to work. Phrases such as "What I can do is transfer you to the person who handles that area" or "What I can do is give you the telephone number of the company that supports this product" enable you to keep the good will of your customer even when you are unable to assist the customer directly.

➤ "That's not the way we do things." — This phrase rejects the customer's request without offering an alternative or positive option. Rather than state the negative, turn this phrase into a positive statement that addresses the customer's request. "I need for you to fill out a form and obtain your manager's signature, and then I can assign those rights to your account."

➤ "There is nothing else I can do." — This phrase, and its counterpart "I don't know what else I can tell you," rejects the customer's request and implies you are unwilling to explore other ways to meet the customer's needs. It also undermines your credibility. Remember that there is always something you *can* do. When in doubt, offer to let the customer speak with your manager. Although you do not want to want to engage your manager in every conversation you have, there are times when management involvement is needed to satisfy the customer.

➤ "You need to look this up in online help." — This phrase begs the response "I don't need to do anything!" A good technique is to replace "you" with "Let me" or "Let's." For example, "Let me show you how to look up that information in online help." Although customers may prefer you simply give them the answer, this technique enhances their self-sufficiency while acknowledging their need to get information quickly.

➤ "You set it up wrong." — There is nothing to be gained by pointing out the fact that a customer has made a mistake. Here is another example of where the "Let's" technique can be used. "Let's look at the system parameters and make sure they are set up correctly." If the customer figures out that he made a mistake, offer empathy. Letting the customer know with an encouraging "It happens to the best of us" will go a long way in restoring the customer's confidence.

➤ "We don't support that. You need to call…" — Stating the negative disempowers you and may alienate the customer. Remember that there is always something you can do. A more appropriate response would be "What I can do is give you the telephone number of the group that supports this product." Using this positively stated phrase leaves the customer with the impression that you have helped. And you have! You have directed the customer to the best possible source of help.

➤ "We're swamped. I can't get to that until later." — We are all busy. The fact that you are busy is not the customer's fault nor does the customer really want to hear about it. While it is appropriate to let the customer know that there are other customers who also are waiting for service, the best thing to do when you can't respond to a customer's request immediately is give an *honest* estimate of how long it will take to satisfy her request.

➤ "What's your point?" — A more appropriate way to ask this question would be "Let me make sure I understand" or "Would you explain that again. I'm not sure I understand." Remember that you are the one not getting the point or you wouldn't be asking that question. If you don't understand, ask the customer in a respectful way to clarify what she means.

➤ "Whoa! Slow down!" — You may be tempted to use this phrase when a customer is speaking very quickly. While it is appropriate to let the customer know you are having trouble following the conversation, a more appropriate approach would be to get the customer's attention, for example, call the customer's name if it has been given, and then respectfully ask the customer to slow down. "Mr. Lee, could I ask you to slow down just a bit so that I can be sure I am getting all of your information correctly?"

➤ "You've got to be kidding!" — This is where the golden rule comes into play. How would you feel if a service provider said this to you? There will be times when you are amazed by what a customer says or requests, but you must always be respectful. Consider the customer's request and positively and respectfully let the customer know what you *can* do.

Choose your words carefully when communicating with customers. The wrong words can not only alienate your customer, they can also disempower you and undermine the credibility of your entire company. Practice using phrases that are positive and respectful.

 When you support a global customer community, it is a good idea to know a few words—such as "Hello," "Could you hold please?" and "Thank you"—in each of the primary languages that your customers speak. This way, you can politely place on hold any customers who do not speak English while you obtain translation services.

ANN COOK
AMERICAN ACCENT TRAINING
AUTHOR / DIRECTOR
VALENCIA, CALIFORNIA
HTTP://WWW.AMERICANACCENT.COM

One of the things that analysts may find difficult in a customer support setting is understanding people who have accents. Conversely, customers sometimes have difficulty understanding analysts who have accents. When you add technical jargon to the equation, communication can quickly break down. Ann Cook, author of *American Accent Training*, answers a few questions about accents, particularly as they relate to American English. Ann Cook is the Director of American Accent Training, an international program that teaches people who speak English as a second language how to speak standard American English. She has developed a diagnostic speech analysis that identifies each aspect of a person's accent and pronunciation.

Question: What is an accent?

Answer: An accent is how we deliver a particular language. An accent has three main parts: the speech music or intonation, word connections, and the actual pronunciation of each sound. If you don't have speech music, your speech will sound flat and monotone: "He. Is. In. A. Dark. Room." With intonation, you'll be able to say, "He is in a DARK room" (developing photographs) or "He is in a dark room" (the room is dark). With intonation, you can also indicate how you feel about something. Think of the difference between "I should CALL him" and "I SHOULD call him." In the first case, it is likely that you will pick up the telephone; in the second case, you are indicating some degree of reluctance.

How you run words together, or word connections, is also very important. A sentence that looks like "He is in a meeting room" actually sounds like "heezina meeding room."

Finally, pronunciation is the difference between phrases such as "I like tennis" and "I like Dennis."

Question: How do people get an accent?

Answer: People learn their original accents in infancy. Babies hear the speech rhythms of the people around them and mimic those rhythms, long before they acquire grammar and vocabulary. When they learn a second language in adulthood, they bring those patterns and pronunciations with them, and that results in a "foreign" accent. For instance, in languages other than American English, the R sounds like a D, the T always sounds like a T, and there are only five vowel sounds. In American English, the R is a kind of growly semi-vowel (ARRR), the T is frequently pronounced as a D ("meeting" sounds like "meeding") and American English has fourteen vowel sounds. The result is that when a person who was not born in America says, "Eet eess hoeddeebel," they are trying to say, "It is horrible." In American English, it would come out "Idiz horrabul."

Question: What perceptions do people have about people who have accents?

Answer: To a large extent, it depends on the accent. If a person's accent is very light, people frequently respond positively. If an accent makes communication difficult, however, the response can be extremely negative, to the point of considering the speaker less capable or less intelligent. Americans and Europeans generally understand each other's accents, as they all speak western languages. Asians, on the other hand, tend to have difficulty both speaking and understanding western languages.

Question: Are there any stereotypes associated with people who have accents?

Answer: Quite sadly, people think that someone with nonstandard speech is speaking with an accent on purpose or isn't quite bright enough to talk "right." Many age-old notions about people from other countries arise, in large part, from the fact that foreign-born people don't use intonation the way a native American English speaker does. For example, to a native speaker, the sentence "Ben has a red pen" can be inflected many different ways:

BEN has a red pen (not Sue)
Ben HAS a red pen (he already has it, so don't offer him one)
Ben has a RED pen (not a blue one)
Ben has a red PEN (but no pencils)

A non–native American English speaker will frequently say BEN HAS A RED PEN, so the listener has to try to imagine which interpretation to make. Also, most other languages don't use the words "A" and "THE," so words that are important in American English may be left out. Think about the difference between:

A teacher bought a book (an unspecified teacher bought an unspecified
  book)
The teacher bought a book (a specific teacher bought an unspecified book)
A teacher bought the book (an unspecified teacher bought a specific book)
The teacher bought the book (a specific teacher bought a specific book)

Given all of those possible interpretations, it is easy to see that if a person were to say, "Teacher bought book," the American listener would have to struggle to interpret what the speaker meant.

Question: What techniques can people use to better understand people who have a strong accent?

Answer: To better understand people who have a strong accent:

1. Speak slowly and clearly, but not loudly.
2. Acknowledge and accept that their speech isn't "perfect."
3. Don't sweat the details: try to grasp their main idea, as opposed to trying to understand each and every word they are saying.
4. Don't try to correct them, even if inadvertently (Oh! THE teacher bought THE book).
5. Listen for a key word, no matter how it's pronounced.
6. Don't interrupt. Make notes and go back to the problem point when the person finishes speaking. The calmer you are, the calmer the other person will be.
7. Avoid colloquial, or conversational, speech. Foreign-born speakers are usually more familiar with longer words rather than the short words Americans prefer. For instance, "postpone" would be more familiar to someone who does not speak American English than "put off," and "arrange" would be more familiar than "set up." When you think about English verbs and prepositions, it's mind-boggling. With the word "get" alone, you have "get up," "get over," "get away," "get away with," "get off," "get on," "get through to," and many, many more. These are very difficult for foreign-born speakers.

Question: Is there one most important thing that people can do to better understand people who have an accent?

Answer: It's like learning a new dance — try to catch the rhythm without being judgmental of how it "should" be.

Question: How is interacting over the telephone with a person who has an accent different than interacting face-to-face with that person?

Answer: There is so much more information available face-to-face. You can point to things, hand things back and forth, and use facial expressions and body language to communicate. Over the phone, you are limited to the sound of the other person's voice.

Question: What techniques can people use to reduce their accent?

Answer: To reduce an accent:

1. Focus on the rhythm of an entire phrase instead of word by word.
2. Learn to "hear." Listen to the radio and write down exactly what the person says based on pronunciation, not spelling. For example, the word "water" would be "wahdr," not "wa-ter."
3. Don't worry about sounding fake—Americans don't tend to notice if a foreign-born person speaks with a heavy American accent. They'll just think that your English has improved.
4. Don't sound too perfect—native American English speakers don't talk that way. Let all your words run together. "I'll get it" should sound like "I'll get-dit." This is not slang; it's perfectly standard colloquial American speech.
5. Take a course that is specifically oriented to "accent training" or "accent reduction," rather than grammar or vocabulary based.

Question: Is there one most important thing that people can do to reduce their accent?

Answer: Imitate and learn the American intonation. One way to do that is to listen to and repeat ballads and children's books on tape.

Question: Is there anything else that you think it is important for students to know about accents?

Answer: For a person to have an accent means that they communicate perfectly in a entirely different language—not that they are deficient in their second language, which is English. Also, English is the hardest language in the whole world. It has more synonyms than any other language. Think of the difference between to tap, to rap, to pat, to pet, to stroke, to caress—these are all very similar words for using your hand to touch something, but look how different and specific each one is.

Nonverbal Communication

Nonverbal communication is the exchange of information in a form other than words. Nonverbal communication can say as much as our words and includes qualities such as our facial expressions, our body language, and even our clothing. When communicating with customers over the telephone or by e-mail, these nonverbal qualities have no impact whatsoever. When communicating face-to-face, however, they make up over half of our conversation. This is because people can read meaning into our nonverbal cues. For example, if you wink while telling a story to a friend, he knows that you are kidding or teasing. If you avoid eye contact and tightly fold your arms across your chest when speaking with a customer, she may perceive that you are not listening or that you are rejecting what she is saying. If you dress sloppily or do not practice good grooming, people may perceive your thinking is sloppy as well and may resist your ideas.

To communicate effectively, learn to use your nonverbal vocabulary in the same positive way you use words. Be respectful, be attentive, and "listen" to what the speaker is telling you with his or her nonverbal cues. If a customer steps back when you approach him to discuss a problem, you may be standing too close. Allow the customer to establish a distance that feels comfortable. You can also observe and consider emulating the nonverbal techniques used by someone that you believe is an excellent communicator. Also, be aware of the culture at the company where you work. Companies are increasingly introducing a more casual dress code, but there is such a thing as too casual. A neat appearance and good grooming will always serve you well.

People in the United States are much more casual in terms of how they speak and dress than are people in other countries around the world. When traveling for business, ask people who have been to the country you are visiting, or ask your co-workers who live in that country, for guidance on how to make a good impression.

Tone of Voice

Figure 2-2 illustrated the dramatic difference tone of voice makes when you are interacting with customers face-to-face and even more so over the telephone. A number of factors, including those listed in Figure 2-4, make up your tone of voice.

- Energy
- Rate of speech
- Volume and pitch

Figure 2-4 Factors that influence tone of voice

2

We all have different voices and we can change our voices by controlling the energy, rate of speech, volume, and pitch we use when we speak.

Energy—Enthusiasm is contagious and the energy in your voice often reflects your personality and your attitude. Answering the telephone with a bored "Yeah" will not impress and instill confidence in customers. Facial expression mirrors mood, and mood mirrors facial expression. One technique that works well is to approach all interactions with customers as if they were standing in front of you. In other words, even if you are speaking to a customer over the telephone, put a smile on your face, focus your attention on what the customer is saying, and be as responsive as possible. Don't overdo it, however. False enthusiasm can be just as offensive and distracting as no enthusiasm. Be yourself! And remember, some days it can be tough getting excited by the prospect of handling one problem after another. Stay focused on the fact that you have chosen the field of customer support because you enjoy helping people. Hang inspiring quotes in your office or sit a funny picture on your desk that will help you put a smile back in your voice on even the toughest days.

> *Everyone smiles in the same language.* Author Unknown

To monitor their facial expressions and posture, some analysts place a mirror on their desk at eye level when they are sitting straight. By taking a quick look in the mirror before they answer the telephone, analysts can ensure they have a relaxed and pleasant facial expression. They can put a smile on their face, give the customer (who they pretend to see in the mirror) their full attention, take a deep breath if needed to get focused, and then answer the telephone. Give it a try!

Rate of speech—A normal rate of speech is about 125 words per minute. Speaking too quickly or too slowly can be distracting to customers and affect their ability to listen. A good technique is to determine your normal rate of speech. You can do this by placing a tape recorder next to you while you are engaged in conversation or while you read aloud casually from a book. The trick is to forget about the tape recorder so you get a more accurate reading of the number of words you speak per minute. Once you have determined your normal rate of speech, strive to adapt your pace to the needs of your customer. Factors to consider include your customer's rate of speech and the information you are delivering. For example, if you tend to speak quickly, and a customer is speaking slowly, you may want to slow your speech slightly as well. Or, if you are walking the customer through an important set of instructions, you may want to slow your speech slightly. You may also want to slow down a bit if you are speaking to a customer in his or her second language. On the other hand, if you are asking a routine set of questions or simply validating information, you can pick up the pace *a little.*

Speaking too quickly at any point in a conversation can cause confusion or alienate the customer. This is particularly true when you are wrapping up a call. There is often a temptation to rush through the closing and move on to the next call. Unfortunately, you can undo any good will you have created by hanging up before the customer is satisfied. Take your time and listen to your customers, their needs will help you adapt and adjust your pace.

Volume and pitch—The volume of your voice should always be loud enough that your customer and any of the other people involved in your conversation can hear you. The volume of your voice should not, however, be so loud that it disturbs the people around you.

Help desks can get loud. All analysts must do their best to be courteous and respectful in terms of keeping the volume of their voice at an appropriate level and utilizing speakerphones appropriately. If things get too loud on any given day, don't be afraid to politely signal co-workers that they need to keep it down. Graciously accept and respond to any such signals you receive from co-workers.

Pitch—Refers to the highness or lowness of vocal tone. Generally speaking, high-pitched voices are viewed as weak. We also tend to associate a high-pitched voice with someone who is excited, possibly even in a state of panic or out-of-control. Low-pitched voices are typically viewed as strong and we tend to associate a low-pitched voice with someone who is confident and in control.

Voice pitch is influenced by the way you hold your head and by the way you breathe. For example, if you tend to have a high-pitched voice, practice lowering your head slightly when you speak. If you tend to have an exceptionally low-pitched voice, practice raising your head slightly when you speak. Your posture could also be influencing the quality of your voice. Good posture enables you to project your voice and makes it easier for customers to understand what you are saying. You can improve your posture by making sure you have a good chair that enables you to sit up straight and by making sure your workspace is ergonomically aligned.

Chapter 8, *Minimizing Stress and Avoiding Burnout*, discusses in detail how to set up an ergonomically aligned workspace.

You can also influence the pitch of your voice by learning to take long, slow, deep breaths, especially when you are under pressure. Most people become shallow breathers when they are under pressure. When this happens, your vocal cords tend to tighten, making your voice go up and sound strained. By slowing down your breathing, you lower the pitch of your voice and create a calmer tone.

2

Coupled with the right words, the tone of voice you use can dramatically change the message you communicate to a customer. Consider the differences between the following two phrases:

> Stated using a frustrated tone of voice: "What do you expect me to do about it?"

> Stated using a calm tone of voice after taking a deep breath: "How would you like to see this situation resolved?"

Both questions ask the customer how they would like to see the situation resolved. The first example not only fails to engage the customer, it also fails to have the speaker take responsibility for the customer's satisfaction. The second example encourages a dialogue with the customer and at the same time avoids false promises. By selecting positive words and using a calm tone of voice, you communicate a completely different message—one that is much more empowering to both you and your customer.

Customers recognize and respond to your "words," whether they are spoken or communicated through nonverbal cues or your tone of voice. Practice using each of these techniques to establish rapport with your customers and gain their trust. Understanding the communication style of your customer is another tool you can use to enhance communications.

Identifying and Understanding Customer Communication Styles

Becoming an effective communicator requires that you acknowledge the fact that customers are people . . . and people are different. They have different personalities, different ways of handling change and stress, and different communication styles. To communicate effectively, you must first identify the communication style of your customer. You can then respond, rather than react, to your customer in a way that is meaningful. Figure 2-5 lists some of the most common communication styles you will encounter.

- Aggressive people
- Chatterers
- Complainers
- Know–it–alls
- Passive people

Figure 2-5   Common communication styles

You determine every customer's communication style by listening to the information they provide and to the responses they give when you ask questions. Use the following techniques to determine which communication style your customers exhibit and how to respond to them.

➤ **Aggressive people** — Aggressive people like to be in control. They are usually unwilling to engage in social conversation and want to get to the point immediately. Aggressive people may be quick to inform you that they don't "have time for this." They can become hostile and will often try to bully and intimidate people, or they will make a scene in order to get their way. For example, an aggressive person may challenge you to "Get someone out here right away" or "Put your Supervisor on the phone." When interacting with aggressive people, give them time to tell their story and then jump into the conversation when they pause or ask you a question. You can also try to get their attention and then take control of the conversation. For example, respectfully call out their name and then state specifically what you *can* do. Always restate the information that aggressive people give you and their opinions of the problem. This technique enables aggressive people to feel that they have been heard.

➤ **Chatterers** — Chatty customers can be fun, but they can also be a challenge when you are busy. The first way to deal with a chatty customer is to avoid encouraging them. For example, resist the temptation to ask a chatty customer how his vacation was. You are asking for a prolonged answer. When a chatty customer asks you a question that lends itself to a prolonged response, reply with a minimum response. For example, if a customer asks if you are busy, you can politely respond "Yes, very. How can I help you?" Another great technique is to take control of the conversation by asking closed-end questions. **Closed-ended** questions prompt short answers such as "yes" and "no." Once you have taken control, you can ask open-ended questions as needed to obtain more information. **Open-ended questions** cannot be answered with a "yes" or "no" response.

> **Closed-ended questions:**
> Have you ever been able to access this system? [Yes/No]
>
> Is there another printer close by that you can use? [Yes/No]
>
> **Open-ended questions:**
> What other applications did you have open when this problem occurred?
>
> When was the last time you were able to use this device?

➤ **Complainers** — Complainers whine and object but cannot always identify reasons why a solution will not work. They cannot or will not take responsibility for problem solving and often deflate the creativity or optimism of

2

others. When interacting with complainers, empathize but do not necessarily sympathize with the customer's complaint. For example, it's okay to acknowledge that computers can be frustrating, but agreeing that they should all be banished from the face of the earth is probably not a good idea. Also, when interacting with complainers, paraphrase their main points and make sure you understand the specific nature of their complaint. Try not to waste time talking about generalities. You can also ask complainers how they would like things to turn out. By empowering them to participate in developing a solution, you enhance their self-sufficiency and increase the likelihood that they will be satisfied with the final outcome.

➤ **Know-it-alls** — Know-it-alls believe they know everything and tend to resist advice or information they receive from others. They may go to great lengths to convince you that they are right. They can be condescending and pompous and in extreme cases take pleasure in making other people feel stupid. When interacting with know-it-alls, suggest alternatives without attacking their opinions. For example, avoid phrases such as "That won't work," which tend to be perceived negatively. Instead, use positive phrases such as "In my experience, this will work." Also, be respectful when asking questions and acknowledge the customers' knowledge. When appropriate, use phrases such as "What if . . ." and "Let's try this." These phrases will engage customers in the problem-solving process without rejecting their perspective.

➤ **Passive people** — Passive people avoid controversy at all costs and they often cannot or will not talk when you need information. They never volunteer opinions or comments and will tend to go along with suggestions from other people whether or not they feel those suggestions are correct. When interacting with passive people, ask open-ended questions in an effort to encourage a prolonged response rather than a "yes" or "no" response. Also, do not feel you have to fill the silence when waiting for a passive person to respond. If you have posed a question, wait for them to answer. Resist the temptation to jump in and put words in their mouth. Listen responsively when passive people are talking. If they perceive you are not listening, they may resume their silence.

Although these are the most common communication styles, they represent only a handful of the different kinds of people that you will encounter during your career in the support industry. It is also important to remember that people can use different communication styles depending on the situation they are facing or the response that they are receiving. For example, a customer who is getting pressure from his boss may tend to be much more aggressive than he normally would when he is experiencing a problem. Or, a customer who perceives that you have been rude may suddenly become very passive and unresponsive. The more carefully you listen and strive to understand the different ways that people communicate, the more effective a communicator you will become.

Speaking the Listener's Language

It may not have occurred to you before, but you and your customers are bilingual. You may not speak French or Spanish in addition to English, but you *do* speak Business and Technology. Customers tend to speak Business. Analysts tend to speak Technology. Table 2-2 lists some examples of how customers and analysts speak different languages.

Table 2-2 Sample translations between business and technology languages

Customers say	Analysts hear
I can't log on.	The system is down.
I can't print.	The printer is down.
Analysts say	**Customers ask**
FPS1 (File and Print Server #1) is down.	Why can't I print?
The mainframe will be unavailable this weekend.	Does this affect Payroll?

To keep communications on track, and to avoid alienating your customers, avoid jargon and acronyms that they may not understand, or worse, may think they understand but actually do not. Recall that jargon is the specialized or technical language used by a trade or profession, in this case, the computer industry. An **acronym** is a word formed from the initials of a name, such as TSC for Technology Support Center. When customers do use jargon or an acronym, ask clarifying questions in an effort to avoid making an invalid assumption that they fully understand what they are saying. We all know it is possible for two people to have a conversation, walk away thinking they agree, only to find out later that they did not communicate. The excessive use of jargon and acronyms increases the likelihood that this will occur.

Remember that most people consider technology a tool. They typically are using it to *do* something, not just for the sake of it. The best way to serve your customers is to understand their business and learn to speak its language. You can then translate that language into your language, the language of technology.

CHAPTER SUMMARY

- Listening is the most important skill for a support person. Active listening involves participating in a conversation by asking questions, responding to the speaker, and verifying understanding. Good listening requires discipline and begins with a willingness to fully comprehend and retain everything that customers are saying both in terms of *what* they are saying and *how* they are saying it. Listening brings many benefits and is a skill that you can use and apply daily in all areas of your life.

■ Communication is the exchange of information. It requires skills such as listening, speaking, and writing. It also requires the desire to convey information in a meaningful and respectful way. What you say—the words you choose to use—greatly influences the response you receive from customers. How you say it—the nonverbal ways you communicate and your tone of voice—can say as much as your words because people can read meaning into your nonverbal cues. You can determine and influence your customers' response by listening and by learning to speak their language.

KEY TERMS

acronym — A word formed from the initials of a name.

active listening — Listening that involves participating in a conversation and giving the speaker a sense of confidence that he or she is being heard.

closed-ended questions — Questions that prompt short answers, such as "yes" and "no."

communication — The exchange of thoughts, messages, and information.

jargon — The specialized or technical language used by a trade or profession.

listening — To pay attention; make an effort to hear something.

nonverbal communication — The exchange of information in a form other than words.

open-ended questions — Questions that cannot be answered with a "yes" or "no" response.

paraphrase — Restating the information given by a customer using slightly different words in an effort to verify you understand.

passive listening — Listening that involves simply taking in information and shows little regard for the speaker.

pitch — The highness or lowness of vocal tone.

speakerphone — A telephone that contains both a loudspeaker and a microphone.

verbal communication — The exchange of information using words.

REVIEW QUESTIONS

1. What is the most important skill a support person must possess?

2. What is a basic human need?

3. You have to _____ to listen.

4. Why is active listening important?

5. What is active listening?

6. What is passive listening?

7. How can analysts use checklists?

8. What are tactful questions?

9. What can you learn about a customer by listening to how the customer uses jargon?

10. When is it inappropriate to ask questions?

11. What are two ways to let a customer know you are listening when you are interacting face-to-face?

12. What is a verbal nod of the head? Provide two examples.

13. How can you obtain the information you need to solve a problem?

14. What are three cues that a customer may give off when confused or unsure?

15. What is paraphrasing?

16. What two things should you listen for when interacting with customers?

17. Why is it important to acknowledge a customer's emotion?

18. What must you do if a customer indicates he or she does not perceive you are listening?

19. List six benefits of active listening.

20. What percentage of our listening capacity do we normally use?

21. List the six distractions that prevent good listening.

22. What should you do if you are speaking to a customer and hear one of your co-workers discussing a similar problem?

23. What are three risks you run when you jump ahead?

24. What information should you capture about a customer's problem or request?

25. What can silence tell you when you are interacting with a customer over the telephone?

26. What factors influence customer perception in terms of what people say?

27. What factors influence customer perception in terms of how people say it?

28. What is a good substitute for "forbidden phrases?"

29. What are three nonverbal ways that people communicate?

30. Name the three factors that influence your tone of voice.

31. What is a normal rate of speech?

32. What three factors influence your voice pitch?

33. How can you lower the pitch of your voice?

34. How can you determine the communication style of your customer?

35. What is an open-ended question?

36. Which language do you need to speak? Business or technology?

HANDS-ON PROJECTS

Project 2-1

Assess your listening skills. Table 2-1 compares the characteristics of active and passive listening. Review these characteristics and identify the active listening characteristics that you possess. Discuss these characteristics with at least three of your friends and family members. Ask them to provide feedback in terms of what kind of listener you are. Review your list, consider the feedback provided by your friends and family members, and then prepare a list of ways you can become a more active listener.

Project 2-2

Discuss the pitfalls of passive listening. Assemble a team of at least three of your classmates. Discuss each of the characteristics of passive listening. Discuss the ramifications of these characteristics in terms of meeting customer needs. Write a brief summary of your conclusions and then discuss them with the class.

Project 2-3

Pay attention when you are the customer. Over the course of a week or two, pay close attention when you are the customer. Note any situations wherein you experienced emotion, such as confusion, frustration, or anger, as a result of a customer service encounter. Keep a list of each situation that occurs. For each situation, answer the following questions:

- How did the service provider treat you?
- Did the service provider acknowledge your emotion?
- How did that make you feel?

Additionally, write a brief paragraph describing the conclusions you can draw from your experiences.

Project 2-4

Avoid distractions. Review the list of distractions that prevent good listening. Select two distractions that you can honestly say have influenced you in the past or continue to affect you in your current job, hobby, or home life. Prepare a list of three things you can do to minimize the impact of each distraction.

Project 2-5

Collect and rewrite forbidden phrases. During the next week, pay close attention to the service you receive (*see* Project 2-3) and keep a list of any "forbidden phrases" that you hear. Refer to Figure 2-3 for a sample list of forbidden phrases. For each phrase, state a more positive, respectful way of delivering the message. Discuss your list with your classmates and have them critique your restatements.

Project 2-6

Determine your rate of speech. Place a tape recorder next to you while you converse or read aloud casually from a book. If you don't have a tape recorder, simply read aloud casually from a book. Document the number of words you speak per minute. Is your rate of speech faster or slower than the average rate of 125 words per minute? Prepare a list of situations when you may want to adjust your rate of speech.

Project 2-7

Assess the effectiveness of nonverbal communication. Over the course of a day, take note of the various nonverbal ways that people communicate. Write a paragraph describing two or three nonverbal cues that you found to be particularly effective. Conversely, write a paragraph describing two or three nonverbal cues that you found to be particularly ineffective or offensive. Write a final paragraph describing any conclusions you can draw from your observations.

Project 2-8

Determine the pitch of your voice. Record your voice and replay the recording, listening for the pitch of your voice. If you do not have a tape recorder, leave a voice mail message somewhere that you can play it back. Do you have an exceptionally low- or high-pitched voice? Prepare a brief list of ways that you can adjust the pitch of your voice to project confidence and strength. Practice changing the pitch of your voice. Record your voice again and replay the recording. Have you improved the pitch of your voice? Consider asking a classmate to listen to your recording and provide feedback.

Case Projects

1. **Asking Open-Ended and Closed-Ended Questions**

   Your boss has asked you to develop a problem-solving checklist that can be used to diagnose printer problems. She has asked you to "keep it simple" and list only a half a dozen questions. Prepare a list of three open-ended and three closed-end questions that can be used to determine why a customer may be having trouble printing a report.

2. **Keeping It Positive**

   You are the team leader for a large internal help desk. Your boss indicated that he was recently walking through the help desk and overheard an analyst ask a customer, using an incredulous tone of voice, "You want it by when?" He has asked you to provide the analyst with some coaching. Speak with the analyst (choose a classmate) and help the analyst determine a more positive, respectful way to respond to a customer's seemingly unreasonable request.

3. **The Business of Listening**

   This exercise illustrates how to be an effective communicator and a good listener.

   a. Select volunteers who are willing to read out loud to the class.

   b. Students who are not reading close their books and prepare to listen.

   c. Each volunteer reads from an article in one-minute sequences.

   d. As a class, discuss how effectively the volunteer communicated, and how well the students listened. For example:

      - Was the volunteer's tone of voice energetic?

      - How was the volunteer's rate of speech? Fast? Slow?

      - Did the volunteer read as fast or slow as the class perceived?

      - How was the volunteer's volume?

      - How was the volunteer's pitch?

- Did any factors influence the students' ability to be good listeners? If so, what factors?
- What were the students listening for?

As a class, discuss the main points of this article.

4. **One-Way Communication**

This exercise illustrates how analysts and customers benefit when they can ask questions and receive responses. In other words they engage in two-way conversation as opposed to one-way communication, which does not allow the exchange of questions and answers.

a. Select one volunteer to describe a diagram to the class.

b. Other students place a clean sheet of paper in front of them and prepare to listen. Students are *not* allowed to ask questions or communicate in any way with the volunteer. Students must remain silent throughout this entire exercise.

c. The volunteer describes the diagram to the class. The volunteer must use only words to describe the diagram. The volunteer cannot use any nonverbal techniques to communicate, such as facial expressions, hand movements, or body movements. The volunteer cannot ask the students if they understand the information that is being communicated.

d. Students draw the diagram the volunteer is describing on their clean sheet of paper. Remember, students cannot ask clarifying or follow-up questions.

e. Once the volunteer has finished describing the diagram to the class, reveal the diagram. Compare the students' drawings to the original diagram.

f. As a class, discuss how effectively the volunteer communicated, and how well the students listened. For example:

- How explicitly did the volunteer describe the diagram?
- Did the volunteer use any jargon that the class did not understand?
- Did the volunteer go too fast or too slow?
- Did any students become confused or frustrated and just quit listening? Why?
- Why was the one-way communication more difficult to follow?
- If the students had been allowed to speak, what questions would they have asked the volunteer?

As a class, discuss the benefits of being able to engage in two-way conversation. Also discuss ways to become better listeners and communicators.

CHAPTER THREE

WINNING TELEPHONE SKILLS

After reading this chapter and completing the exercises you will be able to:

➤ Understand the power of the telephone

➤ Handle calls professionally from the moment you answer the telephone to the close of the call

➤ Avoid the most common telephone mistakes

➤ Use proven techniques to place customers on hold and transfer calls in a positive, professional way

➤ Use a variety of techniques to continuously improve your telephone skills

➤ Consistently convey a positive, caring attitude

For many help desks, the telephone is the primary way that customers obtain service. According to a survey conducted by the Help Desk Institute, 73 percent of its membership indicated that customers request services via the telephone versus 12 percent whose customers use e-mail, and 1 percent whose customers use the Internet (*Help Desk and Customer Support Practices Report*, 1998, p.10). Although e-mail and Internet support services are expected to increase considerably in the coming years, the telephone will always play a role in customer service. Professional telephone skills help to ensure that the help desk handles customer requests in a prompt, courteous, and consistent manner. Consistency is particularly important because it builds trust between the analyst and customer, and it teaches customers what they can expect when they call so they know how to prepare.

To communicate effectively with customers over the telephone, you must understand how to handle calls professionally and how to avoid the most common call handling mistakes. You must also learn to let your caring attitude and personality shine through and use your telephone skills to send a positive, professional message to your customers. How you answer the telephone and handle telephone calls greatly influences how customers feel about your entire company.

CREATING A POSITIVE TELEPHONE IMAGE

Two characteristics of excellent customer support discussed earlier—responsiveness and a caring attitude—are fundamental to a positive telephone image. How long it takes analysts to answer the telephone and the energy and enthusiasm they convey can greatly influence a customer's perception of the analysts and their entire company. Although conducting business over the telephone can be frustrating and impersonal for both analysts and customers, when handled properly, the telephone can be an efficient, effective way to deliver support.

Understanding the Power of the Telephone

The telephone is one of the most common ways that businesses and customers communicate today. In the United States alone, nearly 10 percent of the workforce has a job that involves daily telephone contact with customers and vendors. At a help desk, analysts may handle "incoming" calls, such as calls from customers, or they may handle "outgoing" calls, such as follow-up calls to customers or calls to vendors. Telephone technology automates and facilitates many of these activities. The most common telephone technologies are listed in Figure 3-1.

- Voicemail
- Fax
- Fax-on-demand
- Automatic call distributor
- Voice response unit

Figure 3-1   Common telephone technologies

Help desks use telephone technologies that range from simple voicemail boxes to highly complex, automated systems. Which telephone technologies a help desk selects are determined by a number of factors, such as the help desk's size, the company's goals, the nature of the business it is in, and customer expectations. For example, smaller help desks may opt to use a simple set of telephone technologies, such as voicemail and fax. Larger help desks and those in high-technology industries tend to use more sophisticated technology, such as automated call distributors and voice response units. The technology a help desk uses affects how analysts receive their work and how their performance is measured.

VoiceMail

Voicemail is an automated form of taking messages from callers when no one is available to take their calls. According to a survey conducted by the Help Desk Institute, 82 percent of its members use voicemail. For customers to view voicemail positively, they must be given an idea of when their call will be returned and then they must receive the return call within the promised timeframe (*Help Desk and Customer Support and Practices Report*, 1998, p. 64). The best companies diligently manage voicemail messages and promptly return all customer calls, even if only to let the customer know that (1) the call was received, (2) it has been logged in the company's call tracking or problem management system, and (3) it is being handled. Analysts may also contact customers who have left a voicemail message to verify the accuracy of the customers' information or to gather additional information. Voicemail requests are typically logged in the help desk's call tracking or problem management system in the same way as a telephone call.

Most call tracking or problem management systems automatically assign a "ticket" number or unique identifier to logged customer requests. An excellent practice is to provide customers with that number as assurance that their request will not be lost or forgotten. Also, inform customers that they can reference the ticket number when calling to check the status of a problem or request.

The term "ticket" is a throwback to the days when customer requests were recorded on paper forms or tickets. Today, of course, customer problems and requests are logged electronically, but the term "ticket" is still widely used. Tickets may also be called records, cases, incidents, and logs.

Fax

A **fax** sends or receives printed matter or computer images electronically. Some companies allow their customers to fill out forms or write letters requesting service and then fax the form or letter to the help desk. Occasionally, a help desk analyst may ask a customer to fax information, such as a report that has an error message, to the help desk so that the analyst can see the error and better diagnose the problem. Faxed requests are typically logged in the help desk's call tracking or problem management system in the same way as a telephone call.

Fax-on-demand

With **fax-on-demand**, customers use their touch-tone telephone to request that answers to FAQs, procedures, forms, or sales literature be delivered to the fax machine at the number provided by the customer. Help desks encourage analysts, when appropriate, to inform customers that this type of system is available. Analysts are then free to work on more complex issues, and customers can quickly receive the desired information at their convenience, even if it is after hours and the help desk is closed.

Increasingly, help desks are making available the forms that customers can complete and submit electronically through the help desk's Web site or by e-mail. The information captured using these electronic forms typically corresponds to the problem entry screen of the company's call tracking or problem management system. Once the electronic form has been completed, the information is automatically logged in the call tracking or problem management system. Most companies also have paper forms that can be used as a backup if the system goes down.

Automatic Call Distributor

An **automatic call distributor (ACD)** answers a call and routes, or distributes, it to the next available analyst. If all analysts are busy, the ACD places the call in a **queue**, or line, and plays a recorded message, such as "We're sorry, all of our service representatives are currently assisting other customers; your call will be answered in the order it has been received." Some companies let customers choose between waiting in the queue or leaving a voicemail message. The automatic call distributor determines what calls an analyst receives and how quickly the analyst receives those calls. This technology is very common in large help desks that handle a high volume of calls and is becoming more common in smaller help desks that are experiencing a growing call volume.

The automatic call distributor has become a "must have" technology for many support organizations. This is because ACDs provide a wealth of statistical information that the help desk can use to measure individual and team performance. Also, a recent advance in ACD technology enables companies with newer systems to use this tool to queue and manage e-mail, voicemail, fax, and Internet inquiries along with traditional telephone calls. This feature is very attractive to companies because it enables them to use a single tool to produce statistics about their workload.

Voice Response Unit

A **voice response unit (VRU),** which may also be called an interactive voice response unit (IVRU), integrates with another technology, such as a database or a network management system, to obtain information or to perform a function. A VRU obtains information by having callers use the keys on their touch-tone telephone, or, when speech recognition is available, speak their input into the telephone. For example, a VRU can collect a unique identifier, such as a customer's employee ID or Personal Identification Number (PIN), and then use it to verify that the customer is entitled to service. A VRU can prompt customers to specify the nature of their inquiry or the type of product they are using and then route the call to an analyst skilled in that product. Some companies also use a VRU to automate routine tasks, such as changing a password or checking the status of an order. Other companies use a VRU to provide access to a reduced set of help desk services during non-business hours. For example, after normal business hours a VRU can enable a customer to hear system status information, leave a voicemail message, or page an analyst if the customer is experiencing a critical problem.

When poorly implemented or when used improperly, telephone technology can lead to customer frustration and be perceived negatively. When customers mistrust or dislike technology, it affects how they interact with help desk analysts and how analysts receive their work. For example:

➤ Some companies fail to respond to voicemail and fax messages in a timely fashion. As a result, customers may mistrust that technology and choose to wait in the queue instead. This means that help desk analysts are required to be on the telephone for extended periods of time.

➤ Some companies are not staffed properly, causing customers to spend an extended time waiting in the queue. When customers finally reach an analyst, they may be more upset at having to wait than they were about the problem they were originally calling to report.

➤ Some companies offer long VRU menus with a number of confusing options. Because there may not be any way to reach a human being who can help, customers select the option they *think* most closely matches their need. As a result, help desk analysts occasionally receive calls from disgruntled customers or calls that they are not qualified to handle because a customer inadvertently selected the wrong option or was unsure of which option to select.

➤ Some companies fail to provide customers with the ability to leave a message or reach a human being. As a result, customers are forced to either wait in a queue, hang up and call back later, or seek an alternate form of support.

These negative effects are a result of telephone technology that has been poorly implemented. By listening to customers and help desk analysts and implementing the technology in a way that both perceive is useful and beneficial, companies can minimize these negative effects.

Telephone technology is not a substitute for help desk analysts. Implemented correctly, it is a powerful communication tool that can enhance the services a help desk offers and benefit help desk analysts. For example, tools such as voicemail and fax offer flexibility to customers and time away from the telephone to analysts. Automatic call distributors can broadcast messages at the beginning of the call that inform customers about, for example, a virus that is affecting the network, thus reducing the number of calls that analysts must handle. Automatic call distributors can also use caller ID data or automatic number identification data to provide the analyst with the name of a caller. **Caller identification (caller ID)** is a service provided by your *local* telephone company that tells you the telephone number of the person calling.

Automatic number identification (ANI) is a service provided by your *long distance* service provider that tells you the telephone number of the person calling. ACDs can also use the caller's telephone number or information collected from the caller through automated prompts to route the call to the analyst best suited to handle the customer's request. As a result, analysts receive only the calls they can handle, which reduces their stress.

Increasingly, companies are using computer telephony integration to further enhance the services offered via the telephone. **Computer telephony integration (CTI)** links telephone technology with computing technology to exchange information and increase productivity. Companies use CTI at the help desk to perform functions such as screen pops and simultaneous screen transfers. CTI can also facilitate fax server transmissions and outgoing calls because people can send faxes or dial an outgoing call right from their computer.

A **screen pop** is when information about the caller appears, or "pops" up, on an analyst's monitor based on caller information captured by the telephone system and passed to a computer system. For example, the telephone system can determine the caller's telephone number and the computer system can look up the number in the company's customer database to find additional information, such as the caller's name and address. The computer can add this information to the telephone number and create a new ticket that pops up on the screen of the analyst taking the call. A history of the caller's previous problems and requests can also pop up on the screen, which the analyst can then use to diagnose the customer's problem or provide a status update. A screen pop reduces the amount of data that an analyst must gather to create a ticket and enables the analyst to quickly verify the customer's information and begin determining the customer's need. A screen pop also ensures that the data collected is accurate and complete because much of the information is entered automatically, rather than by an analyst.

When working in a help desk, you must understand the telephone technology that is available and strive to use it properly. Regardless of the technology that is available, there are proven techniques that can facilitate faster and smoother telephone transactions. These techniques enable you to present a positive image to customers and leave them feeling confident that their call has been handled professionally.

Handling Calls Professionally from Start to Finish

Jan Carlzon, president and CEO of Scandinavian Airlines (SAS) refers to service encounters as "Moments of Truth" for a company (*Moments of Truth*, 1989). This means that to be excellent, customer service providers must view each and every customer encounter as critical to the success of the company.

This is particularly true when interacting with customers over the telephone. Over the telephone, customers cannot see an analyst's body language to know that the analyst is ready to assist them or is listening. They cannot see that the analyst is using a tool to determine an answer to their question. All they have to go on is *what* the analyst says and *how* the analyst says it. Figure 3-2 lists some of the most common "Moments of Truth" that occur in the course of a call to a help desk.

3

- Answering the telephone
- Handling calls about unsupported products or services
- Taking a message
- Closing the call

Figure 3-2   "Moments of Truth" during telephone calls

Each of these moments contributes considerably to how customers perceive an analyst and the entire company. The use of a **script**, or standard set of text and behaviors, is a common help desk practice that is particularly useful when providing technical support. Using scripts and turning them into a habit enables you to focus your energy on solving problems and handling unique situations. Analysts may use scripts when they need to find a positive way to say something they do not feel comfortable saying, such as "No" to a customer. Scripts also enable customers to perceive that help desks deliver services consistently. By learning and applying the following proven techniques, you can feel confident that you are providing the best service possible, regardless of the situation.

> *Customer service should flow smoothly, almost effortlessly. Everything about the business is touched and nourished by it. It's not a department, it's an attitude.* Author Unknown

Answering the Telephone
How you answer the telephone sets the tone for the entire conversation. Grunting your last name into the telephone, a common practice followed by some technicians, hardly amounts to good telephone etiquette. When answering the telephone, pick up the telephone promptly, but with composure. Customers like timely service but they also like working with someone who is composed and in control. Put a smile on your face and, if you have one, glance in a mirror to ensure you appear willing and ready to assist the customer.

Remember that your smile, energy, and enthusiasm are communicated to the customer through your tone of voice. Take a deep breath so the customer perceives you are relaxed and in control.

Most companies have a guideline or goal that reflects how quickly the telephone should be answered. For example, most companies strive to answer the telephone within three rings. Companies that have sophisticated telephone technology that places customers in a queue if an analyst is not available may strive to answer the telephone within a goal time, such as twenty seconds.

Answer the telephone using your company's standard script. This ensures that customers are greeted in the same, consistent way. Many companies use the following approach:

1. **Announce the name of your company or department.** This lets customers know they have reached the right place. Some companies place a greeting such as "Hello" or "Good Morning" in front of the department name. This is because customers very often do not hear the first word or two that is stated and so the first thing they do hear is the department or company name. Be careful when using greetings such as "Good Morning" and "Good Afternoon." If you state the time of day incorrectly or if the customer is in a different time zone, the customer may perceive that you are inattentive or insensitive. The best practice is to keep it simple.

A **best practice** is the current best knowledge about how to deliver a service. Companies identify and implement best practices in an effort to enhance the performance of their employees and improve the quality of their service to customers.

> *Quality is never an accident; it is always the result of high intention, intelligent direction, and skillful execution. It represents the wise choice of many alternatives.* Will A. Foster

2. **Give the caller your name.** Say your name slowly, so it can be understood. Providing your name is a simple courtesy and it lets customers know that you are taking ownership of their problem or request. Your company's policy will dictate whether you provide your first name or your title and surname.

3. **Ask the first question.** By asking the first question, you take control of the call and begin gathering needed information. Your company's policy and the technology you use will determine the question you ask. For example, some help desks must determine if customers are entitled to service before they begin handling a call. In this case, you may ask customers

for a Customer ID or a product serial number. You can then use their response to look up information in the company's call tracking or problem management system. Some help desks simply ask customers how they can help. Resist the temptation to ask personal questions or questions that can veer the call off track. This is a common mistake that analysts make when they know customers personally or have established a high degree of rapport. Greeting a customer with a hardy "Hey, Jan, how was your vacation?" will elongate the call and may offend a customer who is experiencing a severe problem and needs immediate help. The best practice is take care of business first and keep personal conversation to a minimum.

The following are a few examples of standard help desk greetings.

> "Help Desk, this is Carmen. How may I help you?"
> "Help Desk, this is Sue. May I have your name please?"
> "Hello, Options Unlimited, this is Leon. May I have your Customer ID?"

Remember to listen carefully to how customers provide their name. If a customer uses a title, such as Professor Brown, Dr. Jones, or Ms. Smith, address the customer using that title until you are given permission to use a first name or nickname.

After greeting the customer, *actively* listen to the customer's request. When asking the customer for the information you need to log the request, ask every customer for the same information *in the same order every time*. For example, if you must determine a customer's name, location, and Employee ID in order to log the request, ask for that information in the same order every time. Over time, customers learn what information they need to provide when they call. Customers can then be prepared and often begin to volunteer the information before being asked. As a result, you will be able to quickly and easily log the customer's request.

If you speak with a customer regularly and know, for example, his address or telephone number, a good practice is to verify the information rather than skipping over that step and assuming that what you have is correct. For example, "Julian, do you still live at 123 Main Street?" You want to verify the information because the customer may have moved or some information may have changed. This also ensures that the customer knows the call is being logged and manages the customer's expectation of how calls are handled no matter who answers the call. Remember that you are usually not the only person on the help desk. Although it may seem that you are making it easier for the customer by skipping steps and failing to ask questions, you are actually doing the customer and your co-workers a disservice. A customer who has gotten used to speaking with you may be dissatisfied when your co-worker follows the standard procedure. As a result, the customer may ask to speak with only you in the future. Although this seems like a compliment, it actually is a disservice to the customer because you may not always be available when that customer needs help. The help desk is a team setting; by being consistent you communicate your company's policies and you convey to customers that anyone on the help desk can assist them.

Handling Calls about Unsupported Products or Services

Few companies are in a position to be "all things to all people." This means that few companies can support every product or service their customers may conceivably use. The costs would simply be too high. As a result, many companies define a list of supported products and services. In an internal help desk setting, the help desk supports those products that are most commonly used by the company's employees and those products that most directly contribute to the company's goals. In an external help desk setting, the supported products and services are limited to those developed or sold by the company. Most external help desks do not support products and services that are developed or sold by another company unless they are being compensated to do so. The help desk receives training, documentation, and procedures related to the products and services it does support. It also typically has a copy of supported software and may have access to a lab environment that contains supported hardware that it can use to replicate and diagnose problems. Thus, the help desk is able to deliver high-quality support.

Help desk analysts often have a hard time referring customers to another group or company when customers need help with unsupported products or are requesting unsupported services. In other words, they have a difficult time saying "No" to customers. This is particularly difficult for help desk analysts who may be familiar with the product the customer is calling about because they supported that product in the past. Analysts want to help. It is important to remember, however, that the number of analysts assigned to the help desk is determined by the help desk's projected workload, which is based on the list of supported products and services. When help desk analysts assist customers with problems related to unsupported products, they are undermining the ability of the entire team to handle work that is within its scope of responsibility. This is why it is the policy of most help desks to simply refer the customer to the correct group or company, rather than contacting that group or company for the customer. Then, help desk resources can be better utilized to assist customers who call about supported products and services. Analysts may also try to help customers only to realize that they lack the ability or authority to handle the problem. This is a disservice to customers because time and effort have been wasted working on the problem, the finding of a solution has been delayed, and the customer may need to start over with another group or company. Assisting a customer with an unsupported product also leads the customer to expect that she can contact the help desk about this product in the future. The customer will become dissatisfied if another analyst refers her to the correct group or company.

Note Referring a customer who needs help with an unsupported product or service to another group or company is different than escalating a problem to a level two support group. Typically, the help desk does not retain ownership of problems relating to unsupported products. This means that the help desk does not follow up to ensure the problem is resolved to the customer's satisfaction. It lets the other group or company assume that responsibility.

Remember that while your help desk may not support some products and systems, there is always something you *can do* for the customer. Many help desks develop scripts that analysts can use to present customers their options.

> "What I can do is provide you with the telephone number of the company that supports that product. They will be able to help you."

> "What I can do is transfer you to the group that supports that product. They will be able to help you."

Sometimes you may not know who supports a product. In that case, let the customer know you will look into the matter and get back to them with an answer.

> "What I can do is research this matter and call you back with the name and telephone number of someone who can help."

While uncommon, a few companies allow an exception to this scenario by establishing a "best-effort" policy. A **best-effort** policy means you do your best to assist the customer within a predefined set of boundaries, such as a time limit. For example, you may try to assist the customer, but if you cannot resolve the problem within fifteen minutes, you refer the customer to the correct group or company. This practice is sometimes found in companies that support PC-based off-the-shelf products. **Off-the-shelf products** are personal computer software products that are developed and distributed commercially. Because these products, particularly Microsoft Windows-based products, function similarly, help desk analysts can sometimes assist customers even though they have not received specialized training on a given product. By setting a time limit, the help desk can assist customers while minimizing wasted effort. A good practice is to let the customer know in advance that you are working under a time constraint or that there is a possibility you will have to refer them to another group or to a vendor.

> "This product is supported by Way Cool, Inc., but what I can do is work with you for fifteen minutes to see if we can resolve the problem. If we can't, I can give you Way Cool's telephone number and they will be able to assist you. Would you like to continue working on the problem or would you like to contact Way Cool?"

If your company does not have a policy of giving "best-effort" support, or if you feel you do not have the ability or authority to resolve a customer's problem or request, the best practice is to quickly refer the customer to the correct group or company. Even though it may seem like you are not supporting the customer when you refer them to another group or company, you are actually helping them obtain assistance from the people who are best suited to support the products or services in question. You are also contributing to the goals of your team by resisting the temptation to devote time and effort to support services that are outside the scope of your mission.

Taking a Message

There may be times when a customer calls the help desk and asks to speak with a specific analyst. If that analyst is unavailable, let the customer know that and ask who is calling. Then, in an effort to ensure that the customer receives service as quickly as possible, ask the customer if you can do anything to help.

Inform the customer of the analyst's availability *before* asking for the customer's name. If you state that the analyst is unavailable after asking for a name, the customer may perceive that the analyst is available but avoiding his or her call.

When communicating to a customer the fact that an analyst is not available, explain the analyst's absence in a positive way. Also resist the temptation to give out too much information. For example, rather than informing the customer that the analyst is meeting with a supervisor, simply say that he stepped away for a couple of minutes or that the analyst is currently not available. Avoid saying things the customer may perceive negatively, such as "I don't know where he went" or "She hasn't shown up yet today."

In the best help desks, any analyst can assist a customer even if that analyst did not handle the customer's problem or initial request. For example, if the customer is inquiring about the status of an outstanding problem, you can look up the ticket in the call tracking system and give the customer a current status. If the customer is calling to provide information, you can log that information in the ticket. If the call is personal, concerns a matter that requires a particular analyst, such as a special project, or if there is nothing you can do to assist the customer, offer to take a message or transfer the customer to the analyst's voicemail box.

When transferring a caller to a voicemail box, be careful to dial correctly so that the call is not disconnected during the transfer.

When taking a message, write down all of the important information. For example, obtain the caller's name, telephone number, the best time for the analyst to return the call, and any message the caller chooses to leave.

> "Joyce has stepped away from her desk. May I ask who is calling? (Get caller's name.) Mr. Brown, Joyce should be back in ten minutes. In the meantime, is there anything that I can help you with? (If not...) I can take a message for you or I can transfer you to Joyce's voicemail box. Which would you prefer? (If a message is preferred, record all important information. Read it back to the customer.) Okay, Mr. Brown, I have written that you would like Joyce to call you at 555-1234 before the end of the day about your printer problem. Is there anything else that I can help you with today? (If not...) Thank you for calling, Mr. Brown. Feel free to call anytime."

Read the information back to the caller and verify that you have gotten everything correct. Place the message where the analyst will see it upon his or her return. You may also want to relay the message to the analyst via voicemail or e-mail on behalf of the customer. If the message is urgent and the technology is available, you may want to page the analyst or contact the analyst by cellular telephone.

Closing the Call

There is always something to do in technical support and a help desk can be a particularly busy place. Because of this, there is often a temptation to rush the closing of a call in an effort to take the next call or move on to the next problem. Trust and customer confidence comes, however, by taking a little extra time and making sure that the customer is comfortable with the steps you have taken, before you hang up the telephone. Ending the call on a positive note leaves the customer with a lasting, good impression.

> *Be quick but do not hurry.* John Wooden

Figure 3–3 lists some points to consider when ending the call. Each of these items is important and helps close the call effectively and professionally.

Let's look at each of these steps in more detail.

Recap. Take a moment to ensure that you have collected all of the information needed to log the customer's problem or request and any information that may be required by level two service providers. Verify that all of the information you have collected is accurate and complete. Provide the customer a ticket number and let the customer know that she can use that number if she calls in the future for a status update.

✓ Recap the call.

✓ Repeat any action steps that you are going to take.

✓ Be specific about the time frame within which the customer can expect a resolution or a status update.

✓ Share any information that will enable the customer to be more self-sufficient in the future.

✓ Ask the customer if there is anything else that you can do.

✓ Thank the customer for calling.

✓ Let the customer hang up first.

Figure 3-3   Steps for effectively closing a call

Repeat any action steps that you are going to take. Provide the customer an overview of what you are going to do. For example, "I need to try to duplicate this problem in our lab" or "I need to check with our marketing group to verify the correct policy." If the problem must be escalated to level two, let the customer know that. Remember to resist the temptation to impart too much information. The customer usually does not need to know the name of the person who will be working on the problem. You may not even know that yourself. Keep it simple.

> "Dr. Rogers, I'm assigning this ticket to the network administration group. They will be able to make this change to your account."

Be specific about the timeframe within which the customer can expect a resolution or a status update. This is one of the greatest challenges you will face in technical support. On the one hand, customers do not want vague timeframes, such as "We'll get to it when we can" or "We'll get to it as soon as possible." On the other hand, level two support groups are sometimes hesitant to commit to deadlines that they may not be able to meet. This is not a problem you can solve. It is up to your management team to establish Service Level Agreements that clearly define the timeframe within which problems must be resolved. Then you can state these guaranteed times to your customers. Within their Service Level Agreements, most companies establish guidelines for target resolution times that consider the problem severity and the combined efforts of service providers in level one, level two, and level three that may be called upon to resolve the problem. A **target resolution time** is the timeframe within which the support organization is expected to resolve the problem. **Severity** is the category that defines how critical a problem is based on the nature of the failure and the available alternatives or workarounds. The help desk analyst and customer typically work together to determine a problem's severity.

In the absence of Service Level Agreements, you can work closely with your level two support groups to gain an understanding of their workload. Then, even if you can't provide the customer an estimated resolution time, you can let him know where his request stands in the backlog. That is, how many requests the support group must handle before they get to this customer's request. If nothing else, you can offer to call the customer at an agreed upon time with a status update. Another approach is to provide the customer a timeframe within which level two will contact him to schedule a time to work on the problem or request.

> "Someone from the field services group will contact you within the next two hours to schedule a time when they can come out and work on your PC."

Share any information that will enable the customer to be more self-sufficient in the future. While the help desk's role is to support customers, help desk analysts best serve their customers when they enable them to help themselves. When appropriate, let customers know that they can use resources such as online help or the Internet to find answers to frequently asked questions (FAQs) or solutions to common problems. You can also let the customer know that there are alternate ways to request support. For example, the customer may not know that she can use e-mail to submit inquiries or that she can download and electronically submit forms from a Web site. If the customer does not have the time to discuss these options, let the customer know that you will send an e-mail message or fax/mail a brochure that describes alternative ways to obtain support.

Ask the customer if there is anything else that you can do. Analysts are sometimes hesitant to ask if they can do more for a customer because they are afraid the customer will say "yes." This is particularly true in a busy help desk where calls are stacking up in the queue. The only alternative is to have the customer hang up and call back. This is neither practical nor good customer service. Although difficult, don't worry about the next call until you have fully satisfied the current customer. If the customer does have another request, politely ask the customer to wait for a moment while you complete his first ticket. Then handle the next request as a new ticket. If the customer has a problem or request that is beyond the help desk's mission, for example, the customer may ask you to have someone come out and repair the soda machine in the break room near his office, use the techniques discussed in the "Handling Calls About Unsupported Products or Services" section of this chapter to direct the customer to the group or company that can handle his request.

Thank the customer for calling. Remember that whether you are supporting internal customers or external customers, they are indeed customers, and you have a job because they need your help. Always thank your customers for calling, and let them know that they should not hesitate to call if they need help in the future.

Let the customer hang up first. We've all experienced the frustration of getting cut off mid-sentence. This frustration is even greater when we must work our way through a series of menu options or wait in a queue to get back to the service provider. By letting the customer hang up first, you avoid rushing the customer or cutting the customer off. If the customer seems to be waiting for you to hang up, tactfully ask, "Is there anything else?" If there is not, then go ahead and hang up the telephone. As a courtesy to the customer, make sure the line disconnects before you begin talking either to yourself, a co-worker, or another customer.

The following examples demonstrate how to close a call that the analyst has not been able to resolve as well as how to close a call that the analyst has resolved.

> After searching unsuccessfully for an answer. "Liz, I am going to assign this ticket to the database administration group. You can expect this problem to be resolved within two hours. Is there anything else that I can help you with today? (If not...) Thank you for calling the help desk. If you need further help, please call us again."

> After finding the answer and giving it to the caller. "Kevin, did you know that you can find similar information on our Web site? (If the customer did not...) The address of our Web site is www.waycool.com. Other information you'll find includes answers to frequently asked questions and information about our other products. Is there anything else that I can help you with today? (If yes...) Okay, please give me a moment while I save your first request. (Update and save the ticket.) Now, what else can I help you with?"

When possible, log all important information in the ticket before you hang up the telephone or, if necessary, immediately after you hang up the telephone. Use the first couple of moments after you hang up the telephone to update the ticket and, if necessary, escalate the call properly. Again, this can be difficult when there are other calls in the queue or other customers waiting, but this is time well spent and it ensures that the customer receives the best possible service.

A common misperception is that help desk analysts and people whose job consists primarily of handling telephone calls are the only ones that must develop professional telephone skills. Managers and level two service providers, particularly highly specialized technicians, often believe that they do not need telephone skills because it is the help desk's job to handle calls. Not true. On any given day, anyone may receive telephone calls and may need to place a caller on hold or transfer a caller to another person or group. In today's business environment where telephones are a common communication tool, excellent telephone skills are indispensable regardless of your position.

Avoiding the Most Common Telephone Mistakes

Two things that most frustrate customers are being placed on hold for an extended period of time and being transferred repeatedly. Pay attention when you are the customer. How do you feel when someone asks, "Can you hold please?" and then puts you on hold without waiting for a response? How do you feel when you have given a service provider a detailed explanation and they transfer you to someone else who asks, "May I help you?" and you have to begin again. When working in a help desk there will be times where it is appropriate to place a customer on hold or transfer the customer to another service provider. The proven techniques that follow enable you to conduct these transactions in a way that engages your customer and minimizes frustration.

Putting a Customer on Hold

At times it will be necessary to put a customer on hold while you look up information or determine if another service provider is available. You may need to put a customer on hold if another customer is in front of you demanding your attention or if another call is coming in, for example, on the help desk's emergency line. Remember that it takes only a little extra time to put customers on hold in a professional manner that instills confidence. It is also important to let customers decide if they would prefer to have you call back rather than being placed on hold. Figure 3-4 lists some points to remember when placing a caller on hold.

The following example demonstrates how to use all of these points to put a customer on hold.

> "Tim, may I put you on hold for approximately two minutes while I obtain more information? (Wait for an answer.) Okay, I will be back with you in a minute or two. (...forty-five seconds pass.) Thank you for holding. What I have learned is that the next release of that product will be available in two months."

✓ Ask the customer if you can put him or her on hold.

✓ Tell the customer why he or she is put on hold.

✓ Tell the customer approximately how long he or she can expect to be on hold. Be realistic when estimating the time it will take you to complete a task. If you tell the customer it will take you "Just a second," the customer will immediately mistrust your estimate. A good guideline is to never ask a customer to hold if you are going to be longer than three minutes.

✓ Wait for the customer to respond. *This is very important.* If the customer does not want to be placed on hold, ask what he or she would prefer. If a call back is preferred, set a time when it is convenient for the customer and when you know you will indeed be able to call.

✓ When placing a customer on hold, use the Hold button on your telephone. Resist the temptation to simply set your headset or telephone down on your desk. The customer may want to read or think while on hold and may find the background noise distracting. The customer may also hear you asking questions or interacting with other customers or service providers who have come into your workspace and preceive that you are neglecting his or her problem.

✓ When you return, thank the customer for holding. Resist the temptation to say, "I'm sorry to keep you holding." Customers may consider such a comment insincere because if you were really sorry, you would not have kept them on hold in the first place.

Figure 3-4 Steps for putting customers on hold

If you find it is going to take you longer than expected to handle a particular task, return to the customer and give the customer an update on your progress and the option of either continuing to hold or receiving a call back. The important thing is to stay in control and remain sensitive to your customer's needs. If you have one customer on hold for an extended period of time and another customer who is receiving only half of your attention, it is likely that neither customer will be satisfied. The best practice is to focus your energies on one customer at a time.

Knowing When and How to Transfer Calls

There are a number of reasons why you may need to transfer a caller to another person or group. The customer may ask to speak with a particular analyst, she may have a problem or question that requires the help of a subject matter expert, or he may simply have called the wrong number and must be transferred to another department. As listed in Figure 3-5, there are a number of different ways of transferring a caller. The method used will depend on the type of call and the needs of the caller.

> - Hot transfer (conference call)
> - Warm transfer
> - Cold transfer

Figure 3-5   Telephone transfer techniques

A primary consideration of which technique to use when transferring calls is the amount of information you have received or given until the point when you determine a transfer is needed. The following examples demonstrate when and how to use the hot, warm, and cold telephone transfer techniques.

Hot Transfer (Conference Call)

A **hot transfer,** or conference call, occurs when you stay on the line with the customer and the service provider whom you are engaging in the call. A conference call may be appropriate when:

➤ You can continue to contribute to the resolution of the customer's request.

➤ You can benefit from hearing how the problem is resolved by another help desk analyst or by a specialist from another group. For example, the problem being described by the customer has been occurring frequently and you want to learn how to solve it in the future.

➤ Time allows; that is, there is no backlog of incoming calls or work in the queue.

Before you establish a conference call, inform the caller that you would like to engage another service provider and ask if it is okay. *This is very important.* If the customer does not want to stay on the line, ask what she would prefer. If a call back is preferred, set a time that is convenient for the customer. Make sure you clearly communicate to the other service provider the customer's expectation of when she wants to be contacted.

When establishing a conference call, put the customer on hold and place a call to the person whom you want to engage in the call. Briefly explain the problem to the service provider along with how you feel he can contribute to the resolution of the problem. Ask the service provider for his permission to bring the customer on the line.

Use common sense when engaging another service provider. If the problem is critical and requires immediate attention, make sure the service provider knows that. If the problem is not critical, ask the service provider whether this is a good time or whether you could schedule a more convenient time for a conference call. Being considerate is in the best interests of your customer and will also enable you to maintain a good relationship with other service providers.

When permission is granted, bring the customer on the line and introduce the customer and the service provider. As a courtesy to the customer, explain the reason for the conference call and relay to the service provider any information the customer has given you thus far in the call. Include any problem determination steps you and the caller have already tried. Resist the temptation to have the customer repeat everything she has told you as this could leave the customer with the perception that you were not listening. You can, however, engage the customer in the call by asking her to let you know if you restated any information incorrectly. You can also encourage the customer to jump in if she would like to contribute additional information. Let the customer and the service provider know you plan to stay on the line. Stay on the line until the call is completed to the customer's satisfaction. Close the call as you normally would.

 When working in a help desk, you can avoid embarrassment and customer frustration by understanding how to use your company's telephone system to put customers on hold and transfer customer calls. Follow available procedures or, when necessary, request the training you need to feel confident that you will not inadvertently disconnect your customers.

Warm Transfer

A **warm transfer** occurs when you introduce the customer and the service provider to whom you are going to transfer the call but you do not stay on the line. A warm transfer may be appropriate when:

➤ There is no perceived value to be gained or given by staying on the line. For example, you do not feel that you can continue to contribute to the resolution of the customer's request. Or, you do not believe you can benefit from hearing how the problem is resolved by another help desk analyst or by a specialist from another group.

➤ Time does not allow you to stay on the line. For example, there is a backlog of incoming calls in the queue or you need to attend a meeting.

Before you warm transfer a call, inform the caller that you would like to transfer him to another service provider and explain why. For example, the service provider may be a subject matter expert who is best suited to answer the customer's question. Or, the service provider is a security administrator and has the authority to provide the customer with the requested access to a confidential system. Ask the customer for permission to transfer him or her to the service provider. *This is very important.* If the customer does not want to stay on the line, ask what he would prefer. If a call back is preferred, set a time that is convenient for the customer. Make sure you clearly communicate to the other service provider the customer's expectation in terms of when he wants to be contacted.

Your company's policy and the role of the service provider to whom you are transferring the call will determine whether you place the customer on hold first, or simply transfer the call. If there is a possibility that the service provider will either not be available or not be in a position to assist, put the customer on hold and place a call to the service provider to whom you want to transfer the call. Ask the service provider for her permission to bring the customer on the line. When permission is granted, bring the customer on the line. If you know the service provider is available and in a position to assist the customer, simply bring the service provider on the line.

Once you have both parties on the line, introduce the customer and the service provider. As a courtesy to the customer, explain the reason you are transferring the call and relay any information you have been provided thus far in the call. Include any problem determination steps you and the caller have already tried and explain how you think the service provider can assist. As was the case when establishing a conference call, resist the temptation to have the customer repeat everything he has told you. This could leave the customer with the perception that you were not listening. You can, however, engage the customer in the call by asking him to let you know if you restated any information incorrectly. You can also encourage the customer to jump in if he would like to contribute additional information. Let the caller and the service provider know that you will not be staying on the line.

> "Mrs. Higgins, I understand your urgency in this matter. Would you mind if I transferred you to our spreadsheet expert for immediate assistance?" (Wait for answer.) "Great. Let me see if I can get her on the line."

Once you feel confident that you have relayed all important information and both the customer and service provider have what they need to proceed, give the customer and the service provider the ticket number assigned to the customer's request for follow-up purposes. Encourage both the customer and the service provider to let you know if there is anything else that you can do and then hang up.

Cold Transfer

A **cold transfer** occurs when you stay on the line only long enough to ensure that the call has been transferred successfully. A cold transfer is appropriate when:

➤ The customer asked to be transferred.

➤ You *quickly* realize that the caller has dialed the wrong telephone number or that the caller should be transferred to another person or department.

A cold transfer is *not* appropriate when the customer has provided detailed information about the nature of her request. For example, if a customer is upset and begins venting as soon as you pick up the telephone, you want to actively listen and collect as much information as you can. When the customer has provided detailed information, use either the hot or warm transfer technique described above.

When a cold transfer is appropriate, acknowledge the customer's request to be transferred and let her know that you are going to transfer her to the correct department. *This is very important.* If the customer indicates that she does not want to be transferred, ask what she would prefer. If a call back is preferred, set a time that is convenient for the customer. Make sure you clearly communicate to the other service provider when the customer wants to be contacted.

When appropriate, provide the customer with the telephone number of the person or group to whom you are transferring the call so that the customer can reach that person or group directly in the future. Make sure that providing a direct telephone number is an acceptable policy at your company. Some companies prefer not to give out the direct telephone numbers of employees. Rather, customers are encouraged to contact a department, such as the help desk, when they need support.

When transferring the customer to another support organization, make sure you let the customer know if they are going to encounter another wait in a queue. Transfer the call, making sure you dial carefully so the customer is not cut off.

> "Please hold one moment while I transfer you to the Benefits department."

Handling a customer call and placing a customer on hold or transferring a customer to another service provider requires the use of common sense and sensitivity. Pay attention when you are the customer so that you can gain an appreciation of how it feels when these techniques are and are not used appropriately. By applying these techniques appropriately, you can ensure that every customer feels that you have fully respected their time and needs.

FINE-TUNING YOUR TELEPHONE SKILLS

Telephone skills, like any other skills, need to be honed. You can always learn new techniques and you can periodically rekindle your skills by attending a refresher course. New best practices are constantly emerging that you can use to improve your skills. Also, sometimes analysts just need to get back to the basics of excellent service: being responsive; demonstrating a caring attitude; acknowledging the fact that customers are living, breathing human beings who have called because they need your help. This last point is particularly important when interacting with customers over the telephone, a technology that can be viewed as very impersonal. Continuously improving your skills enables you to feel more comfortable and confident as a service provider, and also enables your customers to know that you care and that you sincerely want to help.

CLOSE UP

3

SPEAKERPHONE ETIQUETTE

A **speakerphone** is a telephone that contains both a loudspeaker and a microphone. It allows several people to participate in a call at the same time without the telephone receiver being held. In some help desk settings, the use of speakerphones is discouraged for a number of reasons. First, many people don't feel comfortable talking on a speakerphone because they do not know who else may be listening. Second, the quality of some speakerphones makes it difficult for the customer and the analyst to understand everything that is being said. Last, speakerphones can be disruptive to co-workers and may make it difficult for them to hear other customers. There are times, however, when speakerphones are appropriate. For example, when the team is working together to solve a problem or when the team is holding an informal meeting to exchange new information or a new set of procedures. In these cases, steps can be taken to minimize the noise that the conversation being held via speakerphone generates. The following techniques can be used to minimize the negative effects of using a speakerphone:

➤ If possible, use the speakerphone behind closed doors

➤ Ask all callers for permission before using a speakerphone

➤ Introduce each person that is present

➤ Briefly explain why each person is present

➤ Participants who are speaking for the first time or who are unfamiliar to other callers may want to identify themselves before they speak

Speakerphones enable multiple people, regardless of their location, to work together. They minimize the problems that can occur when information is relayed second hand. Speakerphones also free people to use their hands to take notes, consult reference materials, and so forth. Used properly, speakerphones are an effective communication tool.

> *To give real service, you must add something which cannot be*
> *bought or measured with money, and that is sincerity and integrity.*
> Donald A. Adams

- Self-Study
- Monitoring
- Customer satisfaction surveys

Figure 3-6   Techniques to improve telephone skills

Many of these techniques can be used to improve all of your skills—business, technical, soft, and self-management—not just your telephone skills.

Self-Study

There are literally hundreds of books, videotapes, and audiocassettes available that you can use to improve your telephone skills and your skills in general. When you work at a help desk, take advantage of any training programs that are offered. Bring to the attention of your supervisor or team leader any training possibilities that you think will help. You can also engage in a self-study program by checking out books or tapes from your local library.

Appendix A lists books, magazines, and organizations you can use to obtain self-study training materials and additional information about the support industry in general.

Monitoring

Recall that monitoring is when a supervisor or team leader listens to a live or recorded call, or sits with an analyst, in order to measure the quality of an analyst's performance during the call. Used properly, monitoring is an excellent training technique because analysts receive specific feedback on how they can improve their call handling. Monitoring also promotes the consistent handling of telephone calls and provides employees and supervisors specific guidelines that they can use when measuring performance. Some companies use monitoring only for training purposes. Others use monitoring both as a training tool and as a way of measuring performance.

To be effective, a monitoring program must be implemented carefully and analysts must perceive they are being given the opportunity to be successful. Most companies involve the help desk staff when designing their monitoring program so the staff is comfortable with the program and participates willingly. For example, management and staff may jointly define guidelines for how and when employees will be monitored. They may agree to monitor only recorded calls or to silently monitor live calls five times each month. Other guidelines include agreeing not to monitor partial calls or personal calls and placing a higher **weight**, or importance, on items in an effort to ensure analysts are focusing on the right things. For example, companies may assign a higher weight to delivering the correct solution than they assign to transferring a call correctly.

One of the keys to a successful monitoring program is providing analysts with a checklist that describes the specific criteria that supervisors or team leaders are using to measure the quality of a call. This checklist typically reflects all of the "Moments of Truth" that occur during the course of a telephone call. For example, checklist items may include using the help desk's standard script when answering the telephone or waiting for customers to respond before placing them on hold. Checklist items may also include items such as analysts' tone of voice, posture, use of knowledge resources, and so forth, as all of these items influence analysts' ability to deliver great service. Without a checklist, analysts are unsure what supervisors and team leaders are looking for when they monitor calls, and therefore may perceive the results as subjective.

Used properly, monitoring enables you to put yourself in the customer's shoes and objectively assess the quality of your service from the customer's perspective. An effective monitoring program provides specific feedback that you can use and apply day to day.

Customer Satisfaction Surveys

An increasingly common practice is for help desks to solicit feedback from their customers by conducting customer satisfaction surveys. Recall that customer satisfaction surveys are a series of questions that ask customers to provide their *perception* of the support services they received. The two most common customer satisfaction surveys are event-driven surveys and overall satisfaction surveys. **Event-driven surveys** are customer satisfaction surveys that ask customers for feedback on a single recent service event. **Overall satisfaction surveys** are customer satisfaction surveys that ask customers for feedback about all calls they made to the help desk during a certain time period.

Help desk managers use survey responses to measure the performance of the help desk team and to identify improvement opportunities. Survey responses, particularly responses to event-driven surveys, can also be used to measure individual performance and identify training needs. The feedback that customers provide via event-driven surveys is particularly useful to individual analysts because it represents feedback about a specific event that the analyst handled. Analysts can use this feedback to improve their telephone skills.

If the help desk where you work does not have a monitoring program or it does not conduct customer satisfaction surveys, you can still receive feedback. You can listen actively to your customers when you are providing support. For example, if a customer begins to raise her voice, check your tone of voice to ensure that you are remaining calm and making positive statements. You can place a tape recorder on your desk and record your calls so you can hear how you sound and determine ways to improve. You can also ask a trusted co-worker or your team leader to provide feedback. Ask for feedback not only when you need to improve but when you handle a situation efficiently and effectively as well.

Regardless of the method used to obtain feedback, analysts can use the feedback their customers and co-workers provide to identify their weaknesses and determine ways they can improve. It is important to remember that your recollection of an event and another's perception of an event may represent different perspectives. When working in a help desk, you must follow the policies of your company while being sensitive to the needs of your customers, service providers, and co-workers. If a customer perceives that you were rude or disrespectful, you must accept that and determine a more positive way to communicate in the future. If a service provider perceives that you did not relay all important information before you transferred a call, you must accept that and vow to slow down and be more thorough in the future. By working hard, being consistent, and keeping a positive attitude, you can let your caring attitude, shine through.

LETTING YOUR CARING ATTITUDE SHINE THROUGH

It is difficult to handle problems and enthusiastically answer questions day in and day out. Some days it seems as if you have to drag the facts from customers who want their problems solved NOW! It is even harder to be "up" for each call, but that is what is required if your goal is to be excellent. Providing superior customer support is a habit—a state-of-mind that promotes enthusiasm and passion. You have to work at it every day and you have to take care of yourself in the process. Practice relaxing and surround yourself with positive reminders of your commitment to customer satisfaction.

Chapter 8, *Minimizing Stress and Avoiding Burnout,* explores in detail techniques you can use to maintain your energy and enthusiasm and minimize the stress that may take away from your ability to enjoy working in a help desk setting.

Using scripts is an excellent habit-building technique and ensures consistent "Moments of Truth" when customers call the help desk. Scripts are not meant, however, to make you behave like a robot, never deviating from predefined remarks. Try to avoid rushing through scripts or using a tone of voice that implies tedium or boredom. When appropriate and allowed, change the phrasing of your script slightly to make it sound fresh and enthusiastic. For example, rather than always saying "Feel free to call us if you need help in the future," you can say "Give us a call if there is anything else you need." What you say is important and the words you use must be positive, but *how* you say it is equally as important. Be enthusiastic!

Become familiar with all of the scripts used at the help desk where you work and, when needed, suggest additional scripts.

It is also important to remember that help desks that respond to calls in a *consistent* manner are perceived as more professional than those that do not. When help desk analysts respond to calls in different ways, customers may be uncomfortable during the call handling process, or they may begin to mistrust the responses they receive. When working in a help desk, you must understand your company's policies and resist the temptation to deviate from those policies, even when you perceive that doing so is in your customer's best interests. If you feel a policy needs to be changed, provide your team leader or supervisor with the reasons why you believe a change is needed and suggest reasonable alternatives. Until the policy is changed, be a team player, and support the policies of your company in a positive way that acknowledges the needs of your customers. Remember that there is always something you *can do.*

CHAPTER SUMMARY

- The telephone is one of the most common ways that businesses and customers communicate today. Telephone technologies used by help desks range from simple voicemail boxes and fax machines to highly complex, automated systems, such as automatic call distributors and voice response units. Implemented properly, these technologies benefit both customers and help desk analysts.

- To be excellent, support providers must see each and every customer encounter, or "Moments of Truth," as critical to the success of the organization. "Moments of Truth" that occur in the course of a typical help desk call include answering the call, taking a message, and closing the call. Handling calls about unsupported products is also important and represents an excellent opportunity to demonstrate your CAN DO attitude.

- Two things that frustrate customers most are being placed on hold for an extended period of time and being transferred repeatedly. Placing customers on hold or transferring them to another service provider requires the use of common sense and sensitivity. You can minimize customer frustration by listening to your customers' preferences and carefully managing their expectations.

- Telephone skills, like any other skills, need to be honed. Techniques you can use to fine-tune your skills include self-study, monitoring, and customer satisfaction surveys. You can use each of these techniques to obtain feedback that you then can use to improve your skills. You can also record and listen to your calls or you can ask a trusted co-worker or your team leader for feedback. Ask for feedback about what you do well along with what areas you can improve.

- Providing superior customer support is hard work. You have to work at it every day and you have to develop good habits. Scripts are an excellent habit-building technique and ensure consistency when customers call the help desk. It is also important to take care of yourself, stay relaxed, and let your caring, CAN DO attitude shine through!

KEY TERMS

automatic call distributor (ACD) — A technology that answers a call and routes, or distributes, it to the next available analyst.

automatic number identification (ANI) — A service provided by your *long distance* service provider that tells you the telephone number of the person calling.

best effort — A policy that states analysts do their best to assist a customer within a predefined set of boundaries, such as a time limit.

best practice — The current best knowledge about how to deliver a service.

caller identification (caller ID) — A service provided by your *local* telephone company that tells you the telephone number of the person calling.

cold transfer — A way of transferring a telephone call that occurs when you stay on the line only long enough to ensure that the call has been transferred successfully.

computer telephony integration (CTI) — An interface that links telephone technology with computing technology to exchange information and increase productivity.

B

event-driven surveys — Customer satisfaction surveys that ask customers for feedback on a single recent service event.

fax — technology that sends or receives printed matter or computer images electronically.

fax-on-demand — Technology that enables customers to use their touch-tone telephone to request that answers to FAQs, procedures, forms, or sales literature be delivered to the fax machine at the number provided by the customer.

hot transfer — A way of transferring a telephone call that occurs when you stay on the line with the customer and the service provider whom you are engaging in the call; also known as a conference call.

off-the-shelf products — Personal computer software products that are developed and distributed commercially.

overall satisfaction surveys — Customer satisfaction surveys that ask customers for feedback about all calls they made to the help desk during a certain time period.

queue — A line.

screen pop — A CTI function that enables information about the caller to appear, or "pop" up, on an analyst's monitor based on caller information captured by the telephone system and passed to a computer system.

script — A standard set of text and behaviors.

severity — The category that defines how critical a problem is based on the nature of the failure and the available alternatives or workarounds.

target resolution time — The timeframe within which the support organization is expected to resolve the problem.

voicemail — An automated form of taking messages from callers when no one is available to take their calls.

voice response unit (VRU) — A technology that integrates with another technology, such as a database or a network management system, to obtain information or to perform a function; also called interactive voice response unit (IVRU).

warm transfer — A way of transferring a telephone call that occurs when you introduce the customer and the service provider to whom you are going to transfer the call but you do not stay on the line.

weight — a rating scale of importance.

REVIEW QUESTIONS

1. What do professional telephone skills ensure?

2. Why is important that calls are handled consistently?

3. What two characteristics of excellent customer support are fundamental to a positive telephone image?

4. List four factors that influence the telephone technologies that a help desk uses.

5. What two things must be done for customers to view voicemail positively?

6. What technologies are some companies using in lieu of a fax machine to make forms available?

7. Do you need to log customer requests that are received via voicemail and fax?

8. List four of the capabilities that ACDs provide.

9. What recent advance in ACD technology is enabling companies to use a single tool when producing statistics relating to their workload?

10. How does a VRU obtain information?

11. Describe three of the benefits that help desk analysts receive when telephone technology is implemented properly.

12. What are "Moments of Truth?"

13. How can scripts be used by help desk analysts?

14. What are two techniques you can use *before* you answer the telephone to ensure you are ready?

15. What three pieces of information should you provide or ask when answering the telephone?

16. What is a best practice?

17. What should you do when customers provide their name?

18. Why should you ask customers for the information you need to log calls in the same order every time?

19. When there is more than one person in the help desk, why should you avoid encouraging customers to speak with only you?

3

20. Why are help desks able to deliver high-quality support for supported products and services?

21. Describe four pitfalls of assisting customers with problems relating to unsupported products.

22. What should you do if a customer asks to speak with an analyst that is unavailable?

23. What are four important pieces of information that you should obtain when taking a message?

24. List the seven steps you should follow when closing a call.

25. How long should customers be kept on hold?

26. What is an important point to remember before you put customers on hold?

27. Briefly describe the difference between a hot, warm, and cold transfer.

28. Why should you resist the temptation to have customers repeat everything that they have told you before you hot or warm transfer a call?

29. List two ways you can improve your telephone skills through self-study.

30. What does monitoring promote?

31. What can you learn from customer satisfaction surveys?

32. What three things can you do to obtain feedback if your company does not have a monitoring program or they do not conduct customer satisfaction surveys?

33. How may customers respond when analysts handle calls inconsistently?

34. What do you do when there is nothing you can do?

HANDS-ON PROJECTS

Project 3-1

Track telephone technology usage. For one week, keep a record of every time you encounter telephone technology when conducting personal or work-related business. Jot down the name of the company, the technology that you encountered (if you can tell), and a grade, such as A, B, or C, that reflects how well you perceive the company used the technology and the techniques discussed in this chapter. For example, if you were prompted to leave a voice-mail message, were you given an indication when your call would be returned? Briefly comment on any ways these companies could improve their use of telephone technology. Share the results with your classmates.

Project 3-2

Discuss the pros and cons of VRUs. Assemble a team of at least three of your classmates. Discuss the different ways you use voice response units (VRUs) in the course of going about your day. The indictor that you can use to know that you are using a VRU is having to input information using the keys on your touch-tone telephone or speaking into the telephone. For example, you may use the telephone technology at your bank to determine your current balance or if a check has cleared. Or, you may use telephone technology to register for classes at your school. Develop a list that describes the positive benefits of using this technology and the negative or frustrating experiences that you and your teammates have had. Write a brief summary of your conclusions and share them with the class.

Project 3-3

Answer the telephone with a smile. It has been said that if you do something for twenty-one days, it becomes a habit. For the next twenty-one days, practice putting a smile on your face before you answer the telephone, whether at work or at home. To remind yourself to smile, place a note or mirror by your telephone. Strive to convey energy and enthusiasm in your tone of voice. Share with your classmates any feedback you receive from callers.

Project 3-4

Explain an analyst's absence in a positive way. Review the phrases below and suggest ways the statements can be made more positive. Prepare a list of revised statements along with a brief explanation of your suggested revision.

1. I don't know where Jim is. I'll have him call you when he gets back.

2. I think she has gone to the restroom. Can I have her call you back?

3. He's probably still at lunch.

4. I think Louisa is coming in tomorrow. I'll have her call you if she does.

5. Judy went home early today. Can I have her call you tomorrow?

6. Mr. Sanchez has not come in yet. Would you like to try again in an hour or so?

7. Deborah is really busy right now. Would you like to leave a message?

Project 3-5

Take complete messages. When you are required to take a message for someone, whether at work or at home, collect all of the information discussed in this chapter. Ask the recipient of the message for feedback on the completeness of your message.

Project 3-6

Look for a "thank you." For the next twenty-four hours, note how many service providers and customers thank you for your business or for your help. Service providers can include the clerk at a local retail store or the waiter at a restaurant where you dine. Customers can be internal or external to the company where you work, or they can be co-workers or classmates that you are helping with a project. Write a brief summary of your observations.

Project 3-7

Pay attention when you are the customer. During the next two weeks, pay attention any time you are put on hold or transferred to another person or group. Note any situations wherein you experience frustration as a result of the way your call was handled or any times you were cut off. Write a brief summary of your experiences.

Project 3-8

Develop a monitoring checklist. Assemble a team of at least three of your classmates. Develop a simple checklist (approximately 10 items) that can be used to monitor calls. Check for specific behaviors that cover each of the "Moments of Truth" that may be encountered in a typical help desk call. Specify items that you would weight higher than others. For example:

- Answer the telephone within three rings.

- Answer the telephone using a standard script.

Compare your results with the checklists developed by your classmates.

Case Projects

1. **WRK Systems, Inc.**

    You have been hired as a consultant to help a new help desk develop scripts and call handling procedures. Begin by developing a script that analysts can use when answering the telephone. Propose the script to the help desk manager and explain the benefits of having analysts say what you are suggesting.

2. **Operating on a Shoe String**

   You work for a help desk that has a very limited budget. Your boss has asked you to determine what books or tapes can be used to improve the telephone skills of your team. Go to your local library or use the Internet to prepare a list of available books and tapes. Explain why you selected each one.

3. **Miller Brothers, Inc.**

   You are the supervisor for a help desk that supports the internal customers of Miller Brother's Inc., a small manufacturing company that has recently opened a new facility in a different state. Prior to this, all of your customers worked in the same building and usually walked in to the help desk when they needed assistance. Customers from the new facility, however, will be calling the help desk for support. Develop a series of scripts and role-playing exercises that you can use to introduce telephone etiquette to your staff.

CHAPTER FOUR

TECHNICAL WRITING SKILLS FOR SUPPORT PROFESSIONALS

After reading this chapter and completing the exercises you will be able to:

➤ Describe the impact that technologies such as the Internet and e-mail are having on the help desk and how the role of help desk analyst is changing as a result

➤ Understand the characteristics of good technical writing and use proven techniques to improve your writing skills

➤ Describe the tools that companies are using to manage their knowledge resources and understand the skills needed to use these highly sophisticated systems

The technical support industry is undergoing a dramatic change in terms of how it collects information and delivers support. Most companies have implemented call tracking and problem management systems that enable help desk analysts to log and manage customer problems and requests. Increasingly, technologies such as e-mail and the Internet are complementing the telephone and onsite services as ways to communicate with customers. Support professionals are more often using and developing online knowledge bases that contain answers to frequently asked questions, solutions to known problems, and policies and procedures that customers can use as well. All of these changes have prompted the need for support professionals to add technical writing to their list of required skills.

Good writing skills enable you to communicate technical information accurately, completely, and comprehensively to customers and co-workers of varying skill levels. Because customers and co-workers have varying skill levels, good writing also communicates information in a way that customers and others can understand. Written communication conveys emotion just like verbal communication, so your "tone of voice" is equally important when you write or speak. As an analyst, you must also learn to be concise and consistent so that readers can quickly obtain the information they need.

THE EMERGING PARADIGM: TECHNOLOGY-DELIVERED SUPPORT

Historically, customers called the help desk on the telephone or perhaps walked in to the help desk, when they needed assistance or information. Although that still happens, companies are now providing additional ways for customers to obtain support. For example, customers may send an e-mail message or fax a form to the help desk. Companies are also establishing Web sites that customers can use to obtain support without having to wait to speak with a help desk analyst. These alternative ways of delivering support enable the help desk to better prioritize and manage its workload. They also enable the help desk to anticipate and proactively meet its customers' needs. They even enable customers to help themselves.

Because of e-mail, Web technology, and other emerging technologies, help desks are completely rethinking the way they deliver support services. Successful companies understand that effective use of these technologies is not just a matter of installing hardware and software. It also requires that they must diligently capture and disseminate high-quality information. For most help desks, this means rethinking not only the skills that help desk analysts must possess, but also the skills and knowledge that customers must possess.

Used effectively, technology empowers both customers and help desk analysts. Used improperly, technology can frustrate everyone and can alienate customers. Telephone, e-mail, and Internet technologies all play a role in customer support, and as we move into the future, no one technology will replace the others. The telephone provides immediacy and the ability to interact with a human being. Customers will continue to use the telephone when they do not want to wait for an e-mail response or do not have the ability or the desire to access Web-based services. For example, customers will use the telephone when they are experiencing a critical problem or when they have questions that need to be answered before they order a new product. They will also turn to the telephone when Web-based services are not available or the network is down. E-mail provides the ability to send and receive detailed information. Customers will continue to use e-mail when they do not require an immediate response or when they want a written reply. For example, they'll use e-mail when they want a detailed set of instructions or when they have a general inquiry, such as when the next release of a product is due out. Web-based services provide customers with the ability to perform functions, such as filling out forms and downloading software, in addition to interacting with help desk analysts. Web-based services will continue to be used by those customers who feel comfortable using Web technology. For example, they'll use the Web when they want to have a workspace set up for a new employee or when they want to obtain answers to FAQs. Customers who want to work at their own pace and on their own schedule also will rely on Web-based services. As a help desk analyst, you must feel comfortable communicating via all of these methods and must possess or develop the different skills that each of these technologies require.

The Help Desk Analyst's Role in a Technology-Centric World

The availability of technology has dramatically changed the role of help desk analyst. Today's analysts must be extremely flexible in their ability to continuously learn new technologies and adapt those technologies to their work. They need to understand and use a myriad of technologies, including the telephone, e-mail, and Web-based services, to support their customers and communicate with their co-workers. Also, analysts are required to record the results of their efforts, typically in a call tracking and problem management system. All of these technologies extend the help desk's ability to gather, organize, and utilize information. **Information** is data that are organized in a meaningful way. **Data** are raw facts that are not organized in a meaningful way.

The best companies view information as an extremely valuable resource. They rely on their help desk analysts to **capture**, or collect, the high-quality data needed to create accurate and useful information. Consequently, help desk analysts must recognize and embrace the important role they play in capturing data and sharing knowledge. Gone are the days where simply solving a problem is good enough, or where people in a help desk setting can hoard their knowledge or relay knowledge by word of mouth. Today, help desk analysts must capture data that can be reused by other analysts to solve similar problems. They can use that data to produce the information needed to prevent problems from reoccurring. At a minimum, they must capture the data needed to reduce the time it takes to solve problems if they happen again.

Analysts are expected to log tickets, document solutions, develop procedures, and exchange information in a way that can be easily used by customers, managers, and co-workers. As a result, writing skills and typing—or **keyboarding**—proficiency are important assets in the help desk. People with good writing and keyboarding skills can quickly, easily, and accurately capture needed data. Because they are often more productive, they may be given a wider range of responsibilities and offered greater opportunity. For example, people with good writing skills may be asked to prepare recommendations that lead to product improvements, or they may be asked to manage or contribute content to the help desk's Web site. By developing good writing skills, you can position yourself to seize these opportunities when they arise. After all, good writing skills not only enable you to communicate efficiently and effectively with customers, they enable you to communicate your abilities to management as well.

Enabling Customer Self-Service

In our busy society, people have become accustomed to using self-services, such as vending machines, voicemail, automatic teller machines (ATMs), and banking by telephone. **Self-services** are services that enable customers to help themselves. Customers appreciate services that enhance their self-sufficiency and enable them to accomplish tasks at their own pace. Given proof that a new way of obtaining service works, customers will embrace and then demand services that free up their most valued commodity—time. Enabling self-service for technical support is no different.

Many companies are embracing this self-service concept and using technologies, such as fax-on-demand, e-mail, and Web technology, to enable customers to help themselves. Customers use these technologies to order products, obtain product information, and find solutions to problems without speaking with a help desk analyst. Manufacturing companies are also refining the design of their products in an effort to enable and encourage self-service. For example, many companies are providing robust and interactive online Help with their software programs that customers can then access and use to answer questions and obtain step-by-step assistance. Hardware manufacturers and software publishers are also embedding diagnostic software in their products that customers can use to troubleshoot and potentially solve problems on their own.

Both customers and help desk analysts benefit from self-services. For example, customers benefit from self-services, such as lists of frequently asked questions, because they do not have to speak with an analyst to receive the information they need. When lists of frequently asked questions are published, help desk analysts are free to work on more complex problems and contribute to product improvements. Simple self-services, such as providing customers with the ability to submit requests via e-mail, are appreciated by customers because customers are able to use a tool that they are already familiar with to request service. These simple self-services also reduce the time it takes analysts to handle requests because customers are documenting the preliminary customer and incident data themselves. This data can then be logged automatically into the company's call tracking and problem management system.

In fact, today's demanding customers have come to expect self-services. Customers appreciate these services because these services save them time and reduce their frustration. Customers often view companies that fail to provide self-services as out-of-touch and inefficient. For example, aren't you surprised when, in this day and age, you call a company and the telephone rings unanswered? We expect to interact with some technology. At a minimum, we expect to hear a message with the company's business hours. Additionally, we want the ability to leave a voicemail message. We are suspicious when companies do not provide this "basic" service.

4

Customers also increasingly expect companies—particularly companies that provide technical support—to utilize Web technology to enable self-services. Today's savvy customers expect external help desks to have a Web site that they can reach via the Internet. The **Internet** is a global collection of computer networks that are linked together to provide worldwide access to information. Internal help desks often enable their customers to access a Web site via their company's intranet. An **intranet** is an internal collection of linked computers that provide a company's employees and other authorized people, such as customers, access to secured information. In other words, an intranet is a secured portion of the Internet. Self-services that help desks may offer customers via their Web sites include:

➤ Answers to frequently asked questions (FAQs)

➤ Tips, techniques, and helpful hints

➤ Schedules for company-sponsored training classes

➤ Information about new and planned products and services

➤ The ability to update customer information, such as address information and customer preferences

➤ Online forms to submit problems and requests

➤ Current status reports (available without calling the help desk)

➤ A current list of standard products

➤ Purchasing policies and information

➤ A database of solutions that customers can use to solve problems on their own

➤ E-mail links to submit requests and comments

➤ A link to live text chats with help desk analysts

➤ An icon to request a call back

➤ A forum to submit questions and exchange ideas with other customers

➤ Customer satisfaction surveys

➤ Links to other useful Web sites

Links, or hyperlinks, are colored and underlined text or graphics. Clicking a link might open a pop-up window with a definition, instructions, a still picture, or an animated picture. Links can also run audio or video clips, or jump to Web pages.

Functionality and ease of use are the keys to a successful help desk Web site. When accessing a support Web site, customers are not looking for a simple billboard with a telephone number to call for support. They are looking for another way to obtain the information they need, when they need it. Web sites are particularly useful when companies cannot support their customers twenty-four hours a day, seven days a week. Even when the help desk is closed, a Web site can offer basic services and access to frequently requested information. Figure 4-1 shows a sample help desk Web site.

Figure 4-1 Sample help desk Web site

Using E-mail Effectively to Communicate with Customers

It is fairly common for help desk analysts to use e-mail to communicate with their co-workers and managers. Help desks may use e-mail internally to communicate the status of projects and promote awareness of changes to existing procedures, or they may use e-mail to communicate schedule changes and notify staff of upcoming system changes. According to a Help Desk Institute study, 89 percent of help desks use e-mail; however, only 12 percent of help desks provide their customers with the ability to use e-mail to submit requests (*Help Desk and Customer Support Practices Report*, 1998, pp. 64, 10). This implies that e-mail is currently used primarily for internal communication. This is changing, however, as companies realize that e-mail is a fast and easy way to communicate with customers.

Some companies use e-mail to simply inform customers about the status of outstanding problems and requests, while encouraging customers to submit those requests via the telephone or their Web site. Other companies encourage customers to use e-mail to submit problems and requests. An increasing number of companies use e-mail to conduct customer satisfaction surveys. E-mail can also be used to inform customers about a product change or new release that might affect them.

It is important to remember that although e-mail is an easy way to communicate with customers, it does not provide many of the capabilities that a call tracking and problem management system provides. For example, e-mail cannot be used to automatically create trend reports and it cannot be used as a knowledge base. For this reason, help desk analysts must log all e-mail requests received from customers in their company's call tracking and problem management system. Analysts must also record all status updates related to a customer problem or request in the call tracking and problem management system, not in e-mail messages that may be lost or forgotten.

Many call tracking and problem management systems now integrate with most of the standard e-mail packages to allow automation of common tasks. For example, e-mail messages from customers can be automatically logged as tickets. The call tracking and problem management system can then automatically send a return e-mail message to inform customers that their call was logged and to provide a ticket number. Some companies automatically send e-mail messages to customers anytime the status of their problem or request changes. Other companies automatically send e-mail messages with a detailed description of the final resolution when the ticket is closed.

One of the downsides of e-mail is that it can be perceived as impersonal. Another downside is that analysts sometimes find that using e-mail elongates the problem-solving process. For example, if the help desk receives an e-mail that does not contain sufficient information, an analyst may try to contact the customer by telephone. If the customer and analyst do not connect, the analyst must send back an e-mail message that requests the needed details. The analyst must then wait for a response before being able to solve the problem. If the analyst does not communicate effectively and the customer misunderstands the analyst's message, the problem-solving process may be further elongated. To minimize these downsides, help desk analysts must use common sense and courtesy when using e-mail to communicate with customers. The best practices listed in Figure 4-2 are a good place to start.

- Manage customer expectations
- Remember the human
- Be practical and be patient
- Check your grammar, punctuation, and spelling
- Be forgiving
- Avoid lengthy discussions and debates
- Avoid negative and derogatory comments
- Use special characters and emoticons appropriately
- Use forms and templates to save time
- Verify your distribution lists periodically
- Standardize your signature

Figure 4-2   E-mail best practices for help desk analysts

Let's explore these tips for using e-mail effectively in more detail.

Manage customer expectations — Some help desks view the telephone as the primary way of receiving customer requests. Because e-mail is a secondary method, they check it infrequently and sporadically, or they check it only periodically, such as twice per day. If customers don't know how the help desk treats e-mail messages, they may be disappointed with the help desk's response. Therefore, it is important that the help desk communicate its e-mail policies to customers. For example, the help desk must indicate the priority it places on e-mail requests and the timeframe within which e-mail requests will be addressed. It is also important for analysts to encourage customers to send messages to the help desk's e-mail box, as opposed to their personal e-mail box. This helps to ensure that every e-mail request is logged and addressed in a timely fashion, regardless of an individual analyst's workload or schedule.

Whatever your help desk's policy is, communicate it *clearly* to customers so they know what to expect. Some companies publish a Help Desk Quick Reference Card or Newsletter that communicates their e-mail policy. A Help Desk Quick Reference Card can also spell out the information that customers must provide when using e-mail to submit a request. Figure 4-3 shows a sample Help Desk Quick Reference Card.

Help desks must refine their e-mail policy as needed to meet their customer's needs. For example, because some help desks are seeing the volume of e-mail requests growing, they are beginning to have analysts check for new messages regularly throughout the day, as opposed to just periodically.

Remember the human — Because e-mail supports a level of anonymity, people sometimes say things in an e-mail message that they would never say in person. Other times they ignore e-mail messages or fail to respond in a timely fashion. Remember, however, that when you send or receive e-mail, you are conversing with another person. Think about and acknowledge that person just as you would if you were interacting in person or over the telephone. Be considerate. Be respectful. Include only those things you would say if that person were standing in front of you.

Be practical and be patient — There are times when e-mail is not the best way to communicate. Use common sense. If a customer immediately needs information that you have, pick up the telephone and call. Even if you prefer to send an e-mail message because the information is detailed, consider calling to let the customer know it is on the way. Remember, too, that not everyone is online throughout the day, and so may not respond immediately to an e-mail message. Also, if you send a message to someone in another country, it may be delivered outside of business hours or during a holiday in that person's country. If you don't receive an immediate response to an e-mail, be patient. Resist the temptation to re-send the message or perceive you are being ignored. If an immediate response is needed, e-mail may not be the way to go.

HELP DESK QUICK REFERENCE CARD

This handy booklet explains the services provided by the help desk and also suggests better ways to interface with the help desk.

GIVE US A CALL...
(123) 456-7890

Please be advised that our peak times are between 8:00 — 9:30 A.M. and 1:30 — 2:30 P.M. During peak times, our call volumes are greater and callers may encounter a delay before reaching an analyst.

SEND LOW PRIORITY E-MAIL MESSAGES TO
help.desk@ company.com
We guarantee a response to all e-mail messages within 1 business day.

24 HOURS MONDAY ➤ FRIDAY

NOTE: Coverage provided on weekends by data center operations.

WHAT SERVICES DOES THE HELP DESK PROVIDE?

The help desk:

¥ Monitors all systems and network lines to ensure availability.
¥ Serves as a central point of contact for you to report any hardware or software problems.
¥ Assists with your User ID (cancel, print, status, routing, etc.) related tasks.
¥ Broadcasts information about upcoming changes and scheduled or unscheduled system outages.
¥ Logs all incoming calls and facilitates problem resolution to your satisfaction.
¥ Contacts the proper source to correct any problems that we cannot directly solve and provides you with a solution in a timely manner.
¥ Communicates with all IS departments to maintain a high level of system availability.

WHEN CONTACTING THE HELP DESK...

¥ Please give us your name and extension.
¥ Identify the PC you are working at by reading the number on the white label posted in the lower-right corner.
¥ Check your screen for any error messages that may help us determine the cause of the problem.
¥ Give us an estimated time factor when you are experiencing a response time problem (10 seconds, 2 minutes, none).
¥ Indicate which system or software package you are encountering a problem with (e.g., Payroll, WordPerfect, etc.).
¥ Give the model number of the failing device for hardware-related problems.

HOW DOES THE HELP DESK MANAGE CALLS?

The Help Desk manages calls in accordance with its business impact, or severity.

Severity definitions are:

1 - System or component down, critical business impact, no alternative available, notify management immediately, bypass/recover within 4 hours, resolve within 24 hours

2 - System or component down or degraded, critical business impact, alternative or bypass available, resolve within 48 hours

3 - Not critical, deferred maintenance acceptable, circumvention possible with no operational impact, resolve within 72 hours

NOTES:

_____
_____
_____
_____
_____
_____
_____
_____
_____
_____

Figure 4-3   Sample Help Desk Quick Reference Card

Check your grammar, punctuation, and spelling — Unless you are corresponding with a friend or family member, form and accuracy both matter. The quality of an e-mail message constitutes a "first impression" and so requires care. In other words, people will judge the appearance of your e-mail messages just as they would your appearance if you were standing in front of them. They will form an opinion about your competence. Resist the temptation to hastily send a response without regard for grammar and punctuation. And *always* check your spelling. Customers may mistrust or discount an entire response if they find typographical errors. Remember, every message you send to a customer represents your entire company. Take care to avoid errors that will reflect poorly or leave a bad impression. A good habit is to proofread every message to a customer twice before you press the Send button. If you are sending an important message that contains detailed or complex information or a message to a large number of people, ask a co-worker to proofread the message for you.

Be forgiving — Just as you do not want someone to misjudge you if they find a typographical error in one of your messages, be forgiving when you find errors in others' messages. If you believe that you are misunderstanding the person's point or that you need additional information, simply ask for clarification or for the missing details. If you receive a copy of a message that a co-worker sent to a customer or manager that contains an error that you feel could damage the reputation of your co-worker or the company, tactfully bring the error to your co-worker's attention and suggest specific ways the co-worker can improve the message.

Avoid lengthy discussions and debates — E-mail communication some-times requires sending several messages back and forth to resolve an issue. This can be compounded if one of the parties is not "listening" or misunderstands the information. There are times when direct conversation is needed. If a lengthy discussion or debate seems needed, pick up the telephone or schedule a meeting. Remember that when communicating with customers, it is your responsibility to communicate clearly and effectively. If a customer misunderstands you, it is *you* that must clarify your position or clear up the misunderstanding.

Avoid negative and derogatory comments — What you say and how you say it is just as important when using e-mail as it is when communicating in person or over the telephone. Perhaps this is even more so with e-mail because customers may misinterpret your words or interject an inappropriate emotion. In other words, they may *perceive* that you are being rude, even though that is not your intent. Furthermore, if you are rude, they can forward the message to your boss or print it out and hold you accountable. You also want to avoid say-ing negative things about your co-workers or your company. Again, because e-mail messages can be easily forwarded, you may find that negative comment making its way to someone you would prefer not see it. If you do not want the world to see something, you should not be putting it in an e-mail message. Let your caring, CAN DO attitude shine through and you can't go wrong.

Use special characters and emoticons appropriately — Relaying emo-tion and emphasizing a point are two of the most difficult things to do when communicating in the written form. Special characters and **emoticons**, symbols used to convey feelings, can help when used appropriately. In the absence of for-matting features such as bold and underline, you can use special characters, such as asterisks surrounding a word, to emphasize a point.

"Passwords must be at least six characters long and *are* case sensitive."

Include emoticons such as a smiley face — ☺ — or a frowning face — ☹ — sparingly and take care to use them appropriately.

> **Appropriate**: Placing a smiley face at the end of a message that indicates you are looking forward to meeting a customer at next month's user group meeting.

> **Inappropriate**: Placing a smiley face at the end of a message that delivers bad news.

Resist the temptation to be overly cute or to use obscure emoticons or acronyms. Recall that an acronym is a word formed from the initials of a name. Customers may not understand what you are trying to communicate or they may misinterpret your message. When in doubt, leave out special characters and emoticons.

Capital letters can be used to emphasize a point, but try not to overdo it. CAPITALIZING MANY WORDS OR AN ENTIRE SENTENCE IS GENERALLY PERCEIVED AS SHOUTING. Conversely, exclusive use of lowercase letters can be difficult to read. It is best to follow standard capitalization rules.

Use forms and templates to save time — Help desks are increasingly using forms and templates to customize their e-mail messages and to distribute and collect information electronically. A **form** is a predefined document that contains text or graphics users cannot change and areas in which users enter information being collected. Forms save time for both customers and analysts. Customers save time because they know what information they must provide to submit their request. Analysts save time because they get the information they need to begin working on the request. Forms often correspond to the problem entry screen of the call tracking and problem management system so that analysts have the information needed to quickly log customer requests. Some e-mail and call tracking and problem management systems interface so that requests are logged automatically. A **template** is a predefined item that can be used to quickly create a standard document or e-mail message. Templates save analysts time because they can save text and items such as custom toolbars and links to Web sites and quickly reuse those items to create documents and e-mail messages. The time it takes to create forms and templates pays off in time saved down the road.

Verify your distribution lists periodically — Checking for new e-mail messages and responding to messages that you receive on a daily basis can be a challenge. Receiving unnecessary e-mail can be frustrating. To avoid being a source of frustration for your customers, periodically verify your distribution lists. For example, you may be sending a message to someone who no longer works for a company or who has moved into a new position and no longer uses your company's product or services. Conversely, a person who should be receiving your information may not be on the list. Make sure you are sending messages to the correct recipients.

Standardize your signature — Most e-mail packages now provide the ability to automatically insert a "signature" into an e-mail message. A good practice for a help desk is to use a standard format for all analysts' signatures that includes all the ways to contact the help desk. This consistency lends a professional air to messages and ensures customers know alternate ways to get help. Figure 4-4 shows a sample help desk e-mail signature. Remember to put the help desk's telephone number and e-mail address in your signature, as opposed to your personal telephone number or e-mail address, so customers cannot contact you directly.

> Mary Jane Smith
> Help Desk Analyst
> Way Cool, Inc.
> *"Working hard to keep you working!"*
> Web: http://www.waycoolinc.com
> E-mail: help.desk@waycoolinc.com
> Phone: (816) 555-HELP (3257)
> Fax: (816) 555-3255

Figure 4-4   Sample help desk e-mail signature

The effective use of e-mail will gain you the respect of customers and co-workers, and like excellent telephone skills will serve you well throughout life. Common sense, care, good judgment, and good writing skills will enable you to make the most of this powerful communication tool.

IMPROVING YOUR WRITING SKILLS

Well-written materials are simpler to comprehend, provide needed information, and leave a good impression. Writing, like any other skill, improves and becomes easier with practice. Another way to hone writing skills is by paying attention when you are reading, just as you can improve your customer service skills by paying attention when you are the customer. There are also a number of excellent books and classes available. In fact, many universities and community colleges offer classes in technical writing.

Appendix A lists several books you can use as references and to improve your writing skills.

Technical Writing Best Practices

As a help desk analyst, you need good writing skills whether you are logging a problem in the company's call tracking and problem management system, sending an e-mail, preparing a report, or preparing content for the help desk's Web site. Regardless of the type of document, good technical writing requires a coherent, precise style. The best practices listed in Figure 4-5 will help you develop an appropriate writing style and improve your writing skills.

- Know your audience
- Use the active voice
- Use simple language
- Be concise
- Be specific
- Avoid or define jargon, technical terms, and acronyms
- Break up your writing with lists and short sections
- Be consistent
- Check your work for accuracy and completeness
- Check your grammar, punctuation, and spelling

Figure 4-5   Technical writing best practices

These best practices become second nature when practiced consistently. After mastering these principles, you can focus on the important part of writing—your content.

Know your audience — To communicate clearly, you must determine the skill and education level of the intended readers. This is particularly true with technical subjects. Help desk analysts typically prepare written materials that are geared to a particular audience. For example, analysts may use e-mail messages to communicate with customers, problem tickets to communicate with co-workers, and reports to communicate with management. Customers, co-workers, and managers all have varying skill and education levels, and your writing must address each of your reader's needs. Ultimately, every reader should be able to understand your main ideas. For example, regardless of the document and its intended audience, it is appropriate to use technical terms, as long as you define those terms the first time you use them. Strive to strike a balance between a very simplistic writing style and one that is highly technical. Either extreme can alienate your audience.

Use the active voice — Active voice is when the subject of a sentence causes or does the action. When active voice is used, it is clear who is doing the action. Passive voice is when the person or thing performing the action is acted upon. When passive voice is used, it is unclear who is doing the action. Active voice makes your writing style seem more vigorous and your sentences more concise. Active voice also creates the impression the activity is ongoing.

> **Passive voice:** Our Web site is updated every Tuesday by our help desk analysts.

> **Active voice:** Our help desk analysts update our Web site every Tuesday.

Use simple language — Simple language communicates more efficiently and effectively than complex language laced with technical terms. It is becoming more acceptable to use a relaxed, conversational style with customers and co-workers, but, if you would not use a phrase during a normal conversation, do not use it in written documents. Keep it simple. Remember that the ultimate goal is to communicate, not confuse.

> **Complex:** By applying the enclosed instructions you can remedy the situation.

> **Simple:** You can use these procedures to fix the problem.

> **Formal:** It is unfortunate that I was unavailable when you visited the Help Desk two days ago.

> **Informal:** I'm sorry I missed you the other day.

Be concise — The fewer words you use, the better. Unnecessary words waste space, take more time to read, and inhibit comprehension. Reread your first draft, eliminating any words, sentences, or phrases that do not add value to your meaning.

> **Wordy:** Apparently this problem has happened before and was not resolved correctly. Repeated attempts to resolve the problem have not been successful.

> **Concise:** Attempts to resolve this recurring problem have not been successful.

Be specific — By its very nature, technical writing must deal in specifics, not generalities. When customers and managers read a problem description or report, they seek detailed information, such as facts, figures, data, recommendations, and conclusions. Being vague can severely weaken the impact of your writing and the value of the information you are producing. Do not be content to say something is good, bad, fast, or slow when you can say *how* good, *how* bad, *how* fast, or *how* slow. Use words that are specific and concrete.

> **Vague:** We respond to e-mail messages as quickly as possible.

> **Specific:** We respond to e-mail messages within 4 hours.

Avoid or define jargon, technical terms, and acronyms — Good technical writers use terminology that is compatible with their readers' technical background. If a technical term is appropriate and most readers will understand it, use the term. But avoid jargon and technical terms when a simpler word will do just as well. If you must use technical terms or if you want to introduce an acronym, define the term or acronym the first time you use it.

> **Technical:** Maximize the visible spectrum on your CRT.
>
> **Nontechnical:** Turn up the brightness on your monitor.
>
> **Undefined acronym:** Many help desks use an ACD to manage incoming telephone calls.
>
> **Defined acronym:** Many help desks use an Automatic Call Distributor (ACD) to manage incoming telephone calls.

Break up your writing with lists and short sections — Readers want to acquire needed information quickly and tend to have a short attention span. Short sentences and paragraphs help them read and grasp information rapidly. Numbered sequences or lists arranged in a logical order also work well.

 Use numbered sequences only when a specific order is required.

Numbered sequence:
Check the following when a customer has a blank screen:

1. Is the monitor plugged in?

2. Is the monitor powered on?

3. Is the security key turned on?

Bulleted list:
Consider the following when establishing a help desk:

➤ Your company's goals

➤ Your customer's expectations

➤ Your commitment to customer satisfaction

Be consistent — In fiction, varying word choice is appropriate. In technical writing, however, inconsistencies cause confusion. To avoid confusion, once you have used a name or title for something, do not use a different name or title to refer to the same thing.

Inconsistent: A Field Service Representative will be onsite tomorrow afternoon. The technician will fix your printer and your monitor.

Consistent: A technician will be onsite tomorrow afternoon. The technician will fix your printer and your monitor.

To increase the readability of a list, use the same grammatical construction for each item in a list. When lists are presented in a consistent way, readers will find the list easier to understand and remember.

Inconsistent grammatical construction:

Reasons companies establish a help desk include:

➤ To provide customers a single point of contact

➤ Minimization of support costs

➤ Minimize the impact of problems and changes

➤ Increasing end-user productivity

➤ Customer satisfaction enhancement

Consistent grammatical construction:

Companies establish a help desk to:

➤ Provide customers a single point of contact

➤ Minimize support costs

➤ Minimize the impact of problems and changes

➤ Increase end-user productivity

➤ Enhance customer satisfaction

Check your work for accuracy and completeness — Accuracy is extremely important in technical writing because people use the answers, solutions, and procedures to do their work, use software, and operate hardware. Inaccurate or incomplete information may cause your customers or co-workers to waste time or experience additional problems. When documenting solutions and procedures, include each and every step a customer or co-worker must follow, even ones that seem obvious or intuitive to you. Ask a co-worker or subject matter expert (SME) to review complex documents for accuracy and completeness. They can catch typographical errors and may question invalid "assumptions" you have made in the document.

Check your grammar, punctuation, and spelling — Grammar, punctuation, and spelling matter. As a final step, proofread every document to eliminate any grammar, punctuation, and spelling errors. Readers may catch errors you missed, and perceive that you are lazy or uncaring when it comes to your work. The time it takes to make your documents error-free pays off in the reader's trust of the information and leaves the reader with a positive perception of you and your company. Many technologies provide spelling- and grammar-checking utilities that can catch some errors. However, still reread your documents. Some words may be spelled correctly but used inappropriately. When in doubt about grammar, punctuation, or spelling rules, check a style guide or dictionary, or ask an experienced co-worker for feedback.

A style guide is an excellent source for rules of punctuation and grammar usage. Appendix A lists several style guides you can use as references and to improve your writing skills.

Writing Help Desk Documents

The primary goal of help desk writing is to accurately convey technical information in an interesting way that can be understood by your audience. This is true regardless of the type of help desk document. Figure 4-6 lists some of the most common documents help desk analysts prepare. Each of these documents has a different audience and purpose. Before writing a word, it is a good practice to ensure you understand the audience's needs and how they plan to use the information.

- Trouble tickets
- E-mail messages
- Frequently asked questions (FAQs)
- Reports
- Policies and procedures

Figure 4-6   Common help desk documents

The amount of documentation analysts write depends on the technology available to their help desk and the size of their help desk. Analysts at most help desks log trouble tickets and send and receive e-mail messages. They may also be asked to prepare some of these other documents. On the other hand, some help desks have teams of technical writers who prepare FAQs, reports, procedures, and other documents; analysts have little involvement.

Remember all of the writing best practices when you prepare these help desk documents.

Trouble Tickets

Recall that a "ticket" is a description of a customer's problem or request. Help desk analysts typically log tickets electronically in a call tracking and problem management system at the time the request is received. Tickets may also be called records, cases, incidents, or logs. Figure 4-7 shows a sample problem entry screen that help desk analysts may use to log a problem or request.

Figure 4-7 Sample trouble ticket

Well-written tickets provide other analysts and level two service providers with the information they need to solve problems quickly. They also provide a historical accounting of the steps taken to solve a problem.

Help desks are increasingly storing information about how to solve problems in a knowledge base so that analysts can use that information to solve similar or recurring problems. The section "Managing and Disseminating Knowledge" discusses in detail how to build and use a knowledge base.

When documenting problems and requests in a ticket, clearly record all of the information the customer provides. Also include *all* of the steps you have taken to diagnose and resolve the problem. Analysts sometimes leave out problem-solving steps that they perceived as "obvious." Unfortunately, if an action is not explicitly stated, co-workers or level two service providers have no choice but to "assume" the step was not taken. For example, if a ticket does not mention that you verified the customer's monitor was powered on and then you escalate the problem, the field service engineer will most likely ask that question before going onsite. This not only wastes the field service engineer's time, it can also frustrate and even anger the customer who must answer the same question multiple times. Sometimes all of the problem-solving steps are part of an existing checklist; in that case, it is appropriate to simply state that you completed the checklist and then summarize the results.

A good guideline when documenting requests is to collect details such as who, what, when, where, and how.

4

Most tickets are made up of two basic parts: data fields and text fields. A **data field** is an element of a database record in which one piece of data is stored. Most systems can validate data as it is entered into data fields and enforce a standard in terms of what data is entered. This means the system can ensure that a date field accepts only correctly formatted dates, as opposed to words. For example, in the United States, dates typically conform to a MM/DD/YY (e.g., 11/27/01) format. In Europe, dates typically conform to a DD/MM/YY (e.g., 27/11/01) format. Again, when data fields are used, the system enforces the standard in terms of how the data is entered. A **text field** is a field that accepts free-form information. Text fields are used to collect detailed information such as descriptions, status updates, and solutions. Text fields cannot typically validate data as it is entered in the system. In other words, the system cannot enforce a standard in terms of what data is entered.

Many companies establish standards for how to enter certain words or phrases into text fields. For example, a standard may direct analysts to use the term "reboot," as opposed to "cold boot," "warm boot," or "power off and on." Although the system cannot enforce the use of these standards in a text field, the presence of the standard helps analysts to write more consistently and minimizes the confusion that can result from inconsistent terms. Some systems also provide the ability to create a synonym table. A **synonym** is a word with the same or very similar meaning to another word. For example, the words "monitor," "screen," and "computer terminal" are often used interchangeably. When a synonym table exists, the system uses the synonym table to find records that match the specified word and its synonyms when searching against text fields. In other words, if you search the database for records with "monitor" in a text field, the system also looks for records that contain "screen" and "computer terminal" in that field. Optimally, standards are defined that spell out how to enter words or phrases that may be similar or confusing into text fields.

Reports are usually created using the data entered into data fields because the data can be validated. As a result, the person creating the report can predict what data will be present in a data field.

When working in a help desk, strive to understand how the data you collect is being used in a effort to ensure that you are entering information as accurately as possible. For example, many call tracking and problem management systems have a "Date Resolved" field. Analysts sometimes simply enter the current date and time, even though the problem was resolved earlier in the day or week. This field, however, is often used to determine whether the problem was resolved within the target resolution time. Recall that target resolution time is the timeframe within which the support organization is expected to resolve the problem. If an inaccurate date and time is entered, this ticket appears on a report as late, even though it may not have been.

 Accuracy is important and takes only a few seconds more.

Another reason accuracy is important is that help desks are increasingly providing their customers with the ability to check the status of outstanding tickets, usually through the help desk's Web site. This customer access has heightened awareness within the support industry of the need to document requests accurately and professionally, and maintain tickets on as close to a real-time basis as possible. Remember that even when customers cannot access trouble tickets directly, the trouble ticket data is often automatically forwarded to the customer in an e-mail message, so it is important to be accurate and professional.

The data documented in tickets is also used by other service providers to diagnose and solve problems, and by management to create management reports and analyze trends. Effective trend analysis can eliminate recurring problems, thus saving valuable time and, ultimately, increasing customer satisfaction. Many companies use the data captured in their call tracking and problem management system to justify resources and to measure performance of both the help desk team and individual analysts. You may perceive that it takes too much time to create complete and accurate tickets. Remember, however, that management analyzes ticket data to more fully understand your workload and your contributions. They also rely on this information to institute improvement opportunities that may save time in the long run.

E-mail Messages

Every day, more help desks are using e-mail to communicate with customers. Well-written e-mail messages are as short and succinct as possible. When e-mail messages are too long, readers may become bored or miss an important detail. If detailed information must be sent, include the information as an attachment. More preferably, let the recipient know how to retrieve the information. For example, a common practice is to include a link to a directory or Web site.

When writing e-mails, it is best to limit the number of subjects in the message, or, clearly distinguish a change in subjects, for example, by leaving a blank line. This is particularly important when you are requesting responses to different subjects. For long messages, consider restating your requests at the end of the message so the recipient does not need to continuously reread the message to uncover your questions or requests. Conversely, respond carefully when you receive a message. Verify that you have answered *all* of the questions.

Ultimately, e-mail messages should provide as much of the needed information as possible the first time and not prompt additional messages to be sent back and forth. If lengthy discussion or debate is needed, it is best to make a telephone call or schedule a meeting.

Frequently Asked Questions (FAQs)

A common business practice that is particularly relevant to help desks is publishing lists of **frequently asked questions (FAQs)**, well-written answers to the most common customer queries. These answers are then made available to customers. For example, they can be posted on a company's Web site, published in the help desk's newsletter, incorporated into documentation, such as a user's manual, or distributed at a training class. Some companies list the top ten FAQs for a given month, for a specific product, or for a certain type of user, such as those who are new to a product.

The key to a well-written FAQ is to state both the question and answer clearly and in a language that is appropriate to the audience. In other words, phrase the question the way that customers do when they contact the help desk, then explain the answer in language that customers can understand. Remember that it is okay to use jargon and technical terms in the answers, as long as you define those terms for the reader.

FAQs are a basic self-service and enable help desks to proactively address their customers' needs. Analysts can also develop FAQs that provide their co-workers with answers to common questions about their area of expertise. FAQs satisfy customers and co-workers because they are able to find solutions and answers to questions on their own. Many people prefer FAQs because they can find answers to questions they may be reluctant to ask or are afraid may seem silly.

Reports

Entry-level analysts do not usually prepare reports, but senior analysts often do. Although in smaller help desks, where analysts tend to be "jacks-of-all-trades," anyone may be asked to prepare a report. Reports may be statistics or detailed accountings that are produced from the data collected in a call tracking and problem management system. Creating this type of report requires knowledge of the system, the available data, and knowledge of the reporting package used to pull the data out of the system. Reports may also reflect the results of a study, the status of a project, or the analysis of statistics. For example, a report may describe why the volume of calls goes up on Thursdays, or why the number of PC-related problems has gone down in the past two months. Preparing these reports requires writing skills and an understanding of the recipient's expectations. Some common reports a help desk analyst may create include:

➤ **Progress report** — A progress report provides an update on activities, such as a project. Typically a progress report states what activities were completed during the current period and forecasts what activities will be completed during the next period, for example, the activities completed this month and the activities to be completed next month. Progress reports will also point out activities that are overdue and why those activities could not be completed on time. Management will usually designate the timeframe of progress reports. Progress reports can also be used to document any considerations or concerns that require management attention.

➤ **Requirements report** — A requirements report typically provides an assessment of the current environment, a description of requirements that will result in an improved environment, considerations, concerns, and recommendations. A **requirement** is something that is required—a necessity. For example, a customer requirement is a service that customers expect the help desk to offer. Requirements can also be associated with technology. For example, a company must identify its requirements for a new call tracking and problem management system before it begins looking for one. Without determining the requirements, the selected system most likely will not meet the company's needs in the long term. Gathering and documenting requirements is usually the first step taken at the start of a new project.

➤ **Feasibility report** — A feasibility report explores the viability of a proposed project, such as implementing a new system or offering a new service. Feasibility reports typically describe the risks and benefits of continuing with the project and may also describe alternatives.

The first time you are asked to prepare a certain type of report, find out exactly what is expected in terms of format and content. Ask to see a copy of a similar report that you can use as an example. Prepare an outline of the report you plan to prepare and then ask for feedback and approval of the outline before you begin preparing the actual report. These are all ways you can avoid wasted time and effort. Also, be open to feedback. Few reports are perfect the first time. Ask for specific, constructive feedback so you can continuously improve.

Policies and Procedures

Companies more than ever are involving the help desk staff in the development of policies and procedures. These policies and procedures may be used by customers, the internal support organization, or simply within the help desk. A **procedure** is a step-by-step, detailed set of instructions that describes how to perform a task. When writing procedures you must state every step explicitly. Do not "assume" readers will know that they have to log on to the network before they can retrieve their e-mail. While a step may seem obvious to you, it may not be at all obvious to your readers. It is also good to state the result to expect when a task is complete. For example, let readers know that they can proceed when the message "Logon Complete" appears. You can also let the readers know what to do if the message does not appear.

4

> *If any single force is destined to impede man's mastery of the computer, it will be the manual that tries to teach him how to master it.*
> *William Zinsser*

When writing procedures, it is appropriate to include information about what *not* to do. For example, you can inform customers that restarting their PC may not be the best way to solve a problem. Explain that it could result in the loss of data or it could erase the conditions needed to diagnose the problem. Another good practice is to include detailed warnings when needed that communicate important instructions. Figure 4-8 shows a sample warning message.

WARNING: Documents can contain viruses that can infect computer files and have harmful side effects. Always scan your disks to find and remove viruses before transferring documents to the network.

Figure 4-8 Sample warning message

Many help desks create and maintain a Help Desk Analyst's Guide. Some help desks refer to this document as a Technician's Guide, or Procedures Guide. Figure 4-9 shows a sample table of contents for a Help Desk Analyst's Guide.

A Help Desk Analyst's Guide spells out the policies and procedures of the help desk and contains information that help desk analysts need to do their work. A Help Desk Analyst's Guide ensures that the knowledge and experience of help desk management and key help desk staff members is available, even when the managers or staff members are not. In other words, analysts can first consult this guide to determine how they should handle a given situation. A Help Desk Analyst's Guide is often used to orient new help desk staff members in obtaining an understanding of the help desk's policies and procedures. An Analyst's Guide should be considered a "living" document that is updated regularly. Many organizations maintain this guide online to make it more accessible and easier to revise. Help desk analysts often help to create the Help Desk Analyst's Guide because they are the ones that will be using it day in and day out. Helping to create a Help Desk Analyst's Guide is an excellent way to practice and improve your writing skills.

Sample Help Desk Analyst's Guide - Table of Contents

HELP DESK MISSION x
- Help Desk Mission x
- Help Desk Operating Objectives x
- Help Desk Analyst's Personal Objectives x

TRAINING/DEVELOPMENT x
- Help Desk Training Plan x
  - Training Objectives x
  - Training Activities x
  - Training Schedule x
  - References (e.g., Books, Tapes, Magazines) x
- Current Skills Inventory Matrix x

CALL MANAGEMENT x
- Scripts ....
  - Answering the Phone ....
  - Terminating a Call ....
  - Miscellaneous Customer Service Tips ....
- Important/Emergency Phone Numbers ....

CUSTOMER PROFILES ....

PROBLEM MANAGEMENT ....
- Problem Management Introduction ....
- Problem Management Process Owner ....
- Problem Management Indicators and Objectives .
- Problem Management Roles and Responsibilities
- Problem Management Process Flow ....
- Problem Escalation/Notification Guidelines ....
- Problem Management Related Procedures ....
  - Adding a Problem Record ....
  - Assigning a Problem ....
  - Resolving a Problem ....
  - Verifying Customer Satisfaction ....
  - Closing a Problem ....
- Problem Management Reports (e.g., Daily, Week

CHANGE MANAGEMENT x
- Change Management Introduction x
- Change Management Process Owner x
- Change Management Indicators and Objectives x
- Change Management Roles and Responsibilities x
- Change Management Process Flow x
- Change Categories x
- Change Flow By Category x
- Change Management Related Procedures x
- Change Management Reports (e.g., Daily, Weekly, Monthly) x

INVENTORY MANAGEMENT x
- Standard/Recommended Hardware and Software x
- Keyboard Mappings x
- Obtaining Inventory/Configuration Information x

AFTER-HOURS PROCEDURES x
- After Hours Call List x
- Determining What Is an Emergency x

DISASTER RECOVERY x
- Incident Tracking System x
- Phone System x
- Workstation (Toolkit) x

VENDOR MANAGEMENT x
- Service Contract Specifics x

APPENDIX A - GLOSSARY OF TERMS AND ACRONYMS x

APPENDIX B - FREQUENTLY ASKED QUESTIONS x

APPENDIX C - TROUBLE SHOOTING TIPS AND TECHNIQUES x

APPENDIX D - SERVICE LEVEL AGREEMENTS x

Figure 4-9 Sample Help Desk Analyst's Guide table of contents

Writing is an acquired skill that becomes easier when you know the rules. If you do not enjoy writing, consider taking a writing class so that writing becomes easier for you. You may find that you enjoy it. If nothing else, you will be able to write faster and thus have more time for the things you do enjoy doing. The ability to write well is an important skill that technical professionals must possess. In today's digital age, good writing is quickly becoming a critical success factor. Remember that all it takes is practice, practice, practice.

MANAGING AND DISSEMINATING KNOWLEDGE

Few, if any, companies have the resources to recreate a solution each and every time a problem occurs. Also, because technology is increasingly complex and changing very rapidly, many companies are unable to give analysts adequate training. When training is provided, it may not occur when analysts need it most—before the technology is introduced. Consequently, just as customers can use self-services to help themselves, analysts must also help themselves by learning to use and create online knowledge bases. A **knowledge base** is a collection of information sources, such as customer information, documents, policies and procedures, and problem solutions.

Building a Knowledge Base

A knowledge base can be built using sophisticated technology or it can simply be a collection of books and documents used to solve problems. For example, most help desks make available the following knowledge resources:

➤ Class notes, such as those you take at a training class

➤ Internet sites that you can access via bookmarks

➤ Online help

➤ Product manuals

➤ A call tracking and problem management system that you can use to look up similar or related problems

➤ Co-workers and level two service providers

Companies are trying to maximize their human resources and consolidate their knowledge resources by implementing sophisticated expert and knowledge management systems. These systems capture human knowledge and make it readily available to others who are involved in solving problems and requests. An **expert system** is a computer program that stores human knowledge in a knowledge base and has the ability to reason about that knowledge. A **knowledge management system** combines the reasoning capability of an expert system with other information sources, such as databases, documents, and policies and procedures. Although a knowledge management system is, in fact, an expert system, the support industry more commonly uses the term *knowledge management system*.

Knowledge management systems can be used to record newly found solutions and retrieve known solutions and procedures, or they can be used to access existing knowledge bases. Help desks that support custom applications often use these systems to collect and retain their in-house knowledge. Help desks that support standard industry applications from companies such as Microsoft, Lotus, Novell, Netscape, and others can purchase commercially available knowledge bases. Commercially available knowledge bases contain solutions to known problems and can be purchased on a subscription basis. Subscribers receive regular updates that are typically delivered on CD-ROM.

Knowledge management systems benefit help desk analysts considerably because the information they need is available online whenever they need it. They do not have to wait for a co-worker to get off of the telephone or for the resident "expert" to return from vacation or training to access that person's knowledge. Many knowledge management systems can also lead an analyst through troubleshooting steps that help resolve complex problems, which then improve the analyst's problem-solving skills.

Today, companies want people who share their knowledge, cross train their co-workers, and continuously develop new skills. Storing knowledge online enables analysts to achieve all of these goals. In addition, it reduces the time help desk analysts spend answering routine and repeated questions. Analysts are then free to work on more complex problems and pursue new skills.

Authoring Reusable Solutions

Today's sophisticated knowledge management systems have value only if the information stored in the knowledge base is accurate and complete. If the information is accurate or incomplete, the knowledge base will likely deliver an inaccurate or incomplete solution. Unfortunately, once analysts begin to mistrust the information in a knowledge management system, they become hesitant to use the system and may return to the practice of seeking out a human who can assist. To be effective, a knowledge management system must be carefully developed and maintained.

An effective knowledge management system serves as a repository for reusable solutions that are developed by analysts and level two service providers, such as the network management group and development groups. A **solution** is a definitive, permanent resolution to a problem, or a proven workaround. In most systems, solutions are stored as records in a separate file than trouble tickets. This enables the use of one solution to solve many trouble tickets (referred to as a **one-to-many relationship**), as illustrated in Figure 4-10. In other words, the same solution can be used each time a problem recurs without being retyped or cut and pasted into each trouble ticket.

Solutions do not describe things to *attempt* when diagnosing problems or responding to inquiries. Checklists and tip sheets can be used to provide this type of information. A solution represents the known answer to a problem. Solutions also do not contain the details of a single specific problem, such as names, dates, and so forth. These specific data elements would make the solution unusable if the same problem happens in the future. By developing a "generic" solution—one that does not contain specific details—the solution is reusable. Again, this is so that one solution can be used to solve many problems.

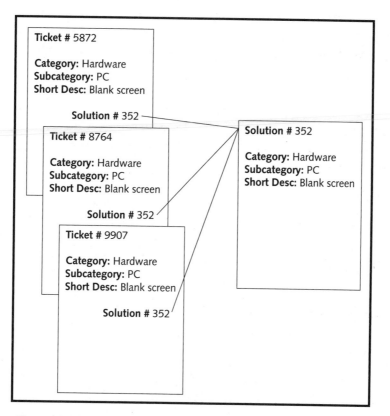

Figure 4-10   One solution to many trouble tickets

SEARCH RETRIEVAL TECHNOLOGIES

Much of the flexibility and power of a knowledge management system comes from (1) the search retrieval technology that it uses to retrieve data and (2) the quality of the data available. Search retrieval technologies include:

➤ Case-based reasoning

➤ Decision trees

➤ Fuzzy logic

➤ Keyword searching

➤ Query by example (QBE)

These retrieval technologies allow users to specify search criteria, which is then used to retrieve similar cases. A **search criteria** is the question or problem symptom entered by a user. Some of these retrieval technologies do very simple data matching while others use highly sophisticated artificial intelligence.

CASE-BASE REASONING

Case-base reasoning (CBR) is a searching technique that uses everyday language to ask users questions and interpret their answers. CBR prompts the user for any additional information it needs to identify a set of possible solutions. CBR finds perfect matches based on user queries but also retrieves cases that are similar to the perfect match. Possible solutions are ranked in order of probability from most likely to least likely to solve the problem.

DECISION TREES

A **decision tree** is a branching structure of questions and possible answers designed to lead an analyst to a solution. Decision trees work well for entry-level analysts because they can walk through a methodical approach to solving problems. Senior analysts often feel that decision trees take too long to identify a solution.

FUZZY LOGIC

Fuzzy logic is a searching technique that presents all possible solutions that are similar to the search criteria, even when conflicting information exists or no exact match is present. Fuzzy logic requires that some part of the search criteria specified is valid. In other words, as long as *part* of the search criteria is valid, fuzzy logic can find a match because it presents all possible solutions.

KEYWORD SEARCHING

Keyword searching is the technique of finding indexed information by specifying a descriptive word or phrase, called a keyword. Keywords must be indexed to be located and an *exact* match must be found. For example, if a user specifies the keyword "computer," only records that contain the keyword "computer" are located. Records that contain the keyword "PC" would not be located.

QUERY BY EXAMPLE

Query by example (QBE) is a searching technique that uses queries, or questions, to find records that match the specified search criteria. Queries can include **search operators**, connecting words such as AND, OR, and NOT. QBE can also find records that *do not* contain the search criteria, or that contain a value less than, greater than, or equal to the specified search criteria.

Today's sophisticated search retrieval technologies have value only if the data stored in the knowledge base is complete and accurate. The expression "garbage-in, garbage out" is appropriate: If inaccurate or incomplete information (garbage) is stored in the knowledge base, then inaccurate or incomplete information will be delivered when a search is performed. In other words, these systems are useful only if *you* enter quality data.

Many help desks develop standards for the ways in which solutions are written. Creating a standard solution format serves many purposes. Analysts with varying skill levels can obtain information at the level of detail that they need. Solutions are presented in a consistent format, so the human mind can very quickly and easily pick out key data elements, such as commands and variables. A standard solution format also makes the writing process easier because analysts know how to present information when documenting solutions. For example, analysts know how to specify words or phrases that may be similar or confusing, such as "monitor" as opposed to "screen" or "computer terminal." Figure 4-11 shows a sample format for a standard solution.

Sample Standard Solution Format

Consider the following guidelines when categorizing solutions:

- <u>Category:</u> Use care when specifying this field. Specifying a very generic category can result in a solution being presented a greater number of times than is appropriate.
- <u>Subcategory:</u> Use care when specifying this field. Specifying this field in too detailed a fashion can result in the solution rarely being presented.
- <u>Solution Short Description</u>: Provide a brief, symptom-oriented description of the solution that is not incident specific.
- <u>Solution Description</u>: Provide a reusable description of the solution. Reusable means that details relating to a single specific incident such as names, dates, and so forth are not included in the solution. While the need for those details may be referenced in the solution, the actual details should reside in the trouble ticket. Include:
    - A technical solution that offers an experienced technician a brief summary
    - A detailed solution that offers a less-experienced technician a more step-by-step approach

The following documentation standards have been developed in an effort to achieve consistency when documenting Solution Descriptions:

- Enclose variable data in brackets. For example, [xxxxxx].
- Enclose specific commands in quotes. For example, "xxxxxxx"
- When attaching another document, specify See *att:document.doc* for additional information where *att:document.doc* represents the name of an attachment.
- When referencing a manual or user s guide, specify Refer to the ***Word Users Guide*** for additional information where *Word Users Guide* represents the complete and accurate name of a reference document. Include the manual s release, version, or volume number when appropriate.
- When appropriate, indicate customers or other service providers to be notified when this solution is implemented.

Figure 4-11   Sample standard solution format

Standard solutions contain two types of information:

1. Fields that are used to index the solution and link it to the type of problem being solved.

2. Text that describes the solution.

The description of a solution may contain links to online documents, or a multimedia presentation of some kind, such as a video or audio clip. This enhances the usability of the information and enables people who are visual learners to receive the information in a meaningful way. Table 4-1 shows a solution that was written using a standard format.

Table 4-1 Solution with a standard format

Technical Solution	Detailed Solution
Delete print jobs with SunOS lp commands.	1. rsh as root to the server where the print queue resides 2. Type **"lpq -P[xxx]"** where 'xxx' is the queue name 3. Find the print job to kill, note the job # and the username 4. Type **"lprm -P[xxx] [job#] [username]"** 5. Use the line printer control utility (lpc) to bring the queue down, restart it, and bring it back up again as follows: **"lpc down [xxx]"** where 'xxx' is the queue name **"lpc restart [xxx]"** **"lpc up [xxx]"**

When working in a help desk, strive to utilize all available knowledge resources and contribute to the creation of your company's knowledge management system. By doing so, you can considerably expand your ability to solve problems and you can help others solve problems by sharing what you know. Respect the fact that your co-workers and level two service providers are just as busy as you are. Rather than interrupting their work to ask a routine question, look in the knowledge base for the answer. If you have difficulty finding a solution or using your company's knowledge management system, seek help from someone who is involved in administering or maintaining the system.

Administering Knowledge Resources

Many companies designate a knowledge base administrator (KBA) or knowledge engineer, to maintain their knowledge management systems. A **knowledge engineer** develops and oversees the knowledge management process and ensures the information contained in the help desk's knowledge base is accurate, complete, and current. It is the knowledge engineer's responsibility to ensure that all available information sources are added to the help desk's knowledge base. The knowledge engineer may also provide training in an effort to ensure that analysts can quickly and easily retrieve information when needed.

In smaller companies, a help desk analyst with excellent writing skills may perform this role on a part-time basis. Larger companies may have one or more full-time knowledge engineers. In larger companies, these individuals are often degreed technical writers. This position is becoming increasingly more important and should emerge as a highly valued position in the twenty-first century.

The practice of building a knowledge base and using all available knowledge resources is not meant to imply that humans are unimportant and we can get by without them. Quite the opposite. Companies want to free human resources to work on unique and complex problems rather than wasting time answering routine questions. Furthermore, most people would prefer to work on interesting new problems rather than handle the same boring problem over and over. Given the rapid pace of change in today's business world, continuing to hold on to knowledge that may soon be obsolete is one of the worst things you can do. By contributing to and utilizing your company's knowledge base, you can expand your knowledge and free yourself to learn new skills.

CHAPTER SUMMARY

- Technologies such as e-mail and the Internet are increasingly complementing the telephone and onsite services as a way to communicate with customers. These technologies extend the help desk's ability to gather, organize, and utilize information. They also enable companies to provide self-services that customers can use to obtain the information they need, when they need it. Information is an extremely valuable resource and people with good writing skills are able to capture it easily and accurately.

- When working in a help desk, good writing skills are needed to log problems in your company's call tracking and problem management system, send e-mail messages, prepare reports, or prepare content for your company's Web site. When preparing these documents, always be aware of grammar, punctuation, and spelling. A coherent, precise style is also important. The primary goal is to convey technical information in a way that is interesting and can be understood by your audience. Good writing takes time and attention to detail. It becomes easier and improves with practice.

- More companies are trying to maximize their human resources and consolidate their knowledge resources by implementing sophisticated knowledge management systems. These systems are used to capture human knowledge and make it readily available to people solving problems and requests. These systems must be carefully developed and maintained. Many companies establish documentation standards and designate a knowledge engineer in an effort to ensure the information captured is accurate, complete, and current. Using and contributing to these systems enable analysts to share their knowledge, cross train their co-workers, and continuously develop new skills.

KEY TERMS

capture — To collect.

case-base reasoning (CBR) — A searching technique that uses everyday language to ask users questions and interpret their answers.

data — Raw facts that are not organized in a meaningful way.

data field — An element of a database record in which one piece of data is stored.

decision tree — A branching structure of questions and possible answers designed to lead an analyst to a solution.

emoticons — Symbols used to convey feelings.

expert system — A computer program that stores human knowledge in a knowledge base and has the ability to reason about that knowledge.

form — A predefined document that contains text or graphics users cannot change and areas in which users enter information being collected.

frequently asked questions (FAQs) — Well-written answers to the most common customer queries.

fuzzy logic — A searching technique that presents all possible solutions that are similar to the search criteria, even when conflicting information exists or no exact match is present.

hyperlinks — *See* links.

information — Data that are organized in a meaningful way.

Internet — A global collection of computer networks that are linked together to provide worldwide access to information.

intranet — An internal collection of linked computers that provide a company's employees and other authorized people, such as customers, access to secured information.

keyboarding — Typing.

keyword searching — The technique of finding indexed information by specifying a descriptive word or phrase, called a keyword.

knowledge base — A collection of information sources, such as customer information, documents, policies and procedures, and problem solutions.

knowledge engineer — A person who develops and oversees the knowledge management process and ensures the information contained in the help desk's knowledge base is accurate, complete, and current.

knowledge management system — A system that combines the reasoning capability of an expert system with other information sources, such as databases, documents, and policies and procedures.

links — Colored and underlined text or graphics, which when clicked might open a pop-up window with a definition, instructions, a still picture, or an animated picture; run video clips; or jump to Web pages; also called hyperlinks.

one-to-many relationship — One solution solves many trouble tickets.

procedure — A step-by-step, detailed set of instructions that describes how to perform a task.

query by example (QBE) — A searching technique that uses queries, or questions, to find records that match the specified search criteria.

requirement — Something that is required—a necessity.

search criteria — The question or problem symptom entered by a user.

search operators — Connecting words such as AND, OR, and NOT.

self-services — Services that enable customers to help themselves.

solution — A definitive, permanent resolution to a problem, or a proven workaround.

synonym — A word with the same or very similar meaning to another word.

template — A predefined item that can be used to quickly create a standard document or e-mail message.

text field — A field that accepts free-form information.

REVIEW QUESTIONS

1. List five ways that customers may be able to obtain support from a help desk.

2. What are the benefits to both help desk analysts and customers for having ways other than the telephone to obtain support?

3. What role does the telephone play in delivering support?

4. What role does e-mail play in delivering support?

5. What role does the Web play in delivering support?

6. How do technologies such as the telephone, e-mail, and the Web benefit a help desk?

7. How are data and information different?

8. Why are writing and keyboarding skills becoming an important asset in the help desk?

9. Describe three ways that technology manufacturers are enabling customers to help themselves.

10. Why do customers appreciate self-services?

11. What is an intranet?

12. What are the keys to a successful help desk Web site?

13. List four ways that companies can use e-mail to communicate with customers.

14. Name two things that customers need to know about a help desk's e-mail policy.

15. Why is "how you say it" important when communicating in the written form?

16. Why is it important to check your grammar, punctuation, and spelling when sending an e-mail message?

17. When should you use characters such as asterisks in an e-mail message?

18. Why do you want to avoid capitalizing entire sentences in an e-mail message?

19. Should you put the help desk's telephone number or your personal telephone number in your standard signature? Why?

20. List three ways that you can improve your technical writing skills.

21. What do you need to know about your readers to communicate clearly?

22. When is it okay to use technical terms in your writing?

23. What is the best style to use when writing about technology?

24. What are the benefits of using simple language when you write?

25. When should you define a technical term or acronym?

26. When should you use a numbered list?

27. Why is it important to be accurate when writing technical documents?

28. What is a style guide?

29. Should you include all of the steps you have taken to diagnose a problem when creating a trouble ticket?

30. How is a data field different than a text field?

31. Name three users of the data entered in a call tracking or problem management system.

32. What should you do if you want to send a customer detailed information via e-mail?

33. What is an FAQ?

34. What is the key to a well-written FAQ?

35. What should you do if you are asked to write a type of report that you have never written before?

36. Is it necessary to state explicitly every step when writing a procedure?

37. How can you practice and improve your writing skills?

38. List three reasons that analysts must learn to use and create knowledge bases.

39. What is a knowledge base?

40. Describe the relationship that exists between an expert system and a knowledge management system.

41. What is a reusable solution?

42. List three benefits of having a standard format for solutions?

43. What is the role of the knowledge engineer?

44. List three ways that you personally benefit by using a knowledge management system?

HANDS-ON PROJECTS

Project 4-1

Identify support options. Select a software or hardware product that you use regularly. Identify all of the ways you can obtain support from the vendor. For example:

➤ Is telephone support available?

➤ During what hours is telephone support available?

➤ Is e-mail support available?

➤ Does the vendor guarantee a response to e-mails within a stated timeframe? If yes, what is the timeframe?

➤ Does the vendor have a Web site?

➤ Are FAQs available on the Web site?

➤ What, if any, other ways can you obtain support?

Prepare a short summary of your findings.

Project 4-2

Identify self-service options. Visit the Web site of a large software or hardware vendor, such as Microsoft, Cisco, Dell, or Gateway. Explore its Web site and identify any self-services it provides in support of its products. Prepare a brief paper describing your findings.

Project 4-3

Develop a standard signature. Using the format suggested in this chapter, develop a standard e-mail signature. Use telephone numbers and addresses related to your job or school.

Project 4-4

Assess your writing skills. Select a report or paper that you have written recently. Read through the report and, given what you have learned in this chapter, note any changes you could make in terms of style to improve the quality of the report. Briefly summarize your findings. Rewrite the report or a few pages of the report using what you have learned in this chapter. Read through the report again. Briefly summarize how the changes you have made improve the readability of the report.

Project 4-5

Document a problem and its solution. Briefly describe a technical problem that you recently encountered or were asked to help with. Include details such as who, what, when, where, and how. Develop a solution for this problem using the solution guidelines described in this chapter.

Project 4-6

Prepare a list of FAQs. Prepare a list of at least five questions and answers that you are frequently asked about an aspect of your life, such as school, your job, a hobby, or a sport that you enjoy.

Project 4-7

Prepare a progress report. Prepare a brief progress report about an important activity you are involved in, such as a project at school, at work, or an upcoming event that you are planning, such as a wedding or a vacation.

Project 4-8

Write a procedure. Write a procedure for a simple task, such as tying a shoe or brushing hair. Pair up with a classmate. Have the classmate follow your procedure and see if he or she can successfully complete the task. Ask the classmate to give you feedback on your writing. For example, are the procedures accurate, complete, and easy to understand? Refine your procedure based on any observations you made while your classmate was following the procedure and based on his or her feedback. Have the classmate follow or review your refined procedure and provide any additional feedback.

Case Projects

1. **Document Requirements**

   Your school's help desk manager has hired you as a consultant. The manager would like to enhance the help desk's Web site and provide students with the ability to use self-services. You have been asked to determine the students' requirements for an improved Web site. Ask three to five of your classmates how the school's Web site can be improved in an effort to provide self-services. Prepare a one-page Requirements Report that describes your findings.

2. **Join us!**

   Your company is holding its first user's group meeting for customers who use its software product. Your boss has asked you to draft an e-mail message that enthusiastically invites customers to attend the meeting. Draft an e-mail message that will meet your boss's approval. Include your help desk's standard signature. Be creative!

3. **Research Knowledge Bases**

You and your help desk teammates would like to implement a commercially available knowledge base that can be used to support industry-standard applications. Your help desk supports products from Lotus, Microsoft, and Novell. Your manager has asked you to provide her with information about the products that are available and to describe the benefits of implementing this type of product. Search the Internet and gather information on three products that offer knowledge bases that contain answers and solutions for the products you support. Briefly describe the features and functionality that each product offers. Summarize your report by describing the benefits of implementing this type of product to both help desk analysts and customers.

HANDLING DIFFICULT CUSTOMER SITUATIONS

After reading this chapter and completing the exercises you will be able to:

➤ Understand why customers sometimes behave in a challenging way

➤ Use proven techniques to handle irate, difficult, and demanding customers

➤ Keep yourself in control by learning to respond, not react, to difficult customer situations

➤ Take positive steps to stay calm and in control

Most customers are pleasant, calm, and appreciative of analysts' efforts. Unfortunately, there are times when customers become upset, angry, and demanding. These difficult situations can be extremely stressful. In one survey, 47 percent of customer service professionals listed calls from irate customers as their number one cause of stress (*TELE-Stress,* 1996, p. 65). As a help desk analyst, you cannot control your customer's behavior. You *can* control your response to their behavior and you can develop the skills needed to handle even the most difficult situations.

When handling difficult customer situations, it is important to be empathetic to your customer's needs. This means you must listen actively and try to understand why the customer is upset or angry. You must then acknowledge and address the customer's emotional state before you begin solving the customer's technical problem. You must also remember that you cannot take difficult situations personally. You must learn to vent your emotions, manage your stress, and stay calm and in control.

HANDLING UPSET, ANGRY, AND DEMANDING CUSTOMERS

Wouldn't it be nice if day in and day out people were pleasant and agreeable? Sure it would. The reality, though, is that we all have bad days. We all can become upset or even angry when things are not going our way—particularly when dealing with technology. Doesn't it seem that the closer the deadline or the greater the importance of an assignment, the bigger and more frustrating a technical problem becomes? Murphy's Law—anything that can possibly go wrong, will go wrong—seems particularly relevant when dealing with technology. Technology can be frustrating, but remember that when customers are having a problem using technology, it is your job as an analyst to help.

Most of the time, customers who contact the help desk are reasonable, pleasant, and grateful for your help. Some customers have a great sense of humor and are fun to work with. Some customers are very interesting and knowledgeable and enjoy working together with you to solve a problem. Some customers may even teach you a thing or two, if you are open and willing to learn. The reality, however, is that some customer situations are more challenging. A customer who is upset may need a caring ear and a calm helping hand. A customer may be angry and want to hear an apology followed by a swift and sound resolution to her problem. A customer may even be demanding, perhaps unrealistically so, and insist that you satisfy his needs—NOW! The important thing to remember is that difficult customer situations are the exception, not the rule.

Because they are so stressful, difficult situations can affect your attitude and even your interactions with other customers. For example, if an irate customer calls first thing in the morning, it can ruin your entire day—if you let it. That is why it is important to avoid the temptation to make sweeping statements, such as "Why is everyone being so difficult today?" or "Why are all of these customers so nasty?" These pessimistic generalizations can cause you to lose your perspective and can even influence your co-workers' attitudes. For example, a co-worker who has been having a great day may begin to view things negatively.

Although it is sometimes hard to do, try to consider and treat each customer and each situation as unique. Try to put yourself in your customers' shoes and strive to fully understand their needs. This perspective will not do anything to change the behavior of angry or demanding customers, but it will enable you to control how you respond to your customers' behavior.

CLOSE UP

RON MUNS
HELP DESK INSTITUTE
CHAIRMAN AND CHIEF MEMBER ADVOCATE
COLORADO SPRINGS, COLORADO

Ron Muns is an internationally recognized authority on the support industry. He founded the Help Desk Institute (HDI) in 1989, and served as its CEO and President until 1994. Ziff-Davis acquired HDI in 1992; Ron Muns reacquired HDI from Ziff-Davis in 1999. HDI is the leading membership organization for support professionals worldwide. Ron Muns shares his views on the traits and skills needed to succeed in the support industry.

5

Customer expectations go up every year. Customers want products and services that are new, better, cheaper, and faster. Companies that are not improving their level of service are getting behind. The help desk plays a strategic role by providing quick responses to customer issues and problems as well as by storing information about those issues and problems in one place. Advanced help desk organizations use this information they collect in their issues and problems databases to better identify quality improvement opportunities. This is one of the reasons why the help desk has gained a more prominent position within the eyes of both the IT and general business worlds.

The ability to be successful in the support industry is a personality trait as much as it is a set of skills. You must like quick action and the fact that a lot of things are happening all at one time. You must develop an awareness of different types of customers and appreciate the fact that each customer needs to be handled in a different manner. Try to understand people and where they're coming from. Try to appreciate the fact that every customer who calls wants to believe that he or she is your only customer. Customers also often want more than can be delivered. You must listen to what your customers are saying and then communicate reality in a way they can accept and understand.

Listening is and always will be one of the most important skills that analysts must possess. Speaking, writing, and problem-solving skills are also important. You must be able to think logically and ask the right questions. You must also be a team player, not an island. Things are simply happening too quickly. You must build tight relationships with the people who are monitoring systems and getting ready for new product rollouts so they let you know what is happening, and vice versa.

The manner in which technology is rolled out, including how it is supported and how people are learning to use it, greatly affects their productivity. The help desk plays an important role in terms of engineering how support is distributed. The help desk must also help people solve problems on their own. This means building knowledge bases, developing and distributing voicemail scripts, and so forth. Increasingly, solutions are being delivered through the Internet and e-mail. "E" is the word, and electronic support is one of the greatest changes currently affecting the support industry.

My challenge to people joining or working in the support industry is that you take seriously the fact that you are impacting the lives of the hundreds of customers who you support. I encourage you to evaluate your performance on an ongoing basis and see how you are impacting those workers. Use surveys, get out and talk to customers, walk through the areas where people are working and gain an understanding of how they are using technology. Try to learn what problems customers are having that they are not calling the help desk about and figure out how you can help with those as well.

Understanding Customer Behavior

To understand customer behavior, you must strive to empathize with what customers are experiencing. **Empathy** involves identifying with and understanding another person's situation, feelings, and motives. Being empathetic does not mean you are responsible. For example, if a customer is screaming at you because he cannot print his report and it is going to be late, you are not responsible for the late report. The customer may have procrastinated writing the report until the deadline was reached, or he may have known there was a problem with the printer and failed to report it to the help desk. Regardless, it *is* your responsibility to acknowledge the fact that the customer is upset and do everything you can to help him get the report printed. Isn't that what you would want if you were the customer?

Put yourself in your customer's shoes and try to relate to the confusion and frustration everyone at times feels when dealing with technology. Figure 5-1 lists some of the situations that may cause customers to become frustrated or angry.

Be aware that your company or department may be responsible for some of these situations. For example, if a customer is angry because past promises have been broken, it is imperative that you keep your promises. Also remember that there is always something that you can do. For example, if customers are complaining that your company's telephone menus are confusing or they had to wait too long for you to answer the telephone, what you can do is pass each complaint on to your team leader or supervisor. You can also let customers know if there are any shortcuts they can use to move more quickly through the telephone menus.

- Broken promises
- Confusing telephone menus
- Confusing user instructions
- Having to call back repeatedly
- Long wait times
- Looming deadlines
- Negative phrases, such as "That's not our policy" or "You're wrong"
- Poor product quality
- Rude analysts

Figure 5-1   Situations that may frustrate or anger customers

Don't think that because you have reported a customer complaint once that there is no need to report it again. Management may not act on a single complaint but often will respond when they receive the same complaint from a number of customers.

On any given day, everyone has more or less patience, awareness, and persistence. The presence or absence of these qualities invariably affects your ability to solve problems. Give your customers the benefit of the doubt; they may just be having an exceptionally bad day, or you may be the one having the bad day. Be honest. Don't blame your customers for your lack of patience or for your negative attitude. Strive to be positive and professional at all times.

Pay attention when you are a customer. Consider how you feel when you receive service from someone who is having a bad day. Consider how you feel when a service provider complains to you about how busy he is or how difficult her job is. Do you care? Typically, no. You just want service. Remember that it is not your customer's fault that you are having a bad day.

Winning Over Difficult Customers

Working with difficult customers requires patience and composure. How you respond to these customers, particularly during the early moments of your conversation, will greatly influence their perception and willingness to work with you. You can make a situation worse by failing to listen or by failing to communicate with positive statements. Figure 5-2 lists a step-by-step approach you can use to handle even the most difficult situation.

1. Get focused

2. Let the customer vent

3. Listen actively

4. Acknowledge the customer's emotional state

5. Restate the situation and gain agreement

6. Begin active problem solving

Figure 5-2   Technique for handling difficult customer situations

Let's explore each of these steps in detail and discuss some important nuances to keep in mind when practicing the steps in this proven technique.

1. **Get focused** — If you sense that an interaction with a customer is going to be difficult, get yourself focused. Take a deep breath. Make sure you have a smile on your face or that you appear eager and caring. Sit or stand up straight and get your notepad ready. These are preparatory steps that you should be following prior to each customer interaction—whether on the phone or face-to-face—but they are sometimes overlooked. For example, you may be particularly busy or you may be relaxed and joking with co-workers when you answer the phone without thinking. Before you know it, the pressure is on. Rather than plowing forward unprepared, take a few seconds to relax and get focused.

2. **Let the customer vent** — An upset or angry customer has a story to tell and you must let the customer tell that story from beginning to end without interruption. If you interrupt the customer at any point in time, it is likely that she will start the story over again. Or, the customer may have rehearsed what he is going to say and have written down several points that he wants to make. Until each point is made, the customer cannot calm down. This venting is necessary for the customer's well-being. Your challenge is to listen actively and look for cues that the customer is ready for you to begin taking control of the interaction. Customer cues include a deep sigh or a challenging statement such as ". . . and what are you going to do about it?"

3. **Listen actively** — Recall that active listening involves participating in a conversation and giving the speaker a sense of confidence that he or she is being heard. When a customer is venting, resist the temptation to ask questions, but still communicate the fact that you are listening. Nod your head

or use a verbal nod of the head to let the customer know you are listening. For example, incorporate non-intrusive verbal phrases at appropriate points in the conversation.

> "Uh-huh."
>
> "Go on."
>
> "I see."
>
> "I understand."

Remember also to pay attention to *what* is being said and *how* it is being said. Listen carefully for the central theme of the customer's problem or complaint. In other words, listen for the "real" problem in the customer's story. Try not to get bogged down by a customer's angry words or by what may be exaggerated statements. Take notes and be prepared to restate exactly what you have heard.

4. **Acknowledge the customer's emotional state** — An upset or angry customer needs to feel that you care and that you fully understand the situation before he or she can calm down. If you fail to acknowledge the customer's emotional state, it is likely that the customer will perceive that you were not listening and then become even more upset. You must acknowledge the customer's emotion, even if you do not understand why the customer has that emotion. Try to empathize with the customer or at least accept that this customer may be having a really bad day and needs your help. This is also an excellent time to respectfully use the customer's name and communicate your desire to do all you can. When appropriate, sincerely apologize to the customer for any inconvenience your company may have caused.

> "Miss Navarro, I'm sorry our field service engineer did not arrive at the time promised. Let me find out what happened. Would you like to hold while I contact his office or would you like me to call you back?"

It is imperative that you be respectful and genuine at this point of the interaction. If you use a snide or derogatory tone of voice when using the customer's name, the customer will most likely be offended. If you use an insincere tone of voice when apologizing, the customer will doubt your apology. If you don't feel that you can apologize using a sincere tone of voice, you must at least acknowledge the customer's emotion.

> "Mr. Sheng, I understand that you are very upset. I will do everything I can to get this printer problem resolved right away."

5. **Restate the situation and gain agreement** — It is imperative that you gain the customer's agreement that you fully understand the situation and the customer's expectations about when a solution will be delivered. Fixing

the wrong problem or failing to resolve the problem in the timeframe the customer expects will just make the situation worse. Begin, when possible, by restating the problem in the customer's exact words. This lets the customer know that you were listening. Ask the customer to verify your understanding of the problem. Use a simple verifying statement to obtain agreement from the customer that you have heard the point he is making.

> "Is that correct?"

> "Did we cover everything?"

6. **Begin active problem solving** — If you have been patient, clearly communicated that you care and sincerely want to help, and have gained agreement from the customer that you understand the situation, the customer should now have calmed down. This means that you can begin diagnosing the problem and developing an action plan or solution. This doesn't mean you can lose your focus. It is likely that the customer is still fragile and you may have to repeat all or some of these steps for handling a difficult customer situation before the problem is fully resolved.

Many analysts want to go straight to problem solving when a customer is upset or angry. Their thinking is that the best and fastest way to calm down the customer is to solve the problem. Solving the problem is important and will be the final outcome, but assisting and satisfying the customer is the ultimate goal. This requires that you strive to understand, acknowledge, and address the customer's emotional needs as well as the customer's technical needs. Remember that you are supporting people—living, breathing human beings—not just technology.

Calming Irate Customers

People experience varying degrees of anger. Typically, people first experience a lesser emotion, such as frustration or confusion, which builds to anger. In some cases, these emotions can be avoided by the proper handling of "Moments of Truth," such as placing customers on hold, transferring customers, and so forth. Some people are very slow to anger; others seem to become enraged by the slightest inconvenience. If a customer's problem or concern is addressed quickly, by using the technique for handling difficult customer situations described above, she may not become irate. On the other hand, bypassing one or more of the steps in this technique can cause the customer to become increasingly upset or angry. It is important to listen carefully so you can accurately assess and address a customer's level of emotion.

Initially, a customer describes the inconvenience of the problem he is experiencing or his frustration with the current situation. By acknowledging the customer's frustration and communicating that you will do all you can to remedy the situation, you can calm the customer and gain the customer's confidence.

Customer: "I've had to wait twenty minutes to get through. Why can't you people learn to pick up the telephone?"

Analyst: "I'm sorry to keep you waiting. How can I help you?

Customer: "This is the third time I've called about this printer this week. Why can't you get someone out here that will fix it right?"

Analyst: "I'm sorry that your printer is still not working correctly. Let me pull up a history of the problems that you have been having so we can determine the best course of action."

5

If you fail to acknowledge the customer's emotion or the source of frustration, the customer may become even angrier. Very often a customer becomes angrier because he perceives that you do not understand and are not addressing his concern. In other words, he perceives that you are not listening.

Customer: "You're not listening. Let me say it again."

Customer: "I don't seem to be getting anywhere with you. Let me talk to your supervisor."

At this point, the customer may be starting to mistrust you. Even though you may have been listening very carefully, you have not *communicated* that fact to the customer. You may have acknowledged *what* the customer said, but not *how* the customer said it. The customer is either going to give you one more chance or he is going to ask to speak with someone else. Make sure you understand how to engage help at this point, if you need it. For example, some telephone systems have a "panic" button that analysts can press to get their team leader or supervisor's attention. Some analysts stand up and wave or somehow signal to a co-worker or team leader that they need assistance. Do your best to handle the call, but don't be afraid to ask for help when you need it.

Finally, some customers will become irate even if you have done your best. Remember that some people have unrealistic expectations or they may simply be under so much stress that they are incapable of calming down. Your challenge is to ensure that your actions do not drive customers to their irate state. It is very important to understand that customers may be responding to your behavior, or what they perceive is your behavior, when they become increasingly angry. For example, you may be using negative phrases, such as "That's not our policy" or "We don't do that," without offering the customer any options or alternatives. Keep it positive and focus on what you *can* do.

Repairing a Damaged Customer Relationship

Even the most dissatisfied customers will continue doing business with a company if their problems and complaints are *consistently* handled quickly and cheerfully. Companies that provide world-class customer service understand this fact and work hard to establish policies aimed at maintaining their customer's good will, even in difficult situations. As a help desk analyst, the best thing you can do is stay focused on what you can do for the customer. The worst thing you can do is make promises that you cannot keep.

You cannot assume that just because a customer seems to be happy when you hang up the telephone that you have regained that customer's trust. Customers often feel they have to fight for their rights and even the slightest misstep can cause a customer to once again become defensive and distrusting. Patience and consistent follow-through are required to repair a damaged relationship. **Follow-through** means that you keep your promises, including calling the customer back when you said you would—even if you don't have a resolution to the problem. Follow-through means that a field service engineer arrives onsite when promised—or calls *before* she is late to arrange a new arrival time. The key here is to keep customers informed and be sure they know and are comfortable with exactly what is being done to resolve their technical problem or complaint.

Keep the customer informed, keep the customer!

Once the problem has been resolved, it is important that you or someone from your help desk or company follow up to ensure that the customer is fully satisfied. **Follow-up** means that a help desk or company representative verifies that the customer's problem has been resolved to the customer's satisfaction and that the problem has not recurred. For example, some companies have the help desk manager or the customer's sales representative contact a dissatisfied customer in an effort to show that the company values the customer's business. In some cases, you may be the company representative contacting the customer.

Although you may feel uncomfortable following up with a customer who was very angry and perhaps, from your perspective, unreasonable, it is the only way to repair the relationship. Repairing the relationship enables both you and the customer to feel comfortable when working together in the future. For example, some analysts report that when they have called angry customers to follow up, the customers apologized for their behavior. A customer may indicate that he was getting pressure from his boss or she was having one of those days where nothing seemed to go right. When difficult situations are handled properly, even the most disgruntled customer can become the help desk's greatest advocate.

KEEPING YOURSELF IN CONTROL

Difficult situations are inevitable when interacting with customers, so it is important to be prepared. By practicing the techniques listed in Figure 5-3, you will gain the confidence needed to stay calm and in control. You will also begin to consider these situations less stressful as you develop a track record of handling them successfully. Remember that you are a professional, and your job is to serve and support your customers.

```
• Learn to respond, not react

• Stay calm under pressure

• Get ready for your next call
```

Figure 5-3   Techniques for staying in control

By responding to difficult situations in a positive, professional manner, you will gain personal confidence as well as your customers' trust and respect.

Learning to Respond, Not React

Reacting is easy, especially in a difficult customer situation. Without thinking, you say or do the first thing that comes to mind. Very often, you mirror the behavior, even bad behavior, of your customer. For example, if a customer shouts, your instinct may be to shout back. If a customer is rude, you may be tempted to be rude in return. When you react without thinking, situations can quickly spiral out of control and you may say or do things you will later regret. Remember that a customer who is angry or upset needs your assistance just as badly as a pleasant customer who asks you nicely for help. Try to think rationally about what the customer needs and respond calmly to that need.

Learning to respond involves making a conscious choice to control *your* behavior. Practice using the proven techniques discussed in this chapter to get and keep even the most difficult situation under control. Recall that getting focused is the first step in handling a difficult customer situation. It is easy to lose your focus, so take a few seconds to calm yourself any time you feel that you are losing control. By thinking rationally and staying calm at all times, you can *respond*, rather than react, to your customers.

Staying Calm Under Pressure

People experience stress and pressure differently. Some analysts can "go with the flow" and rarely become upset. Other analysts feel threatened and may panic when facing even a slightly difficult situation. Learning to stay calm under pressure requires that you learn to control *your* behavior. It is your job to stay in control and handle even the most difficult situations in a professional, positive manner.

Difficult situations are tough. As a human being, you can "lose your mind" on any given day in much the same way that your customers can lose theirs. This is because different sides of our brains handle logic and emotion. As is illustrated in Figure 5-4, the left side of our brain absorbs memorized data and handles linear and logical thinking. The right side of our brain handles emotion.

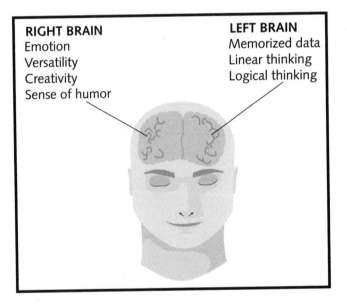

RIGHT BRAIN
Emotion
Versatility
Creativity
Sense of humor

LEFT BRAIN
Memorized data
Linear thinking
Logical thinking

Figure 5-4   How our brains handle logic and emotion

The two sides of our brain work together, although, in most people, one side dominates the other. When we are extremely upset or angry, however, the right brain takes over. You may have heard the expression "he's not in his right mind," which implies that someone is not thinking clearly. Well, the truth is that when we are extremely upset or angry we *are* in our right mind. As a result, we are incapable of thinking logically as that is an activity handled by our left brain. Given the way our brains work, you can understand why you must avoid the temptation to focus only on problem solving when someone is in an emotional state. In other words, you must resist the temptation to engage the customer in left-brain activities when the customer's right brain is in control. You must first acknowledge the customer's emotional state and let the customer know that you empathize and understand his or her needs and expectations. Then, and only then, will the customer regain the capability of his or her left brain and as a result be ready to respond logically and rationally.

Recall that in most people, one side of the brain dominates the other. Determining the dominant side of your brain may be helpful to you as a help desk analyst. For example, if you are predominantly a "left-brained" person, you will tend to be a very logical thinker and may have a difficult time understanding why other people become emotional. As a result, you may try to go straight to problem solving without addressing the customer's emotional needs. Remember that this can cause the customer to become even more upset because the customer may perceive that you are not listening. Predominantly left-brained thinkers must learn to listen for and acknowledge emotion.

If you are a very "right-brained" person, you may find that you become emotional fairly quickly in a difficult situation. For example, you may find that you tend to become upset or angry when you encounter someone who is upset or angry. Remember that reacting in a negative way can cause a difficult situation to quickly escalate out of control. Predominantly right-brained thinkers must learn to control their own emotions.

Whether you are left- or right-brained, it is important that you remain calm and in control at all times. This is essential when you are interacting with a customer who is extremely upset or irate. In other words, you must maintain control of your ability to think logically. If you become upset or enraged, then neither you nor the customer is going to be able to bring the situation under control or solve the problem. One way to remain calm and in control is to learn the symptoms that you experience when you are getting upset or angry, such as the ones listed in Figure 5-5.

- Headache

- Grinding teeth

- Concentration loss

- Nausea

- Reddening face

- Strained tone of voice

- Neck and shoulder tension

Figure 5-5   Common symptoms of being upset or angry

Whether on the phone or face-to-face, your customer will most likely notice these symptoms, and the customer's perception of these symptoms could, in fact, make the situation worse. If your voice becomes strained, the customer may perceive that you are raising your voice or shouting, or the customer may perceive that you are being rude or curt and begin to respond in a similar manner. Condition yourself to stay focused on what you have to do, and not how you feel. Figure 5-6 lists some of the techniques you can use to stay calm under pressure.

- Take a deep breath

- Sip water

- Use positive imagery

- Use positive self-talk

Figure 5-6   Calming techniques

Each technique has a different benefit, so you may want use two or more of these techniques in combination.

➤ **Take a deep breath** — Tension causes your chest to tighten up, which in turn causes your breathing to become shallow. This can also affect your voice. For example, your voice may become high-pitched or raspy. Taking a deep breath or a series of deep breaths will lessen the tension and enable you to resume a normal breathing rate. Breathe in deeply—inhale— through your nose so that you fill your lungs and feel the release of ten- sion, then breathe out—exhale—fully through your mouth. Remember, however, not to exhale audibly or the customer may perceive your deep breath as a sigh of weariness or a sign of frustration. For example, you may want to mute the telephone for a second or two while you take your deep breath, or, when facing a customer, you may want to take a series of smaller, less obvious breaths.

➤ **Sip water** — Taking a sip of water will lubricate your throat and help restore your voice to its normal pitch. It will also buy you the few seconds you may need to calm yourself before you speak. Sipping water is compa- rable to the practice of "counting to ten" before you speak.

➤ **Use positive imagery** — **Positive imagery** is the act of using mental pic- tures or images to influence your thinking in a positive way. For example, some analysts envision themselves standing next to the customer, looking at the problem. Rather than imagining that you are pitted against the customer, this positive image enables you to remember that you and the customer are pitted against the problem, as shown in Figure 5-7. Some analysts replace the image of an angry customer with the image of someone they love and care about. Analysts who use this technique find that it enables them to remain empathetic and to better understand their customer's perspective.

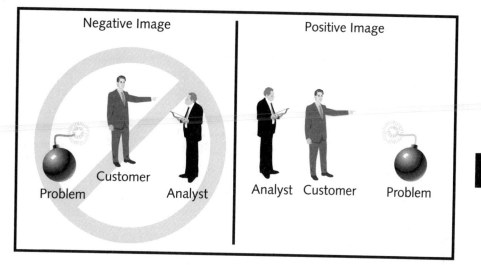

Figure 5-7   Using positive imagery

➤ **Use positive self-talk—Positive self-talk** is the act of using words to influence your thinking in a positive way. The words people use, even when they are talking to themselves, influence their thoughts and attitudes. It is normal for people to talk to themselves throughout the day. Whether people are conscious of it or not, the words people use affect how they think about themselves and how they experience situations. By watching the words that you use, you can begin to notice which of your thoughts are positive and which are negative. Once you become aware of how your self-talk sounds, you can practice eliminating negative thoughts and attitudes by using positive words.

> **Negative words:** "I can't handle this."

> **Positive words:** "I know what to do."

When facing a difficult customer situation, use positive self-talk to remind yourself that you cannot take this situation too personally. Tell yourself that you know what to do and coach yourself to use the proven techniques discussed in this chapter to calm your customer and begin solving the problem. Train yourself to replace negative thoughts about the customer with positive thoughts. Try to maintain a positive perspective.

> **Negative perspective:** "What a jerk."

> **Positive perspective:** "This person is really upset. What can I do to help?"

Practice will enable you to make each of these calming techniques a habit that you will do without conscious thought. Techniques you can use to practice staying calm under pressure include role-playing with another analyst or with your supervisor or team leader. You can also record your calls and listen to them afterward, listen to other analysts' calls to learn what you can, and review a difficult call in a staff meeting to see how it could have been handled better.

Difficult situations do not occur only when you are at work, so practice these techniques any time you find yourself losing control. For example, if someone is rude to you or you find yourself becoming angry, think about how you are feeling and make a conscious effort to calm yourself and regain control. The more you practice these techniques, the more confidence you will have when handling difficult customer situations.

Customers tend to respond positively when you are calm, confident, and in control. Learn to control your own emotions so that you can focus on meeting your customers' needs. Remember that you must meet your customers' emotional needs as well as their technical needs, which requires active listening and empathy.

Getting Ready for Your Next Call

It is likely that you will find some difficult situations more draining than others. What time of day the situation occurs, your level of preparedness, and even your personal mood all influence your ability to recover from a difficult situation. Take the time you need to compose yourself before answering your next call or meeting your next customer. Give yourself the opportunity to let your positive, CAN DO attitude shine through. In most cases you may just need to stand up, take a deep breath, and stretch a bit. Then you'll be ready to go. In some cases, however, you may need to follow all or some of the steps listed in Figure 5-8.

- Inform your team leader or supervisor

- Take a short break

- Avoid caffeine or other stimulants

- Employ stress-coping mechanisms

Figure 5-8   Steps for recovering from a particularly upsetting situation

You will need to follow these steps only when you feel a situation has been particularly upsetting.

➤ **Inform your team leader or supervisor** — If you are upset, it is likely that the customer may still be upset. Your team leader or supervisor needs to be informed to determine what, if any, additional steps should be taken to satisfy the customer. This will also enable you to present the facts of the situation from your perspective, enabling your team leader to have a balanced view in case the customer perceives the situation differently.

➤ **Take a short break** — Leave the area and catch your breath for a few moments. Take a short walk outside if you can to get some fresh air. If a walk is not possible, take a minute to look out the window and observe nature. If the day is dismal, look at art or go somewhere that you can hear music. Engage as many senses as you can and try to clear your mind of negative thoughts.

➤ **Avoid caffeine or other stimulants** — Caffeine is a stimulant and can increase your anxiety or exacerbate your feelings of frustration or anger. Caffeine is found in coffee, tea, cola, and chocolate. If you feel compelled to eat or drink something after a difficult situation, keep it simple. Drink a big glass of water or eat a simple snack, such as whole wheat crackers or a bagel. Give your body the time and fuel it needs to unwind.

➤ **Employ stress-coping mechanisms** — Just as people experience stress in different ways, people also employ varying techniques to manage and cope with stress. For example, some analysts keep a stress ball at their desk. Some help desks have a punching bag that analysts can use. Some analysts turn to a co-worker or seek out a friend who they can talk to about the situation. Try these or other stress-coping mechanisms.

Chapter 8, *Minimizing Stress and Avoiding Burnout,* will explore in detail the causes of stress and ways to minimize its negative effects.

Remember that each and every difficult situation you handle will increase your confidence and your ability to handle future situations. As time passes, you will find these situations less stressful because you have developed the skills needed to calm your customers and gain their confidence. You will also have learned how to take care of yourself and prepare yourself for the next customer. Difficult situations are inevitable. By practicing the techniques discussed in this chapter, you can handle these situations with confidence.

CHAPTER SUMMARY

- Most customers are pleasant, calm, and appreciative of your efforts, but there are times when customers become upset, angry, and demanding. Although difficult customer situations are the exception, not the rule, these situations can be extremely stressful and can affect your attitude—if you let them.

- Proven techniques enable you to understand, acknowledge, and address the emotional needs of your customers as well as their technical needs. Consistent follow-through and follow-up enable you to maintain your customer's good-will and repair a damaged relationship. When difficult situations are handled properly, even the most disgruntled customer can become the help desk's greatest advocate.

- Difficult situations are inevitable, so it is important to be prepared. By thinking rationally and staying calm at all times, you can learn to respond, not react, to these situations when they occur. One way to stay calm and in control is to learn the symptoms, such as headaches, nausea, or neck and shoulder tension, that you experience when you are under pressure. You can then use techniques, such as taking a deep breath or sipping water, to relieve these symptoms, enabling you to focus on meeting your customer's needs. Taking the time to compose yourself before you take a new call or meet with the next customer is also important.

- Each and every difficult situation you handle will increase your confidence and your ability to handle future situations. In time, you will find these situations less stressful because you have the skills needed to calm yourself and your customer and to stay in control at all times.

KEY TERMS

empathy — Identifying with and understanding another person's situation, feelings, and motives.

follow-through — The act of keeping your promises, including calling the customer back when you said you would—even if you don't have a resolution to the problem.

follow-up — The act of having a help desk or company representative verify that the customer's problem has been resolved to the customer's satisfaction and that the problem has not recurred.

positive imagery — The act of using mental pictures or images to influence your thinking in a positive way.

positive self-talk — The act of using words to influence your thinking in a positive way.

REVIEW QUESTIONS

1. Can you control your customer's behavior?

2. Do difficult customer situations happen often?

3. Why is it important to avoid the temptation to make sweeping negative statements about your customers?

4. What is empathy?

5. Does being empathetic mean that you are personally responsible for another person's situation?

6. What influences an upset or angry person's willingness to work with you?

7. What is the first thing you should do when handling a difficult situation? Briefly explain your answer.

8. Why is it important to let an angry customer vent?

9. What should you be listening for when a customer is venting?

10. What can happen if you do not acknowledge a customer's emotional state?

11. What tone of voice should you use when using a customer's name or when apologizing to a customer?

12. Why is it important to gain agreement from customers that you understand their needs?

13. When handling a difficult situation, when can you begin active problem solving?

14. Briefly describe the three stages customers go through on the way to becoming irate.

15. How can you ensure your behavior is not driving a customer into an irate state?

16. How do customers want their problems and complaints to be handled?

17. Describe two ways to regain a dissatisfied customer's trust and repair a damaged relationship.

18. Why is it important to follow up with a customer who was angry?

19. How is *responding* to a difficult situation different than *reacting*?

5

20. What is the key thing you must do in order to respond, rather than react, to difficult customer situations?

21. What does the left side of the brain do?

22. What does the right side of the brain do?

23. What side of the brain takes control when you are extremely upset or angry?

24. What do you need to do if you are a predominantly left-brained service provider?

25. What do you need to do if you are a predominantly right-brained service provider?

26. List three symptoms a person may experience when he or she becomes upset or angry.

27. List four techniques that a person can use to stay calm when facing a difficult situation.

28. What physical benefits do you derive from taking a deep breath when under pressure?

29. What benefits do you derive from taking a sip of water when under pressure?

30. What is positive imagery?

31. What kind of words can you use to eliminate negative thoughts and attitudes?

32. Why is it important to inform your team leader or supervisor that you have just handled a particularly difficult situation?

33. Why should you avoid caffeine after a stressful situation?

34. What are three things you can do in an effort to find difficult customer situations less stressful?

HANDS-ON PROJECTS

5

Project 5-1

Practice being empathetic. For the next week, note any situations you encounter or observe where someone becomes upset, angry, or demanding. Then, try to think of situations you were involved in that enable you to relate to what the people who have become upset, angry, or demanding are experiencing. For example, if the driver behind you beeps the horn as soon as the traffic light turns green, try to think of a situation when you may have been late for work or school and as a result experienced frustration with the driver in front of you. The point of this project is to simply acknowledge the fact that we are all human beings and we can all lose our cool on any given day. Briefly summarize the situations you observed and the personal experiences you used to empathize with each situation.

Project 5-2

Discuss situations that cause frustration or anger. Assemble a team of two or three classmates. Discuss the list of situations presented in this chapter that may cause customers to become frustrated or angry. As technology users—and therefore at times customers yourselves—discuss these situations and answer the following questions:

- What are the top five situations that cause technology users frustration?
- What other situations that cause frustration or anger can your team add to this list?

Select the three situations that your team feels are the greatest causes of frustration. Brainstorm a list of ways that companies can minimize the frustration that customers may experience when facing these situations. Present your ideas to the class.

Project 5-3

Discuss a difficult customer situation. Assemble a team of three to five of your classmates. Ensure that you or one of the classmates on your team has, as a service provider, faced a difficult customer situation. For example, the customer may have visited your workplace, or the customer could be a family member for whom she cooked dinner, a neighbor whose lawn he mowed, a friend to whom she sold candy or greeting cards, parents whose children he baby-sat, or strangers whose car you washed at a fundraiser. Have the classmate describe the difficult situation to the best of his or her recollection. Discuss and document your team's answers to the following questions:

- What emotion was the customer experiencing?

- How, if at all, can you empathize with the emotion the customer was experiencing?

- Constructively assess the response of your classmate (the service provider) to the customer's emotional state.

- What, if anything, could the company have done to prevent this situation?

- Given what you have learned in this chapter, what can you learn or what conclusions can you draw from this scenario?

Project 5-4

Be objective. Unfortunately, everyone has experienced a difficult customer situation from the viewpoint of the customer. Think of a situation where you were the customer and you became upset or angry. For example, you may have received poor service in a restaurant or you may have waited on hold for an extended period of time before a customer service representative answered the telephone. Consider what you have learned in this chapter about why customers behave the way they do and how service providers can best handle difficult situations. Describe in a paragraph or two the situation and how you (the customer) or the service provider could have handled the situation better.

Project 5-5

Become aware of "broken promises." It is not uncommon for service providers to make promises to their customers that they cannot realistically keep. For example, a waiter in a restaurant may tell you he will be "back in a second" with your check. Realistically speaking, that is impossible because the "second" is up before he has even turned to retrieve your check. For the next week, pay attention to the promises that service providers make to you. Select two or three situations and briefly note your perceptions in terms of the following:

- When the promise was made, did you consider it realistic?

- Was the promise kept?

- How did you feel when the promise was or was not kept?

- Given what you have learned in this chapter, what conclusions can you draw from this exercise?

Project 5-6

Learn the predominant side of your brain. Use the following two exercises to learn whether you tend to be predominantly left or right-brained. The first exercise is simple, while the second is more comprehensive.

Exercise One—Simple Left-Brain, Right-Brain Exercise

This exercise uses the relationship between your thumbs and your brain to determine if you tend to be left- or right-brained.

1. Fold your hands together with your fingers intertwined (the way people often do when they are preparing to pray).

2. Look at your thumbs and determine if your left or right thumb is resting on top.

If your right thumb is resting on top, it is likely that you are predominantly right-brained. If your left thumb is resting on top, it is likely that you are predominantly left-brained. A fun way to validate this preference is to reverse your thumbs. That is, put the thumb that had been resting on the bottom on the top. You will typically find that it feels uncomfortable.

Exercise Two—Comprehensive Left-Brain, Right-Brain Exercise

This exercise uses your answers to a series of questions to determine if you tend to be left- or right- brained (*Brain Builders!*, 1995, pp. 332-3). Check one answer for each question.

Question	Answer	Score
1. In your opinion, is *daydreaming* (a) a waste of time, (b) an amusing way to relax, (c) helpful in solving problems and thinking creatively, (d) a good way to plan your future?		
2. What's your attitude about *hunches*? (a) Your hunches are strong and you follow them. (b) You are not aware of following any hunches that come to mind. (c) You may have hunches but you don't trust them. (d) You'd have to be crazy to base a decision on a mere hunch.		
3. When it comes to *problem solving*, do you (a) get contemplative, thinking it over on a walk, with friends; (b) make a list of alternatives, determine priorities among them, and take the one at the top; (c) consult the past by remembering how you handled something similar to this situation before; (d) watch television, hoping the problem will go away		
4. Take a moment to relax, put this book down, close your eyes, and put your hands in your lap, one on top of the other. Which hand is on top? (a) Your right hand; (b) your left hand; (c) neither, because they are parallel?		
5. Are you goal oriented? (a) True (b) False		
6. When you were in school, you preferred algebra to geometry? (a) True; (b) False		
7. Generally speaking, you are a *very organized* type of person, for whom everything has its proper place and there is a system for doing anything. (a) True; (b) False.		
8. When it comes to speaking or writing or expressing yourself with words, you do pretty well? (a) True; (b) False.		
9. When you're at a party, do you find yourself more natural at listening rather than talking? (a) True; (b) False.		
10. You don't need to check your watch to accurately tell how much time has passed. (a) True; (b) False.		
11. When it comes to athletics, somehow you perform even better than what you should expect from the amount of training or natural abilities you have. (a) True; (b) False.		
12. If it's a matter of work, you much prefer going solo to working by committee. (a) True; (b) False.		
13. You have a near photographic memory for faces. (a) True; (b) False.		
14. If you had your way, you would redecorate your home often, take trips frequently, and change your environment as much as possible. (a) True; (b) False.		
15. You are a regular James Bond when it comes to taking risks. (a) Yes; (b) No.		
Total Score		
Score divided by 15		

Scoring Key:

1. (a) 1 (b) 5 (c) 7 (d) 9

2. (a) 9 (b) 7 (c) 3 (d) 1

3. (a) 7 (b) 1 (c) 3 (d) 9

4. (a) 1 (b) 9 (c) 5

5. (a) 1 (b) 9

6. (a) 1 (b) 9

7. (a) 1 (b) 9

8. (a) 1 (b) 7

9. (a) 6 (b) 3

10. (a) 1 (b) 9

11. (a) 9 (b) 1

12. (a) 3 (b) 7

13. (a) 7 (b) 1

14. (a) 9 (b) 1

15. (a) 7 (b) 3

1. Score each answer using the scoring key above.

2. Total your points.

3. Divide your total points by 15.

The lower the number, the more left-brained you are; the higher the number, the more right-brained. For example, if your score is 1, you are an exceptionally left-brained person. On the other hand, if your score is 8, you are exceptionally right-brained. A score of 5 means that there is regular traffic between your left and right brain.

5

Project 5-7

Learn the symptoms you experience under pressure. For the next week, record the symptoms you experience anytime you are upset or angry at home or at work. Remember that you do not have to be extremely upset or irate to experience symptoms. For example, you may simply be frustrated or perhaps confused. Keep a log of the situations you encounter and the symptoms you experience. Assess how you relieve these symptoms and identify any techniques you can use to stay calm in these situations. Share your experiences with your classmates and discuss how you can use the techniques discussed in this chapter to stay calm and in control.

Project 5-8

Assess your habits. Staying calm when faced with a difficult situation requires that you have good habits in place for dealing with pressure. Briefly describe a technique or techniques you use to calm yourself when facing a difficult situation. For example, is it your habit to take a deep breath or use positive self-talk? Briefly describe the benefits you derive from this habit. Given what you have learned in this chapter, what additional techniques can you incorporate as a habit?

Case Projects

1. **Role Playing**

   You have been hired as a consultant to a company that wants to (1) improve its customer service, and (2) reduce the stress its staff experiences when handling difficult situations. Drawing from your experiences both as a customer and as a service provider, develop a script that illustrates a difficult situation. Prepare a series of questions you can use to prompt empathy for the customer's situation, constructive feedback for the service provider's handling of the situation, and tips and techniques for handling this situation better in the future.

2. **Planting a Positive Image**

   Your boss has asked you to develop a poster to hang on the bulletin board in the help desk where you work. He wants this poster to illustrate the techniques that can be used to handle difficult customer situations and techniques that analysts can use to stay calm and in control when faced with difficult customer situations. Prepare a creative illustration for his review.

3. **Showing a CAN DO Attitude**

A co-worker has just had to handle a difficult customer situation. She thinks she could have handled the situation better and has asked for your feedback. Also, the customer hung up, in disgust, before the analyst was able to assist and she doesn't know what to do. Here's how your co-worker describes the call to you:

5

> **Customer:** "This is Jane Apponte. Let me talk to Suzie Peters."
>
> **Analyst:** "I'm sorry Ms. Apponte, Suzie is on another call right now, is there something I can do to help you?"
>
> **Customer:** "No, I can't wait. Interrupt her and tell her that I am waiting to speak with her."
>
> **Analyst:** "I can't do that Ma'am, but I can take your telephone number and have her call you back when she gets off the phone."
>
> **Customer:** "That's not good enough. I have been waiting two hours for someone to get out here and fix my PC."
>
> **Analyst:** "Did you call the help desk about your PC?"
>
> **Customer becoming irritated:** "Of course I called the help desk. Suzie told me a technician would be here within the hour and no one has shown up or called. I have a meeting in ten minutes and I want this problem taken care of before I leave. You need to get someone out here right now!"
>
> **Analyst:** "Do you know your ticket number?"
>
> **Customer Shouting now:** "I don't care what the ticket number is. Get someone out here now!"
>
> **Analyst:** "Ms. Apponte, there is nothing I can do until I know your ticket number. Please hold while I look it up." [Places customer on hold.]
>
> **Customer:** [Hangs up in disgust.]

First, write out the steps that must be taken immediately to address this customer's concern. Then, write out a sample script that shows how the analyst could have handled the call better. Include in the script examples of how analysts can let their CAN DO attitude shine through. Share and discuss your recommendations with your classmates.

SOLVING AND PREVENTING PROBLEMS

After reading this chapter and completing the exercises you will be able to:

➤ Use proven techniques to methodically solve problems

➤ Take ownership when problems cannot be solved immediately and ensure that customers and management are kept informed about the status of problem resolution activities

➤ Manage your workload and maintain a positive working relationship with other support groups

➤ Prevent problems by determining the root cause of problems and by performing trend and root cause analysis

To be successful, help desk analysts must be able to solve problems efficiently and effectively. A **problem** is an event that disrupts service or prevents access to products. Common problems include a broken device, an error message, or a system outage. Solving problems efficiently and effectively involves more than simply searching a knowledge base for known solutions. It requires a methodical approach through which analysts gather all available information, determine the probable source of a problem, and then decide upon a course of action.

As a help desk analyst, you need effective questioning skills and superior listening skills to be a good problem solver. Persistence is also important, because proficient problem solving requires going beyond the "quick fix" to find a permanent solution. By analyzing trends and suggesting ways to eliminate problems, you can help reduce the number of problems that customers experience and even prevent problems altogether. Problem solving is an innate skill, but it is also a skill that you can improve with practice. Improved problem-solving skills will enable you to resolve more problems, resolve problems more quickly and accurately, and, ultimately, satisfy more customers.

How to Solve Problems Methodically

Studies indicate that a high percentage of technical problems are recurring. In other words, many technical problems show up repeatedly and have already been reported to the help desk or to the product's hardware or software manufacturer. As a result, plenty of information is available for finding solutions to problems. As a help desk analyst, you can draw from your experience, access available knowledge bases, or use tools in an effort to find a solution. You can also engage other analysts or level two service providers who may have experienced the same or similar problems in the past.

The Problem Management Process

Most help desks develop processes and procedures in an effort to ensure problems are handled quickly, correctly, and consistently. A **process** is a collection of interrelated work activities—or tasks—that take a set of specific inputs and produce a set of specific outputs that are of value to the customer. A **procedure** is a step-by-step, detailed set of instructions that describes how to perform the tasks in a process. Each task in a process has a procedure that describes how to do that task. In other words, processes define *what* tasks to do, while procedures describe *how* to do the tasks. When multiple groups are involved in solving a problem, processes and procedures provide the framework that enable each group to understand its role and responsibilities.

Table 6-1 Flow chart symbols

Symbol	Name	Purpose
(A)	**On Page Connector**	Represents an exit to, or entry from, another part of the same flow chart.
Task	**Task**	Shows a single task or operation.
Predefined Process	**Predefined process**	Represents another process that provides input or receives output from the current process.
Decision	**Decision**	Represents a decision point and typically has a "yes" branch and a "no" branch.
—No—→	**No result**	Used in conjunction with a decision to show the next task or decision following a "no" result.
Yes ↓	**Yes result**	Used in conjunction with a decision to show the next task or decision following a "yes" result.
Terminator	**Terminator**	Shows the end or stopping point of a process.

Flow charts are often used in business to outline processes. A **flow chart** is a diagram that shows the sequence of tasks that occur in a process. Table 6-1 describes the purpose of each symbol used in flow charts. Flow charts are a good way to show how all the procedures involved in a process are interconnected. Consider a common help desk process—**problem management**, the process of tracking and resolving problems. The goal of problem management is to minimize the impact of problems that affect a company's systems, networks, and products. Figure 6-1 shows a fairly simple problem management process. This process varies from one company to the next and may be much more complex.

Sometimes called **incident management**, problem management typically also includes answering customer's questions and inquiries. **Questions**, such as "How do I…?", are customer requests for instructions on how to use a product. Questions occur when a product is not broken, but the customer simply needs help using it. **Inquiries**, such as "When will my equipment arrive?", are customer requests for information. Inquiries, like questions, usually occur when the product is not broken, but the customer wants a current status report. Most companies distinguish between problems, questions, and inquiries because they represent varying degrees of impact and speak differently to product and company performance. For example, a customer calling to inquire about the date for the next release of a software package may not be dissatisfied with the existing product and is just looking forward to the new version. On the other hand, a customer who gets error messages or loses data when trying to use a software package is clearly dissatisfied, and the company must try to resolve the problem quickly or risk losing that customer.

Note

Most companies also distinguish between problems and requests. A **request** is a customer order to obtain a new product or service, or an enhancement to an existing product or service. Common requests include moves, adds, and changes, such as enhancing an application, installing a new PC, moving a printer, installing new software, or upgrading existing software. A different process, the request management process, is typically used to handle requests. This chapter provides a brief overview of the problem management process, but focuses on problem-solving skills.

6

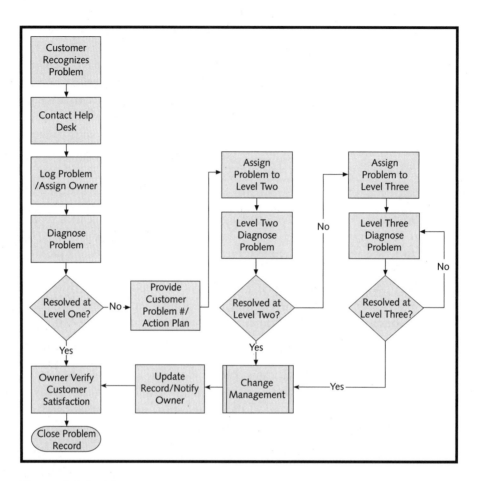

Figure 6-1 Problem management process

Solving Problems

The problem management process describes the overall approach to be used when handling problems within a company. Within the boundaries of the problem management process, analysts need problem-solving skills to handle each problem. The most efficient and effective way to find a solution to any given problem is to take a methodical approach. Figure 6-2 shows the basic steps to follow when solving problems.

1. Gather all data needed to create information

2. Diagnose the problem

3. Develop a course of action

Figure 6-2   Steps to follow when solving problems

The best problem solvers condition themselves to gather and analyze all available information before drawing a conclusion.

Step 1. Gather All Data Needed to Create Information

How well you perform the first step in the problem-solving process will greatly influence your ability to quickly find the correct solution. The first step is obvious: gather all available data to create information. It takes time and effort to capture the data needed to create accurate information. It is not enough to gather data and store it in your head. You must log the data accurately and completely in a call tracking and problem management system so managers, other help desk analysts, and level two service providers can use it. Some help desks view information as a valuable resource and they use comprehensive call tracking and problem management systems in an effort to capture as much data as possible. They can then use this data to create the information needed to justify resources, increase customer satisfaction, enhance productivity, improve the quality of products and services, deliver services more efficiently and effectively, and create new products and services. On the other hand, some help desks are so overwhelmed with their responsibilities, or so understaffed, that they capture little or no data. As a result, they have trouble creating the information needed to measure their performance and make improvements. The information needs of the help desk where you work and the complexity of the problem will influence the amount of data you are required to gather. Data to be gathered includes:

➤ **Customer data** — identifying details about a customer, including the customer's name, telephone number, department or company name, address or location, customer number, and employee number or user ID. All of the data and text fields that describe a single customer are stored in a **customer record** in the call tracking or problem management database. (Recall that a data field is an element of a database record in which one piece of data is stored. A text field is a field that accepts free-form information. A **record** is a collection of related fields.)

➤ **Problem data** — the details of a single problem. They include the problem category (such as hardware or software), affected component or system (such as a printer or monitor), symptom, date and time problem occurred, date and time problem was logged, analyst who logged problem, problem owner, description, and severity. These data are also stored in fields, and all of the fields that describe a single problem are stored in a **problem record** in the call tracking or problem management system. These fields can be used to track problems, research and track trends, or to search the knowledge base for solutions.

Customer records are linked to problem records by a unique *key* field, such as customer name or customer number.

When gathering data about a problem, capture details such as who, what, when, where, and how.

One of the pieces of information you must collect from customers is a description of the problem. Many help desks capture two types of problem descriptions: a short description and a detailed problem description. A **short problem description** succinctly describes the actual results a customer is experiencing. The short description is sometimes called a problem statement.

> Error msg H536 displays when customer is logging on to account-
> ing system. Customer is bounced back to main login screen.

> Spreadsheet package abends when customer runs new macro.

Stating the short problem description is an excellent way to obtain agreement from customers that you understand the problem they are experiencing. The short problem description is often used in reports or online queries to provide an "at a glance" overview of the problem. The short problem description may also be used to search a knowledge base for solutions.

Be succinct when creating the short description, but not to the point of making the description illegible. Resist the temptation to abbreviate words unless the abbreviation is widely recognized. For example, "msg" is a known abbreviation for message. Avoid acronyms and jargon unless the terms are well known to your audience. You can also eliminate words such as "and" and "the" unless they contribute considerably to the readability of the short description.

A **detailed problem description** provides a comprehensive accounting of the problem and the circumstances surrounding the problem's occurrence. The detailed problem description should contain a number of items, including:

➤ The result the customer expects. For example, the customer expects a report to appear on the printer.

➤ The actual result the customer is experiencing. For example, the report is not printing.

➤ Steps the customer took to get the results. For example, the customer issued a print command.

➤ The history or pattern of the problem. For example, this is a new report and the customer has never tried printing it before. To determine the history or pattern of the problem, you can ask the customer questions such as:

- Does the problem occur every time the customer performs this step?

- Does the problem only occur in certain circumstances? What are those circumstances?

- Does the problem only occur intermittently? Under what conditions?

➤ Whether the problem is part of a larger problem. For example, the printer is attached to a portion of the network that is currently down.

Notice that one of the first parts of the detailed problem description is the result the customer expected. When determining the expected result, you are in essence determining the answer. You may be thinking, "If I knew the answer, there wouldn't be a problem." Not true. The answer, or the expected result, is what the customer *expected* to happen. What the customer expected did not happen, hence the problem. Problem solving involves asking questions until you determine *why* the customer's expected result did not happen.

6

Step 2. Diagnose the Problem

When diagnosing the problem, you are trying to determine the probable source of the problem and, ultimately, the root cause of the problem. The **probable source** of the problem is the system, network, or product that is most likely causing the problem. The **root cause** of the problem is the most basic reason for an undesirable condition or problem, which, if eliminated or corrected, would prevent the problem from existing or occurring. Determining the probable source of a problem can be extremely difficult, particularly when dealing with complex technology, such as the technology found in a client-server computing environment. **Client–server** is a computing model where some computers, known as clients, request services, and other computers, known as servers, respond to those requests. For example, consider the earlier scenario where the customer issued a print command and the report did not appear. Figure 6-3 illustrates all of the computing components that must be working correctly for the customer's report to print.

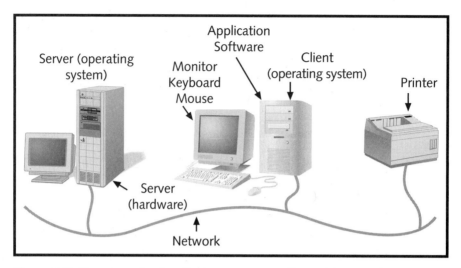

Figure 6-3 Components of a client-server computing environment

This is, of course, a very simple diagram, but it is designed to show that any number of potential points of failure may need to be considered when determining the probable source of a problem.

There are many techniques that are used to diagnose problems and determine the probable problem source. Figure 6-4 lists the most common of these techniques.

- Asking questions
- Simulating the customer's actions
- Using diagnostic tools

Figure 6-4   Problem diagnostic techniques

Each of these techniques is useful. You may use more than one of these techniques in the course of diagnosing a problem.

Asking Questions

Asking questions is an extremely effective way to diagnose problems. Asking questions enables you to continue gathering the data needed to identify a solution. You gain insight as to why the problem is occurring. You also gain insight about the customer. For example, the customer's ability to answer your questions and her use of terminology when answering will provide you with insight about the customer's skill level.

When asking questions, you must listen actively to both the response your customer is giving and the emotion with which your customer is giving that response. Remember that you must acknowledge and address any strong emotions before you begin or continue active problem solving. Remember, too, that your questions must be appropriate to the customer's communication style. For example, recall that you can ask open-ended questions as needed to obtain more detailed information. To take control of the conversation, you can ask closed-end questions that prompt short answers such as "yes" and "no."

Brainteasers and puzzles are an excellent way to improve your problem-solving skills. They teach you to ask questions, view problems from many different angles, and go beyond the obvious in search of a solution.

To become an efficient problem solver, you must condition your mind to ask and obtain answers to a basic set of questions. These basic questions can help you isolate the probable source of the problem. Figure 6-5 lists these basic questions and provides a series of additional questions that you can use to obtain the data you need.

Time may not allow you to ask all of these questions in the course of diagnosing a problem. Usually, you won't have to. The goal is to condition your mind to run through these questions as the customer is relaying information. In other words, you may not need to actually ask a question in order to receive an answer. The customer may simply provide the answer while describing the problem. You will then need to ask only those questions that have not yet been explicitly addressed but still need to be answered.

You may also have checklists available to you that provide questions more specific to the actual problem. For example, Figure 6-6 shows a problem-solving checklist that can be used to diagnose printer problems.

These checklists may be available to you online in the form of a knowledge management system, or you and your co-workers may develop paper checklists for the different types of problems that you encounter. For example, you may have a checklist for each of the software packages that you support or for each of the types of hardware that you support, such as monitors, printers, and so forth. These checklists will help you avoid letting customers lead you to an incorrect course of action. For example, if a customer calls and indicates that his printer will not print and that he has powered it on and off and checked the paper and toner, you might "assume" that a hardware failure has occurred and escalate the problem to the field services group. By asking additional questions, you may learn that the customer was routing his report to a different printer.

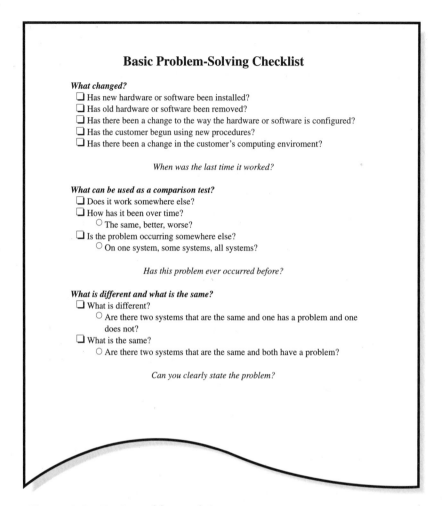

Basic Problem-Solving Checklist

What changed?
- ❏ Has new hardware or software been installed?
- ❏ Has old hardware or software been removed?
- ❏ Has there been a change to the way the hardware or software is configured?
- ❏ Has the customer begun using new procedures?
- ❏ Has there been a change in the customer's computing enviroment?

When was the last time it worked?

What can be used as a comparison test?
- ❏ Does it work somewhere else?
- ❏ How has it been over time?
    - ○ The same, better, worse?
- ❏ Is the problem occurring somewhere else?
    - ○ On one system, some systems, all systems?

Has this problem ever occurred before?

What is different and what is the same?
- ❏ What is different?
    - ○ Are there two systems that are the same and one has a problem and one does not?
- ❏ What is the same?
    - ○ Are there two systems that are the same and both have a problem?

Can you clearly state the problem?

Figure 6-5   Basic problem-solving questions

Ask your level two service providers to help you develop problem-solving checklists so that you can solve problems at the help desk, rather than escalating them to level two.

Some of the questions in this chapter may seem obvious and almosttoo simplistic. It is often the simple question, though, that reaps the most information. For example, if you ask a customer "When was the last time the printer worked?" and she responds with, "Yesterday before I moved it," you may have a good lead on why the problem is occurring. Asking these seemingly simple questions will enable you to quickly eliminate obvious causes before moving on to more complex diagnostics.

Printer Problem-Solving Checklist

✔	Have you ever had this problem before?	Yes/No
✔	Have you ever been able to use this printer before?	Yes/No
✔	Is this a network printer?	Yes/No
✔	Are you properly attached to it?	Yes/No
✔	Have you checked the print queue status?	Yes/No
✔	Has the printer been moved recently?	Yes/No
✔	Is the printer plugged in?	Yes/No
✔	Is the printer powered on?	Yes/No
✔	Do you see a power indicator light?	Yes/No
✔	Do you see an on-line indicator?	Yes/No
✔	Does the printer have paper in it?	Yes/No
✔	Does the printer have an error code?	Yes/No
✔	Have you ever successfully printed this report?	Yes/No
✔	Has it ever printed on this paper?	Yes/No
✔	Can you route the report to another printer?	Yes/No

Figure 6-6   Printer problem-solving checklist

Chapter 6

Simulating the Customer's Actions

Some help desks provide analysts access to the systems or software packages that their customers are using. Some help desks also have lab areas where analysts can access systems that match customers' hardware and software configurations. Analysts can use these systems to simulate a customer's actions in an effort to determine the probable source of a problem. If an analyst can perform an action successfully that a customer cannot, then the probable source of the problem is more likely in the customer's computing environment. For example, if you can access the accounting system but the customer cannot, the accounting system can be eliminated as the probable source of the problem.

The usefulness of this technique depends on the access that you have to the systems your customers use and on the policies of the company where you work. Some companies provide analysts with limited access to the systems being used by customers, in which case analysts may not be able to fully simulate customers' problems. Companies may limit access because customers are working with highly confidential information or because they are performing highly secure transactions. For example, a customer may be authorized to transfer funds in a banking setting or to change grades in an academic setting. In these situations, you may only be able to verify that the system is up and running. If the system is up and running, and you believe that the problem is occurring within the system, you will escalate the problem to a level two specialist who has the authority to perform further diagnostics within the system.

The policies of some companies include very strict standards that determine what technologies customers use. In an internal help desk setting, these standards determine the technologies available to the company's employees. In an external help desk setting, these standards represent the minimum hardware and software recommended to run your company's products without incurring problems.

The help desk is often involved in developing these standards. As a result, the help desk can become very familiar with the technologies it supports. For example, the help desk may be involved in testing and selecting the systems to be used within a company so they will be familiar with the systems' strengths and weaknesses. It also typically receives copies of the systems, documentation, and training, so it can simulate and solve problems more quickly.

Some companies also establish standards that determine what changes customers can make to the systems they use. For example, some companies do not allow customers to change the way their systems are configured or install personal software, such as games, on their business computers. By tightly controlling the changes that customers make to systems, the company can prevent problems that may occur as a result of an inappropriate change.

Without standards, customers may install equipment or software without the help desk's knowledge. As a result, the help desk does not have a copy of the system that can be used to simulate problems. The installation of the new system may, in fact, be causing the problem. For example, a customer may download software from the Internet that contains a virus, which may corrupt files on the customer's PC or may even destroy portions of the customer's PC. Also, without standards, customers may be able to make changes to their systems that cause problems. For example, a customer may change the PC's display settings in such a way that portions of the screen are no longer visible. Unfortunately, the customer may not remember making the change or may not recall exactly what change was made. In these cases, trying to simulate the customer's actions may be a waste of time or even impossible.

When technology standards exist, whether and how strictly those standards are enforced will vary from one company to the next. Some companies encourage customers to comply with its standards by having the help desk provide a high level of support for standard systems and little or no support for nonstandard systems. In other words, customers who choose to use nonstandard systems may be "on their own" if they have questions or problems. Although this policy of letting customers opt to use nonstandard systems without support may benefit the help desk—it is not getting calls about nonstandard systems—the company does not typically benefit in the long run. This is because the problems still occur; they are just not being reported to the help desk. When standards are enforced, the productivity of all of the groups that use and support the systems benefit. These standards benefit technology users as they receive the training they need and the number of problems they encounter is minimized. These standards benefit the help desk and other support groups, such as level two service providers, because they are supporting a limited set of systems and can acquire the training, tools, and talent needed to provide high-quality support.

ESTABLISHING TECHNOLOGY STANDARDS

Many companies establish standards that determine what hardware and software systems are used by their internal employees and, when appropriate, by their external customers. It is common for a committee to select the standard systems and define the policies that govern how the systems are used and supported. The committee typically includes representatives from all of the groups that will use and support the standard systems: Customers, the help desk, and any level two and three groups needed to support the systems are represented.

Systems undergo rigorous testing before they are selected to ensure they meet the selection criteria defined by the standards committee and to ensure the new systems are compatible with other standard systems. This testing also enables the standards committee to illustrate the benefits of implementing standard systems. Benefits of establishing technology standards include:

➤ **A less complex environment.** Rather than using two or more word processing products, such as Microsoft Word and Corel WordPerfect, the product that best meets the company's needs is selected and implemented. As a result, customers, the help desk staff, and level two service providers are able to gain a high level of expertise in the chosen systems.

➤ **Improved ability to share data and exchange information.** Rather than converting data from one system to another, such as from a Microsoft Excel spreadsheet to a Lotus 1-2-3 spreadsheet, a single system is used. As a result, many of the problems that can occur when converting data are prevented.

➤ **Effective training programs can be developed.** Because there are fewer systems, companies have more resources available to develop and deliver high-quality training programs. The help desk receives the training it needs to support the systems, and customers receive the training they need to use the technology as efficiently and effectively as possible. Consequently, customers have fewer questions and problems, and the help desk can quickly handle questions and problems that do occur.

➤ **Proactive support can be provided.** With fewer systems, the number of isolated random problems decreases—because you have reduced the number of potential points of failure—and more common, predictable problems occur. By using trend and root cause analysis to proactively identify the likely source of potential problems, problems can be prevented. Or, their impact is minimized.

➤ **Costs are controlled.** Companies that have standards can negotiate discounts with vendors because they are purchasing software licenses and hardware for a greater number of people. For example, companies can purchase a site license, which enables all users at a given location to use a software package, rather than purchasing more costly individual licenses. Also, the costs associated with abandoning technology that does not work correctly are eliminated, as are the problems that accompanied that technology.

➤ **The company is positioned to take advantage of state-of-the-art technology.** Allowing customers to use any system they want often makes it difficult for a company to implement new technology. For example, customers who are using DOS must be transitioned to a Windows operating system before the company can implement Windows-based applications. Although the customers may be comfortable using the systems they have, those systems may not fit the long-term needs of the company and may be causing problems. The standards committee stays on top of industry trends and selects systems that will benefit the company now and into the foreseeable future.

It is sometimes perceived that establishing technology standards decreases the user's ability to take advantage of the latest technology trends. While that may be true to some extent, it is equally true that the latest technologies are often plagued with problems. Establishing technology standards enables companies to create a computing environment that is more stable and less complex. That is, they create a computing environment that has fewer problems and is easier to support.

6

Using Diagnostic Tools

Some help desks, particularly those that support remote customers, provide analysts with tools, such as remote control systems, they can use to diagnose problems. A **remote control system** is a technology that enables an analyst to take over a customer's keyboard, screen, mouse, or other connected device in order to troubleshoot problems, transfer files, provide informal training, and even collaborate on documents. The customer authorizes the analyst to access his or her system by keying a password. Because the analyst may be able to observe or access confidential information or transactions, some companies prohibit the use of these systems. When these systems are used, analysts can resolve many problems that would previously have required a visit to the customer's site. Most customers appreciate this technology because they do not have to wait for a field service representative to arrive. Not all customers feel comfortable with this technology, though, so it is important to ask permission and respect your customer's feelings on this matter.

Newer hardware and software systems have built-in diagnostic tools. For example, the system may come with a disk that contains a diagnostic program customers can run if they encounter a problem. Some software packages include wizards that step customers through a series of diagnostic questions. Help desk analysts can prompt a customer to use these tools either while they are working with the customer or, in some cases, before the customer contacts the help desk. For example, the help desk can suggest customers use these tools on their Help Desk Quick Reference Card, or customers can be prompted to use these tools when they access the help desk's Web site. These tools can provide help desk analysts with the information they need to solve a problem, but they also can provide customers with the ability to solve problems on their own. When customers solve problems on their own, help desk analysts are freed to work on more complex and unique problems.

Diagnostic tools are an effective way to diagnose problems. Keep in mind that using these tools may not always be an option. For example, if the network is down, access to a customer's system using a remote control system may not be possible. Or, if a hardware failure occurs, having a customer run a diagnostic program may not be possible. When diagnostic tools are not available, you can ask questions or simulate the customer's actions in an effort to identify the probable problem source.

Analysts often feel pressure to resolve or escalate problems as quickly as possible. Because of this pressure, they may draw conclusions based on insufficient information or without understanding all of the facts. You must take the time needed to fully diagnose the problem and identify the correct probable problem source. Otherwise, you can waste time developing a course of action that will not permanently solve the problem. Incorrectly identifying the probable source can also damage your relationship with level two service providers. For example, a level two service provider who spends time diagnosing a problem only to learn that the problem should have been assigned to another group will often resent the interruption and may mistrust you or the entire help desk in the future.

Step 3. Develop a Course of Action

Once the correct probable source is identified, you then can begin to develop a course of action or action plan. The course of action may involve researching the problem further, developing a solution, escalating the problem to a level two service provider, or simply letting the customer know when to expect a more up-to-date status. It is important to note that the course of action taken will not be correct if an incorrect probable source was identified. When the correct probable source is identified, an analyst can:

➤ Consult printed resources, such as manuals, user's guides, and procedures, in an effort to research the problem, identify a solution, or implement a solution

➤ Consult online resources, such as online help, Web sites, and so forth, in an effort to research the problem, identify a solution, or implement a solution

➤ Determine if a workaround is available that can satisfy the customer's immediate need

➤ Escalate the problem to the correct level two service provider or subject matter expert

➤ Search a knowledge base for solutions to known problems or for policies and procedures that can be used to develop a solution

➤ Search the call tracking or problem management system for past problems that are similar or related to the current problem, which can then be used to further develop a course of action

➤ Use personal knowledge to develop a solution

➤ Use tools, such as remote control systems, to further diagnose the problem, identify a solution, or implement a solution

It is important to review the course of action with the customer and ensure that the customer is comfortable with it and with the timeframe within which it will be executed. If the customer is not comfortable, determine what the customer would prefer and, if possible, accommodate that preference. If you cannot accommodate the customer's preference, determine if there is an alternate course of action that will satisfy the customer's need in the interim.

Knowing When to Engage Additional Resources

6

Most help desks strive to solve as many problems as possible at level one. There are times, though, when a level one analyst needs to consult a co-worker or escalate a problem to a level two service provider. For example, a customer may be reporting a very complex or unique problem, or a customer may be having a problem with a product that you have not yet been trained to support. Your first course of action is to use resources such as online help, product and procedure manuals, or a knowledge base. If these resources do not prove useful, you may turn to a co-worker or level two service provider for help.

To ensure problems are solved as quickly as possible, many companies establish a **target escalation time,** which is a time constraint placed on each level that ensures problem resolution activities are proceeding at an appropriate pace. For example, a help desk's policy may state that level one should escalate problems to level two within thirty minutes. Management typically asks that analysts exercise their best judgment in following this guideline. In other words, if an analyst feels that she is close to resolving the problem, she should proceed. On the other hand, if an analyst believes that he has exhausted his capabilities and that he has utilized all available resources, it is time to escalate the problem.

As an analyst, you should consider the following points as the target escalation time approaches but before you escalate the problem to another service provider.

➤ Do I have sufficient information to clearly state the problem? Have I collected pertinent details such as who, what, when, where, and how?

➤ Have I determined the probable source of the problem? Have I eliminated all other possibilities?

➤ Have I gathered the information that is required by level two? If level two has provided a problem-solving checklist, has the checklist been completed and the results documented?

➤ What is the problem severity? Is this a problem that must be solved right away or can the customer wait?

Problem **severity** is a category that defines how critical a problem is based on the nature of the failure and the available alternatives or workarounds. The help desk and the customer usually work together to determine a problem's severity. The problem severity typically dictates the target resolution time of the problem. Then, a problem priority is assigned by the help desk or by the level two or level three group designated to work on the problem. **Problem priority** identifies the order for working on problems with the same severity. Factors that may influence the priority assigned to a problem include the number of times a problem has recurred, how long a customer's system has been down, or the terms of a customer's Service Level Agreement (SLA). For example, a customer, via an SLA, may be paying for premium service that requires a quicker resolution time. Management may also increase the priority of a problem when, for example, the customer affected is a company executive, the customer has had a similar problem before that was not resolved to the customer's satisfaction, or management simply makes a judgment call and prioritizes one problem over another.

Remember that when you consult with a co-worker or escalate a problem to a level two service provider, that person will expect you to be able to provide the answers to the questions listed above. If you cannot give these answers, you may need to ask a few more questions before you seek help. With the answers to just a few additional questions, you may find that you can solve the problem on your own.

TAKING OWNERSHIP

Not every problem can be solved immediately. Contrary to how it may seem at times, most customers *do* understand this fact. What customers expect when a problem cannot be solved immediately is that someone take responsibility for ensuring the problem will be resolved in the time frame promised. When a help desk analyst cannot resolve a problem in the course of the initial telephone call or a problem must be escalated to a person or group outside of the help desk, a problem owner is designated. The **problem owner** is an employee of the support organization who acts as a customer advocate and ensures a problem is resolved to the customer's satisfaction. When a problem owner is designated, the customer shouldn't have to initiate another call. Nor should the customer have to call around to the different groups involved in solving the problem to find out the problem's status or progress. The problem owner does that for them.

In many companies, the person who initially logs the problem is the owner. In other words, the help desk analyst who first handles a problem continues to follow up, even when the problem is escalated to level two or level three.

Often, the analyst (problem owner) is the only person who can close the problem and does so only after verifying that the customer is satisfied. In other companies, the problem owner changes as problems are escalated from one level to the next. The person designated to work on the problem must accept responsibility and agree to assume ownership of the problem before the previous problem owner transfers responsibility (ownership) to him or her.

Regardless of how the problem owner is established, from a customer satisfaction standpoint, it is vital that for every single problem, one person serves as an advocate for the customer. This practice ensures that problems are not lost or forgotten and that customers' needs are considered at all times.

Problem Owner Responsibilities

Taking ownership of a problem comes with specific responsibilities. The problem owner accepts responsibility for proactively ensuring that a problem is resolved to the customer's complete satisfaction. A problem owner:

➤ Tracks the current status of the problem, including who is working on the problem and where the problem is in the problem management process

➤ Proactively provides the customer regular and timely status updates

➤ When possible, identifies related problems

➤ Ensures that problems are assigned correctly and are not passed along from level to level or group to group without any effort being made to identify a resolution

➤ Ensures that appropriate notification activities occur when a problem is reported, escalated, and resolved (discussed below)

➤ Before closing a problem, ensures that all problem-solving activities are documented and that the customer is satisfied with the resolution

➤ Closes the problem ticket

Problem ownership does not mean that analysts focus only on problems that they own. To satisfy customers, each and every member of the help desk team must do all they can to ensure customer satisfaction. Sometimes, that means sharing ownership responsibilities. In other words, analysts:

➤ Help other owners when they can. For example, an analyst may have recently been to training or may be a subject matter expert and can share his or her knowledge with others.

➤ Update a ticket if a customer contacts the help desk to provide additional information and the owner is unavailable. A good practice is to leave the owner a note if the information recorded is time sensitive.

➤ Update a ticket if a customer contacts the help desk for an up-to-date status and the owner is unavailable. A good practice is to note the date and time that the customer requested a status update and the information given in the ticket.

➤ Negotiate a transfer of ownership for any outstanding tickets if the analyst is going to be out of the office for an extended time, such as for training or vacation. A good practice is to ensure all tickets are up-to-date and that all resolved tickets are closed before the tickets are transferred to another analyst.

Ownership is critical to the problem management process. Without it, problems can slip through the cracks and customer dissatisfaction invariably occurs. The concept of ownership ensures that everyone involved in the problem management process stays focused on the customer's need to have the problem solved in a timely fashion and to be informed when the problem requires more than the expected time to resolve.

Providing Status Updates to Customers and Management

A problem owner has the extremely important responsibilities of promoting awareness that a problem has occurred and regularly communicating the status of problem resolution activities. These activities are known as problem notification. **Notification** informs all of the stakeholders in the problem management process, including management, the customer, and help desk analysts, about the status of outstanding problems. Notification can occur when a problem is reported or escalated, when a problem has exceeded a predefined threshold, such as its target resolution time, or when a problem is resolved.

Notification to each of the stakeholders occurs at different points and has different goals. For example, *management* notification is appropriate when:

➤ The problem is extremely severe

➤ The target resolution time has been or is about to be reached

➤ Required resources are not available to determine or implement a solution

➤ The customer expresses dissatisfaction

In each of these cases, notification keeps management aware of problems that might require management intervention. The goals of management notification are to ensure that:

➤ Management knows the current status of problems that are in an exception state, meaning that the problems have exceeded a predefined threshold. For example, the target resolution time has been exceeded, or a level two support group is not acknowledging a problem that has been assigned to it.

➤ Management has the information needed to oversee problems that involve multiple support groups. For example, resources from the network support and development groups are needed to resolve a problem.

➤ Management has sufficient information to make decisions (such as add more resources or re-assign responsibilities), follow up with the customer, or call in other management.

➤ Management actions are recorded in the problem record so that everyone affected by or involved in solving the problem knows what decisions management has made or what steps they have taken to follow up with the customer or involve other management.

6

These goals make sure that the customer's problem is being addressed and responded to in an appropriate time and way. Like management notification, *customer* notification is appropriate in specific situations, such as when:

➤ The analyst has told the customer that he or she will provide a status at a given time, even if there has been no change in the problem's status

➤ The target resolution time will not be met

➤ Customer resources are required to implement a solution

➤ The problem has a high severity and justifies frequent status updates

➤ The customer was dissatisfied with earlier solutions

Customer notification keeps the customer informed about the progress of the problem resolution. The goals of customer notification are to ensure that:

➤ The customer knows the current status of the problem

➤ Customer comments or concerns are recorded in the problem record and addressed

These goals make sure that the customer knows that the problem is being addressed and responded to in an appropriate time and way.

Three ways that help desks deliver value are by: (1) making it easy for customers to report problems; (2) delivering solutions; and (3) taking ownership and ensuring that problems that cannot be resolved immediately are addressed in the required timeframe. One of the most common complaints that help desks hear from customers is that they were not kept informed. It is important to remember that even bad news is better than no news at all. Calling customers to let them know that the target resolution time cannot be met, and perhaps explaining the reason for any delays (such as having to order parts), is far better than having the customers hear nothing.

Keep the customer informed . . . Keep the customer!

The help desk can notify management, customers, and others by telephone, in person, with an e-mail message, through a paging device, or automatically via the problem management system. How notification occurs and who is notified varies based on conditions such as the severity of the problem, who is affected by the problem, and when the problem occurs. Many help desks have documented procedures that spell out who to notify and how to notify them.

BILL ROSE
SOFTWARE SUPPORT PROFESSIONALS ASSOCIATION
FOUNDER, SSPA
SAN DIEGO, CALIFORNIA

Bill Rose has established himself as one of the world's leading authorities on the process of delivering world class software support. He founded the Software Support Professionals Association (SSPA) in 1989 and served as its Executive Director for seven years. SSPA is a membership organization that provides a value-added forum where service and support professionals in the software industry can share ideas, discuss developing trends, and network with their peers. Bill Rose talks about the skills needed in the support industry and trends affecting the industry.

In the support industry, three sets of skills are needed: (1) technical, (2) interpersonal, and (3) administrative. By far, the people who are most successful are those with strong interpersonal skills, particularly those people who can communicate effectively and appropriately with managers, co-workers, and customers.

When interacting with managers, analysts must represent the customer in a realistic fashion. When communicating customer issues to managers, analysts must demonstrate an appropriate sense of urgency. Managers don't want analysts to panic and overstate the impact of an issue; nor do they want analysts to relay an issue in a very casual manner, only to find out later that it is a big problem.

When interacting with co-workers, analysts need to remember that they are part of a team. Sometimes they need to interrupt their co-workers to ask questions. Sometimes they are interrupted and asked questions. Sometimes they have to deal with the stress of the person sitting next to them. Sometimes they have to ask for help dealing with stress. It's like family therapy. You have to stick together.

When interacting with customers, analysts must determine the customer's "level of learning," and then proceed accordingly. We have found that there are four levels of learning:

➤ unconscious incompetence

➤ conscious incompetence

➤ conscious competence

➤ unconscious competence

At the lowest level, *unconscious incompetence*, customers typically cannot articulate their problem. They will use very basic terminology or incorrect terminology, for example, "I can't get this 'doohickey' to work right." The more experienced analysts become, the more difficult it is for them to assist customers at this level. They have to be extremely patient. Customers at the *conscious incompetence* level know what they don't know. They will try to start using terminology but may use it incorrectly. Customers at this level benefit greatly when analysts reassure them and walk them through the problem-solving process step-by-step. Customers at the *conscious competence* level are often the easiest to support. They use terminology correctly and they can often clearly and correctly articulate their problem. They can also work with analysts to solve the problem. At the highest level, *unconscious competence*, customers are often known as "power users." They can be a challenge to support because they often feel they know more than the analysts do. They are often impatient and resent being asked "basic" questions.

You must learn to quickly assess the customers' level of learning so you can communicate effectively with them. It is also important to know your level of learning so that you know when it's time to ask for help.

Many of today's young people have grown up working with computers. They have the technical skills that are needed. The question is, do they—do you—have the interpersonal skills, particularly the skills needed to support customers who are "charged up" because they are frustrated, confused, upset, or angry. Nurture your communication skills. Obtain training or attend programs such as Toastmasters and Dale Carnegie. These skills can be developed and are worth acquiring.

Technical support is definitely a career that is here to stay. People who have the ability to communicate effectively one-on-one, over the telephone, and in writing can reap the greatest rewards. We are seeing a real shift in the way companies generate revenues. Today, greater than 80 percent of a software publisher's revenue comes from customer services. This means that CEOs are becoming very interested in customer service and they are putting programs in place to attract and retain good people. We are seeing more career advancement opportunities and compensation is increasing. Even entry-level salaries are on the rise.

6

Building Good Relationships with Other Support Groups

Although most help desks strive to solve as many problems as possible at level one, there are times when a level one analyst needs to interact with people from other support groups, such as a field services group or a network support group. An analyst may need to escalate a problem to the support group or obtain a status update on a ticket previously assigned. The analyst may be asking for informal training or help developing a problem-solving checklist. A good relationship between the help desk and other support groups ensures that all groups can fulfill their roles and responsibilities.

It takes time and effort to build a strong relationship between the help desk and other support groups. Level one analysts must strive to continuously increase their knowledge and the efficiency and effectiveness of their problem-solving skills. This includes ensuring that all available information has been gathered and that all checklists have been completed before a problem is escalated to level two. Level two service providers must respect the help desk's role as a front-line service provider. They must acknowledge the fact that the help desk's efforts are freeing them from the need to answer the same questions or solve the same problems over and over again. They must be willing to impart their knowledge to the help desk. This enables the help desk to solve more problems at level one, while also reducing the number of problems the help desk escalates to level two. The help desk must be willing to receive that knowledge and seek level two's assistance only after utilizing all other available resources, such as manuals, knowledge bases, and so forth.

The following techniques can be used to foster a strong relationship between the help desk and other support groups so that all groups can reap the benefits.

➤ **Review and understand your company's Service Level Agreements (SLAs)** — Recall that an SLA is a written document that spells out the services the help desk will provide the customer, the customer's responsibilities, and how service performance is measured. These agreements are critical in defining the roles and responsibilities of all of the support groups represented in the company's customer service delivery chain. These agreements contain information such as the services to be delivered, service hours, performance metrics, and so forth. These agreements are integral to the relationship that exists between level one and level two. For example, if there is a critical problem and the company guarantees a customer that the problem will be resolved in two hours, the help desk must notify level two immediately so that the level two service provider has an adequate amount of time to respond. Conversely, the help desk must not insist that level two drop everything else to work on a non-critical problem that does not need to be resolved for several days. The help desk must resist the temptation to "cry wolf," or level two may become unresponsive. Understanding your company's Service Level Agreements is an excellent way to ensure everyone's expectations, including those of other support groups, are being met.

➤ **Provide mutual feedback** — An excellent way to enhance the relationship between the help desk and other support groups is to ask the members of each group for feedback. You will get more benefit from improving or addressing known problems than from addressing what you "think" the problems are. You can solicit feedback informally by getting feedback from someone in the support group that you know and that you trust will be constructive. The help desk team also can solicit feedback formally by, for example, preparing a survey, such as the one shown in Figure 6-7, that asks the members of other support groups for feedback. When the help desk is open to feedback, it will often find that other support groups begin to solicit and respond to constructive feedback in return.

➤ **Job shadowing** — **Job shadowing** involves working side-by-side with another person in an effort to understand and potentially learn that person's job. Job shadowing provides excellent benefits to both the help desk and support groups because each group is given the opportunity to "walk in the other's shoes." This enables both groups to gain a better understanding of the other's perspective and priorities. Job shadowing is a particularly effective way to improve your problem-solving skills. For example, job shadowing may give you the opportunity to work with a specialist to solve a complex or unique problem, or it may give you the opportunity to learn how to use new tools or to develop new checklists. As with providing mutual feedback, you can job shadow someone informally on your own, or your help desk may have a formal program in place.

➤ **Review call tracking system information** — A common complaint from level two service providers is that they cannot understand the information that help desk analysts provide in the tickets escalated to them, or they feel the information is incomplete. Conversely, help desk analysts often complain that level two service providers do not thoroughly document the steps taken to resolve a problem. As a result, the help desk is unable to reusethe resolution when a similar problem occurs. Periodic reviews of call tracking system information by a team of level one and level two service providers can pinpoint areas that that need to be improved. A good practice is to use real tickets during this review to illustrate and discuss examples of both poorly documented and well-documented tickets. The conclusions drawn during these reviews and the examples of well-documented tickets can be used to create new or enhanced ticket logging procedures.

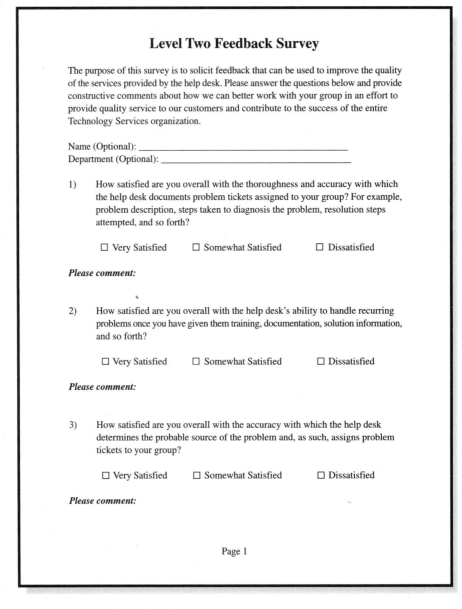

Figure 6-7 Level two feedback survey

➤ **Communicate** — When strained relations exist between the help desk and other support groups, it is often because of poor communication. The help desk and the support groups must make sure that they communicate all appropriate information in a timely manner. For example, the help desk must let the support groups know when it typically receives its highest volume of calls or when it is receiving an unexpectedly high volume of calls. This information enables the support groups to understand the current

Level Two Feedback Survey

4)   How satisfied are you overall with the help desk's efforts to diagnose the problem prior to seeking assistance from your group?

☐ Very Satisfied   ☐ Somewhat Satisfied   ☐ Dissatisfied

Please comment:

5)   How satisfied are you overall with the help desk's ability to record and assign the appropriate severity to problems that are reported to or discovered by it?

☐ Very Satisfied   ☐ Somewhat Satisfied   ☐ Dissatisfied

Please comment:

6)   How satisfied are you overall with the partnership that exists between your group and the help desk?

☐ Very Satisfied   ☐ Somewhat Satisfied   ☐ Dissatisfied

Please comment:

7)   Do you feel comfortable giving constructive feedback directly to the help desk in an effort to enhance the working relationship that exists between the two groups?

☐ Yes   ☐ No

Please comment:

8)   What improvements have been made and what areas do you feel could be further improved between your group and the help desk?

Please comment:

Thank you for taking time to complete this important survey.

Page 2

Figure 6-7   Level two feedback survey (continued)

capabilities of the help desk and the factors that influence its performance. Support groups must, in turn, let the help desk know when they are working on a large project or when they are going to be shorthanded. This information will enable the help desk to appropriately manage its customers' expectations and may influence when and how the help desk escalates problems. Everyone is busy in today's business world. Timely and regular communication will circumvent misunderstandings and promote a spirit of partnership.

➤ **Give praise** — One of the things that makes technical customer support so tough is that you rarely hear good news. In fact, for all intents and purposes, your job is to deal with bad news. Just as you hope to receive thanks for your efforts, you can let the people who work in other support groups know that you appreciate the job they are doing. For example, if a level two service provider develops a problem-solving checklist, a representative of the help desk can send an e-mail message to the service provider's supervisor or team leader that expresses the team's appreciation. Some help desks maintain a "goody" drawer filled with snacks or toys, such as stress balls, that they can hand out to level two service providers who provide training or in some way go the extra mile. While giving praise may seem like a small thing, it is easy to do, costs little to no money, and encourages continued goodwill. Giving praise also encourages praise in return. Praise is something we all appreciate.

Level one analysts and level two service providers must work together to ensure that problems are solved quickly and accurately. All of the support groups within a company, including the help desk, have a role to play and each must respect the other's role and responsibilities. While it is the problem owner's responsibility to act as a customer advocate and ensure a problem is resolved to the customer's satisfaction, each and every member of the customer service delivery chain must do all they can to ensure problems are solved quickly, correctly, and permanently.

FOCUSING ON PREVENTION

Once a solution has been identified and implemented, there are still questions that need to be asked and answered. These include:

➤ Did the resolution solve the problem?

➤ Is the customer satisfied?

➤ Has the root cause of the problem been identified?

➤ Was the corrective action permanent?

If the answer to any of these question is "No," the problem cannot be considered resolved. At this point, the problem owner, assisted by co-workers, level two or level three service providers, and when appropriate, management, must determine the next steps to take.

If the answer to all of these questions is "Yes," the problem ticket can be closed once all pertinent information is captured. It is particularly important to identify the root cause. Without this information, trend and root cause analysis cannot be performed.

Performing Trend and Root Cause Analysis

Trend analysis is a methodical way of determining and, when possible, forecasting service trends. Trends can be positive, such as a reduction in the number of "how to" questions the help desk receives after an improved training program, or trends can be negative, such as a dramatic increase in call volume after a new product appears on the market. Trend reports provide help desk management and staff with the information needed to formulate improvement plans and communicate achievements. Figure 6-8 illustrates that trend reports can also be used to monitor and measure performance.

	Problem Count	Resolved @ Level One	% Resolved @ Level One	Avg Monthly Volume
Dec	534	265	50	534
Jan	635	295	46	584
Feb	601	234	39	590
Mar	556	241	43	597
Apr	710	319	45	622
May	735	356	48	648

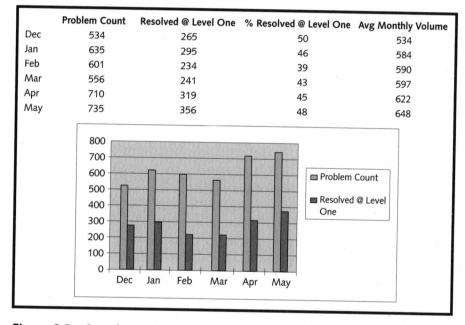

Figure 6-8 Sample trend report

This report shows a consistent rise in the number of problems logged by the help desk. A positive trend worth noting is that the help desk has been able to steadily increase the number of problems resolved at level one, despite an increase in its workload. This may be the positive result of recent training efforts or the addition of improved diagnostic tools. If the percentage of problems resolved at level one was decreasing, as opposed to increasing, it could mean that the level one help desk is understaffed and, as such, does not have adequate time to diagnose problems. It also could mean that a new product has been introduced and the help desk has not received adequate training. Complementary reports, such as the types of problems being reported to the help desk and the types of problems that must be escalated to level two, can be used to identify additional ways the help desk can improve.

Root cause analysis is a methodical way of determining the root cause of problems. If the root cause of problems is not eliminated or corrected, it is likely that they will recur. Root cause analysis enables management to determine *why* problems occur so that the company can take steps to prevent similar problems from occurring in the future. Figure 6-9 shows a sample root cause report.

	Closed Problems by Root Cause From: January 01 To: January 31		
Category	**Root Cause**	**Problem Count**	**% By Root Cause**
Hardware	[All]	20	100%
	Hardware Failure	14	70%
	Installation Error	6	30%
Software	[All]	102	100%
	Insufficient Resources	54	54%
	Configuration Error	36	36%
	Incompatible Software	10	10%
	Human Error	2	2%

Figure 6-9 Sample root cause report

This report shows a breakdown of problems by root cause for a given month and is arranged by problem category. It reveals that a high percentage of hardware problems are caused by hardware failures. Such a statistic should prompt the company to revisit its product evaluation process and perhaps select a different brand of hardware. This information can also be used to show hardware manufacturers the extent of the problems the company is experiencing. A complementary report could show a breakdown of problems caused by hardware failures that is arranged by product or manufacturer.

Charts and graphs are an excellent way to organize data and present information. They help your audience to visualize, compare and contrast, and analyze the information you are presenting. Types of charts and graphs include line, bar, and pie. The type of chart or graph you use depends on the information you are trying to present. For example, if you want to show how parts relate to a whole, pie charts work well. If you want to show how data varies over time, a line or bar graph is best. Effective charts and graphs share three main characteristics: they are easy to understand, visually memorable, and, most importantly, accurate.

Trend and root cause analysis work hand-in-hand. They can be used together either reactively to prevent problems or proactively to identify improvement areas. Help desks that use trend and root cause analysis only reactively rarely have the resources needed to handle problems efficiently and effectively. They simply do not have the information needed to predict their workload. Help desks that use these analysis techniques proactively are able to justify and acquire the resources they need, when they need them. They are also able to better manage their workload, and even reduce their workload, by eliminating problems. Root cause analysis is the more difficult of the two disciplines, and so not all companies determine and document root cause. These companies fail to take the extra time needed to determine *why* the problem occurred once they have "fixed" it. Unfortunately, by not capturing and then eliminating root cause, these companies put themselves at risk for the problem to happen again. As a result, they may waste time rediscovering a solution or retrieving and implementing a solution from the knowledge base. Remember, the fact that there is a solution in the knowledge base does not make it okay for a problem to occur. Ultimately, customers would prefer that problems be prevented.

6

Determining the Root Cause

When customers contact the help desk with a problem, they are typically experiencing a symptom. A **symptom** is a sign or indication that a problem has occurred. Recall that a problem is an event that disrupts service or prevents access to products. Using the information that the customer provides, the help desk analyst diagnoses the problem in an effort to determine the probable source and a possible solution. The root cause of the problem cannot be identified until a solution to the problem is found, implemented, and proven successful. In other words, the root cause cannot be identified until the problem is solved.

Determining the root cause takes a little extra time and it requires the analyst to look beyond the obvious and seek an answer to the question, "Why?" A failing of some analysts is that they think of root cause only in terms of technology. For example, if a customer experiences a problem using a word processing package, the analyst may indicate that the root cause of the problem was software related. The actual root cause may be the fact that the customer has not received adequate training and is using the word processing package incorrectly. Until the root cause is identified and eliminated, that is, until the customer receives training, it is likely that the customer will continue to experience problems.

It is important to distinguish symptoms and the probable source of a problem from the root cause. Each can be different. For example, if a customer contacts the help desk and indicates that she is receiving an error message each time she tries to print a report, the error message is the problem symptom. The analyst may determine that the probable source of the customer's printing problem is the software package that she is using to print. The analyst could determine this by routing a report to the printer himself to see if it prints. If it does, the analyst can eliminate the printer as the probable source. Further discussion with the customer may lead the analyst to conclude that the root cause of the problem is not, in fact, the software package that the customer is using, but the incorrect set of procedures that she is using to issue the print command.

Root cause is captured in a data field when problems are closed and is typically supplied by the person who identified the resolution. For example, if the help desk resolves a problem, an analyst will enter the root cause. If level two resolves a problem, the level two service provider will enter the root cause. Figure 6-10 provides a short list of common root cause codes for technology-related problems.

Root Cause: The basic reason for an undesirable condition or problem that, if eliminated or corrected, would have prevented it from existing or occurring.	
Code	**Description**
Communications Failure	For example, network or telephone line down
Configuration Error	PC/System configured incorrectly
Database Problem	For example, database full or generating errors
Environment	For example, power outage
Hardware Failure	Hardware malfunction
Human Error	Problem caused by human error
Incorrect Data	Incorrect input produced incorrect output
Incorrect Documentation/Procedures	Inaccurate or incomplete documentation/procedures
Incompatible Hardware	Incompatible/nonstandard hardware
Incompatible Software	Incompatible/nonstandard software
Installation Error	Hardware/Software installed incorrectly
Insufficient Resources	For example, memory
Lack of Training	For example, for use with "how-to" type inquiries
Other	For use when no other response is appropriate.
Planned Outage	For example, customer is unable to access a system due to a planned outage
Procedure Not Followed	Complete and accurate procedure not followed
Result of Change	Problem caused by a change to the system/device
Request for Information	For example, for use with inquiries
Software Bug	Incorrect software code
Unknown	Problem could not be duplicated

Figure 6-10   Sample root cause codes

Notice that many of the root cause codes listed are not related specifically to hardware products or software systems. They are related to how people are implementing or using the technology. In many companies, the technology itself is actually quite stable. The bulk of the problems that help desks handle are caused by changes made to the technology or factors such as inadequate training and insufficient documentation. Root cause analysis provides the information needed to address these issues.

Taking Preventative Action

Although some help desks have highly skilled statisticians perform trend and root cause analysis, any or all members of the help desk team can perform the analysis. Very often the front-line staff can identify trends simply by considering the calls they are receiving. For example, the help desk might notice that it is receiving a lot of calls about a certain system or product and bring that fact to management's attention. A trend report can then be created to validate statistically the help desk's hunch.

When working in a help desk, do not hesitate to suggest ways that problems can be eliminated. Be persistent and act on your hunches. Go beyond the quick fix and take the time to resolve problems correctly the first time. If, as a problem owner, you believe a problem has not been permanently resolved, leave the problem ticket open and engage the resources needed to determine and eliminate the root cause. Your co-workers, managers, and customers will thank you.

6

> *If you can't find the time to do it right, where are you going to find the time to do it over?* Author Unknown

To solve problems efficiently, effectively, and permanently, the help desk must be diligent in its efforts to capture and utilize information. This means that help desk analysts must log all problems and capture accurate and complete data about those problems, including the root cause. Without the data captured by help desk analysts, trend and root cause analysis is not possible. When trend and root cause analysis is not performed, it is likely that existing problems will recur and that new problems will appear. When trend and root cause analysis is performed, recurring problems are eliminated, problems are predicted and, in turn, can be prevented, and analysts are freed to work on more complex problems and pursue new skills.

Given the rapid pace at which technology changes, it is unlikely that trend and root cause analysis will enable a company to prevent *all* problems. This analysis will enable the help desk to eliminate common problems and avoid major problems by addressing problems when they are minor. The end result of these efforts is that the help desk will enhance its productivity, its customers' productivity, and its customers' satisfaction—all of which are very positive results.

When working in a help desk, an understanding of your company's problem management process and strong problem-solving skills are essential to your success. The problem management process and the problem-solving process both require that you systematically gather information, diagnose and solve problems, and, when necessary, engage additional resources. The problem management process also ensures that customers and managers are proactively kept informed about the status of problem resolution activities. Handling problems efficiently and effectively is important, but, ultimately, customers prefer that problems be prevented. Trend and root cause analysis can be used to prevent problems, but only if you capture accurate and complete data. When problems are prevented, you will have the opportunity to work on more complex problems and pursue new skills.

CHAPTER SUMMARY

- To be successful, a help desk analyst must be able to solve problems efficiently and effectively. Most help desks develop processes and procedures, such as the problem management process, in an effort to ensure that problems are handled quickly, correctly, and consistently. The goal of problem management is to minimize the impact of problems that affect a company's systems, networks, and products.

- Within the boundaries of the problem management process, analysts use their problem-solving skills to handle each problem. The best problem solvers condition themselves to gather all available information and methodically diagnose the problem before developing a course of action. Effective diagnostic techniques include asking questions, simulating the customer's actions, and using diagnostic tools.

- When problems cannot be solved immediately, customers expect someone to take responsibility for ensuring the problem is resolved in the timeframe promised. The problem owner assumes that responsibility. The concept of ownership ensures that everyone involved in the problem management process stays focused on the customer's need to have the problem solved in a timely fashion and to be informed when the problem requires more than the expected time to resolve. Ownership is critical to the problem management process. Without it, problems can slip through the cracks and customer dissatisfaction invariably occurs.

- Before a problem can be considered resolved, all pertinent information must be captured, including the root cause. This is because information is needed to perform trend and root cause analysis. Trend and root cause analysis work hand-in-hand. They can be used reactively to prevent problems or proactively to identify improvement areas. Root cause analysis is the more difficult of the t wo disciplines. It requires that service providers take the time to determine why the problem occurred once they have "fixed" it. Until the root cause is identified and eliminated, it is likely that problems will recur.

- When working in a help desk, you must log all problems and capture accurate and complete data about those problems to create information. Also, do not hesitate to suggest ways that problems can be eliminated and prevented. Your co-workers, managers, and customers will thank you.

KEY TERMS

client-server — A computing model where some computers, known as clients, request services and other computers, known as servers, respond to those requests.

customer data — Identifying details about a customer, including the customer's name, telephone number, department or company name, address or location, customer number, and employee number or user ID.

customer record — All of the data and text fields that describe a single customer.

detailed problem description — A comprehensive accounting of the problem and circumstances surrounding the problem's occurrence.

flow chart — A diagram that shows the sequence of tasks that occur in a process.

incident management — *See* problem management.

inquiries — Customer requests for information, such as "When will my equipment arrive?"

job shadowing — Working side-by-side with another person in an effort to understand and potentially learn that person's job.

notification — An activity that informs all of the stakeholders in the problem management process (including management, the customer, and help desk analysts) about the status of outstanding problems.

probable source — The system, network, or product that is most likely causing a problem.

problem — An event that disrupts service or prevents access to products.

problem data — The details of a single problem, including the problem category (such as hardware or software), affected component or system (such as a printer or monitor), symptom, date and time problem occurred, date and time problem was logged, analyst who logged problem, problem owner, description, and severity.

problem management — The process of tracking and resolving problems; also called incident management.

problem owner — An employee of the support organization who acts as a customer advocate and ensures a problem is resolved to the customer's satisfaction.

problem priority — Identifies the order for working on problems with the same severity.

problem record — All of the fields that describe a single problem.

problem statement — *See* short problem description.

procedure — A step-by-step, detailed set of instructions that describes how to perform the tasks in a process.

process — A collection of interrelated work activities—or tasks—that take a set of specific inputs and produce a set of specific outputs that are of value to the customer.

questions — Customer requests for instructions on how to use a product, such as "How do I…?"

record — A collection of related fields.

remote control system — A technology that enables an analyst to take over a customer's keyboard, screen, mouse, or other connected device in order to troubleshoot problems, transfer files, provide informal training, and even collaborate on documents.

request — A customer order to obtain a new product or service, or an enhancement to an existing product or service.

root cause — The most basic reason for an undesirable condition or problem, which, if eliminated or corrected, would prevent the problem from existing or occurring.

root cause analysis — A methodical way of determining the root cause of problems.

severity — A category that defines how critical a problem is based on the nature of the failure and the available alternatives or workarounds.

short problem description — A succinct description of the actual results a customer is experiencing; also called problem statement.

symptom — A sign or indication that a problem has occurred.

target escalation time — A time constraint placed on each level that ensures problem resolution activities are proceeding at an appropriate pace.

trend analysis — A methodical way of determining and, when possible, forecasting service trends.

REVIEW QUESTIONS

1. What is a problem?

2. Are most technical problems unique?

3. Define the term process.

4. Explain the relationship that exists between processes and procedures.

5. Draw the symbol that represents a task in a flow chart.

6. Draw the symbol that represents a decision point in a flow chart.

7. Why do most companies distinguish between problems, questions, and inquiries?

8. Is the problem management process typically used to handle requests?

9. List two types of data you must gather before you can begin diagnosing a problem.

10. What is a problem statement?

11. Briefly describe the items that should be included in a detailed problem description.

12. What are you trying to determine when diagnosing a problem?

13. Define the term root cause.

14. List three benefits that are derived by asking questions.

15. List three ways that help desks provide analysts with the ability to simulate their customers' actions.

16. Describe two situations in which you may not be able to use diagnostic tools.

17. Why is it important to determine the correct probable problem source?

18. What typically dictates the target resolution time of a problem?

19. Describe the responsibilities of a problem owner.

20. What can happen if no one takes ownership of a problem?

21. When can problem notification occur?

22. What are the goals of management notification?

23. What are the goals of customer notification?

24. Complete the following phrase: Keep the customer informed . . .
    _____.

25. What are two things that help desk analysts can do to build a strong relationship with their level two support groups?

26. What are two things that level two support groups can do to build a strong relationship with the help desk?

27. What four questions must be answered "Yes" before a problem can be considered resolved?

28. What are two ways that help desk management and staff can use the information that trend reports provide?

29. What is a problem symptom?

30. When do you determine the root cause of a problem?

31. What question is answered by determining the root cause of a problem?

32. List three ways you can help eliminate problems when you work in a help desk.

33. What must help desk analysts do to provide the information needed to perform trend and root cause analysis?

34. List two of the benefits of trend and root cause analysis.

HANDS-ON PROJECTS

Project 6-1
Develop a process flow chart. Assemble a team of three to five classmates. Develop a flow chart that shows all the steps for attending a movie the entire team agrees upon. Begin the process by deciding to go to the movies and end the process by having all of the members of the team return home safely.

Project 6-2
Tease your brain. The following letters represent something that you learned early in life, most likely before you attended first grade. Add the next two letters to the sequence and explain how these letters fit into the sequence.

O
T
T
F
F
S
S
?
?

Project 6-3

Develop a problem-solving checklist. Select a piece of computer hardware or a software package that you use regularly. Develop a problem-solving checklist that contains at least ten questions that analysts can use to diagnose problems customers may encounter when using the selected technology.

Project 6-4

Learn about remote control software. Search the Internet and access the Web site of two companies that manufacturer remote control software. Some popular vendors include Intel, Microcom, Netopia, Network Associates, Stac, and Symantec. For each of the two companies you select, summarize in a paragraph or two what you were able to learn about remote control software. Briefly describe the benefits of using these systems for both the customer and help desk analysts.

6

Project 6-5

Customer notification. A level two field service representative has just informed you that he will not meet the target resolution time for a problem that you own because another problem he is working on is taking longer than expected. The only other person who could work on the problem is in training this week. Briefly describe who you would notify and how you would minimize customer dissatisfaction in this situation.

Project 6-6

Learn about using charts and graphs. Search the Internet or go to your local library and learn more about how to effectively use charts and graphs to present information. For example, how can you use color to enhance your charts and graphs? How can you use labels to provide additional information about the data being presented? Prepare a list of ten tips for creating effective charts and graphs. Share your tips with the class. As a class, develop a list of the fifteen best tips.

Project 6-7

Report on a trend. Everywhere you look studies are being conducted that produce a trend. It seems you cannot watch a news show or read a magazine without hearing or seeing the phrase "Studies show that. . . ." Select a topic in which you are interested—it could be sports, cooking, gardening, the Internet, and so forth. Search the Web or read a magazine that specializes in the subject you have selected and find a trend. Prepare a brief report that describes the trend and explains your perspective on factors that are influencing the trend.

Project 6-8

Identify and prevent root causes. Get together with one or two of your classmates. Brainstorm and prepare a list of root causes for hardware problems, software problems, or network problems. You can use the list of sample root causes presented in this chapter as a starting point. For each root cause your team listed, identify at least one proactive way to prevent the problem from recurring. Compare your list to the lists developed by other teams in your class.

Case Projects

1. **Mind Games**

   You are the manager of a medium-sized help desk and have decided that you would like your staff to have some fun while they improve their problem-solving skills. Go to the library and look in books or magazines for brain-teasers and puzzles that can be used to challenge your staff and encourage logical thinking. Select three brainteasers and distribute them to your staff (choose three classmates). Discuss with your staff the techniques you learned in this chapter that could be useful in solving the brainteasers. For example, what information is available? What is the expected result? What questions can you ask in an effort to determine the expected result?

2. **Brownstein, Popp, and Hepburn**

   You work for a small law firm and have been chosen to work on a committee that will develop standards for the technologies the lawyers will be authorized to use. The lawyers where you work are very autonomous, and they resist any rules that they perceive are unnecessary. For the first meeting, each attendee has been asked to prepare a list of benefits that customers will derive as a result of establishing standards. The committee chairman hopes that promoting the benefits will lessen resistance to the new standards. Prepare for the meeting by listing the benefits that you perceive the entire company, not just the help desk, will derive by establishing technology standards.

3. **Eckes Office Supplies, Inc.**

   You have been hired as a consultant to help the internal help desk at Eckes Office Supplies, Inc. improve the relationship it has with its level two support groups. In an effort to understand the dynamics of the current relationship, you have decided to survey the help desk staff and members of the level two support groups. The help desk escalates a fairly high number of problems to the network support group, so you have elected to work on that relationship first. Prepare a survey that can be used to solicit the help desk's perception of its relationship with the network support group. Your goal is to formulate questions that, when answered, will help you determine if the network support group is meeting the help desk's expectations. (*Hint:* Use the level two feedback survey presented in this chapter for ideas.)

TEAMS AND TEAM PLAYERS IN A HELP DESK SETTING

> **After reading this chapter and completing the exercises you will be able to:**
>
> ➤ Describe the characteristics of a successful team
>
> ➤ Describe the stages of growth that teams go through
>
> ➤ Explain how successful teams manage the conflict that is inevitable and normal in a team setting
>
> ➤ Understand your role in the help desk and in your company's support organization
>
> ➤ Understand how to contribute to your team's goals
>
> ➤ Develop the skills needed to have positive working relationships with your teammates

In the frenetic setting of a technical help desk, no single person can know everything about all the products supported and provide all the support customers need. The demands are too great. As a result, the members of the help desk must work together as team. A **team** is a group of people organized to work together toward the achievement of a goal. To be successful, all team members must understand how their efforts contribute to the attainment of that goal.

Working in a group that calls itself a team does not make a person a team player. A **team player** is a person who contributes to the team's success by cooperating freely and communicating openly with his or her teammates. An effective team is made up of team players who contribute special skills or a unique personal style to the team. To be a team player, you must understand your role in the help desk and your role in the company's support organization. You must know how you can contribute to your team's goals and you must support and respect the abilities of other team members and acknowledge their contributions.

WORKING AS A TEAM

Not all work requires the efforts of a team. For example, the sales profession is usually an individual endeavor. Although a sales person's efforts may benefit the sales "team" or company, the sales person's compensation is typically based on personal achievements. As a result, a company's sales people often compete with one another to enhance their personal standing. In a team setting, competition is eliminated, and team members work together toward a common goal.

Technical support lends itself to a team setting for a number of reasons. These reasons include:

➤ **The sheer number of available products.** The technology marketplace is jammed with vendors looking to sell their product and become a market leader. Users or potential users may be tempted to say, "A printer is a printer," but each product has unique features and functionality that a help desk analyst must understand in order to support it. Although an analyst may be able to become proficient in a single product line or family of products, no one can master all of the products available today.

➤ **The constant and pervasive rate of technological change.** It has become virtually impossible for a single individual to be aware of and understand the changes occurring within a single market segment, such as hardware-, software-, or network-related products, much less the integration of these products throughout an entire company. Simply reading and assimilating all of the information offered in trade magazines and on Web sites could constitute a full-time job. This doesn't even include putting that information into action.

➤ **The need for business knowledge.** Technical support is about helping people use technology to achieve business goals. Increasingly, help desk analysts are being challenged to understand the business goals of their customers so that they can help their customers use technology to achieve those goals. This means that, in addition to technical skills, analysts may possess skills and knowledge that are unique to the profession they support, such as accounting skills or banking knowledge. It is not possible or practical for all members of the help desk team to acquire every business and technical skill needed to support their customers. Rather, team members specialize in different areas of the business and then work together to solve problems that span multiple specialty areas.

➤ **The increasing complexity of the business world.** Help desk analysts work with people of varying skill levels, education levels, and cultural backgrounds. Furthermore, help desks increasingly partner with vendors and service agencies in the course of delivering services. For example, more companies are outsourcing help desk services in an effort to deliver high-quality support services at a reduced cost. It would be extremely difficult for one help desk analyst to manage these diverse relationships and speak the many technical and nontechnical languages associated with them.

➤ **The need to use resources efficiently and effectively.** Managers in today's business world demand high productivity and high quality. Help desk analysts must handle requests and solve problems correctly the first time because little to no time exists to do things over. Also, analysts who lack the skills or training to perform a task that their job requires do not have the time it would take to "figure things out" on their own. As a result, help desk analysts must collaborate with teammates and other service providers to get the job done as quickly and correctly as possible.

Technical support lends itself to a team setting because the demands of the environment are simply too great for a single analyst. Instead, the members of the help desk need to work together as a team. Each analyst must maintain a high level of knowledge about the products and systems for which he or she is recognized as an expert, and at the same time show respect and support for the other members of the team. In other words, a member of the help desk team who is highly skilled in one particular product cannot discount the efforts of another team member who is not familiar with that product. That other team member may be highly experienced in another product, or may have business skills, soft skills, or self-management skills that contribute to the goals of the team.

Characteristics of a Successful Team

Just as working in a group that calls itself a team does not make a person a team player, assembling a group of team players does not make a successful team. To be successful, a team must share the characteristics listed in Figure 7-1. Teams that do not exhibit these characteristics are often ineffective and suffer negative side effects, such as low morale, low productivity, and high stress.

- A clear sense of purpose
- Diversity
- Openness and trust
- Positive relationships with other support groups

Figure 7-1   Characteristics of a successful team

Let's explore each of these characteristics in detail.

➤ **A clear sense of purpose** — For a help desk to be successful, the mission and goals of the team must be clearly defined and accepted by all of the team members. A help desk's **mission** is a written statement of the customers the help desk serves, the types of services the help desk provides, and how the help desk delivers those services. In other words, a mission defines *who* the help desk supports, *what* it supports, and *how* it provides that support. The mission then determines the type, size, and structure of the help desk. **Help desk goals** are measurable objectives that support the help desk's mission. Most help desks establish specific goals each year in an effort to clarify what analysts are supposed to focus on, eliminate conflicting goals, and encourage analysts to produce the desired results. Individual performance goals further define how help desk analysts contribute to their team's goals. **Individual performance goals** are measurable objectives for people who support the help desk's mission. Without a clearly defined mission and goals, a help desk can fall prey to the "all things to all people" syndrome. When the help desk tries to be "all things to all people," its resources can quickly be stretched too thin and its team spirit can quickly decline.

> *The achievements of an organization are the result of the combined effort of each individual.* Vince Lombardi

➤ **Diversity** — A common misconception is that to be successful, all of the members of a team must be "alike." They must agree on everything and get along at all times. The reality is that the most successful teams are made up of players who have unique skills and exhibit varying approaches to teamwork. In a baseball team, for instance, each team member performs different tasks. One plays first base, another specializes in pitching, and so on. Each player has an area of expertise and may actually not perform well if asked to perform in an area other than his or her specialty. (Pitchers, for example, are notoriously poor batters.) Each player must also at times be a leader, and at other times follow the leader. What makes these people with varying talents a team? Their desire to play together in order to win the game. In business terms, team players must be willing to work together in order to achieve the team's mission and goals.

> *Together Everyone Achieves More.* Author Unknown

➤ **Openness and trust** — Communication within a team setting is just as important as communicating with customers. Team members must be willing to share their knowledge, give and receive constructive feedback, and freely express their feelings. Effective communication requires that team members are not only willing to talk, but also willing to listen. If a team member does not understand a point a co-worker is making, that person must ask for clarification, paraphrase, or summarize his or her teammate's point of view to ensure understanding. Team members must also be able to rely on each other to get the job done. Although it is human nature to have a bad day now and then, team members must not impose their personal moods and problems on their co-workers. This does not mean that team members should not ask for help when they need it. In the most effective teams, members feel comfortable stating their weaknesses and looking to teammates for strength.

➤ **Positive relationships with other support groups** — When working in a team, members are accountable not only to the other members of the team, but also to the "greater team" that constitutes the service delivery chain within their company and that includes external service providers. Successful teams have positive working relationships with other groups, such as level two support groups, the training group, the sales and marketing department, external service providers, and so forth. The help desk must rely on these groups to provide knowledge, tools, and credibility. When the help desk lacks credibility, customers may contact these groups directly, circumventing the help desk all together. As a result, the help desk is unable to gain the confidence of its customers and of the other groups in its service delivery chain. Without the support of other parts of the company, it is unlikely that the help desk's potential will be realized and its contribution recognized.

A team leader to whom members are loyal is another characteristic of a successful team. Although a successful team can work around a poor team leader, an effective leader enables the team to achieve its full potential by removing obstacles and by sharing leadership responsibilities as needed to get the job done.

Building a Solid Team

To perform at maximum efficiency and effectiveness, each team member, including the leader, must embrace the characteristics of a successful team. That is, the team must have *a clear sense of purpose*. The team leader cannot simply choose a direction and instruct the team to follow blindly. Members of successful teams are committed to the goals of the team and to each other's ability to grow and be successful. To grow, team members must embrace *diversity*. Team members must acknowledge their weaknesses and take steps to improve, or rely upon the strengths of their teammates, to get the job done. As a team, members must acknowledge the unique skills that each player contributes and seek out and accept into the team people who can fill the team's voids. When people work together this way, the sum of their efforts is invariably greater than the efforts of any one person acting alone. This is because the combined experience of the team is greater than the experience of any one team member.

> *No one can be the best at everything. But when all of us combine our talents, we can be the best at virtually anything.* Don Ward

One of the greatest challenges that a team faces is establishing methods of communication that promote *openness and trust*. This is because the team must have in place ways of communicating within the team, between individual team members, and with groups outside of the team. No team stands alone. Teams must have *positive relationships with other support groups* who can provide the funds, equipment, training, and information the team needs to succeed.

A group of people cannot become a team overnight. It takes time, an open, pleasant working environment, and a willingness to work through the stages of growth that all groups experience on their way to becoming a team. Figure 7-2 introduces the Tuckman Teamwork Model. Developed by Bruce W. Tuckman, Ph.D. (*Psychological Bulletin*, 1965, pp. 63, 384-399), this model is often used to describe the developmental stages that all teams experience.

---

1. Forming

2. Storming

3. Norming

4. Performing

Figure 7-2   Tuckman Teamwork Model

Let's discuss the four stages of team development reflected in the Tuckman model.

Stage 1. Forming

During this first stage, the team members are selected and the process of becoming a team begins. The team's mission and goals are defined along with the team member's roles and responsibilities. Team members often experience a range of emotions during this stage, including excitement, anxiety, and, perhaps, even fear. Little is achieved while a team is in this stage as team members get to know each other and as the team's purpose is defined. During the forming stage, team members are often on their "best behavior" and try to avoid conflict. The team leader is actively involved in this stage and provides the direction and resources the team needs to progress.

Stage 2. Storming

During the storming stage, the team begins to face the reality of turning its mission and goals into executable action plans. Team members often begin to feel the team's goals are unrealistic and they may doubt the leader's ability to provide the team with what it needs. As the team members get to know each other, the polite facade begins to fade and they are more willing to disagree. Team members may experience frustration and self-doubt during this stage and some defensiveness and competition may occur. The team leader coaches and counsels the team during this stage and repeatedly reminds the team to stay focused on its goals.

Stage 3. Norming

This stage represents the "calm after the storm." Team members begin to take ownership for the team's performance and they begin to have confidence in the team's abilities. They begin to feel a sense of camaraderie and they begin to exhibit team spirit. Conflict is, for the most part, avoided as team members accept and welcome feedback rather than viewing it as criticism. The team leader steps away from the team during this stage and gets involved only when the team asks for support.

Stage 4. Performing

At this stage of the team's development, the team is achieving its goals and the team's members are participating fully in team activities. A spirit of cooperation and collaboration prevails, and team members trust each other and their leader. Team members feel a sense of pride and satisfaction, and the team has become a close-knit community. The team leader serves as head cheerleader and encourages the team to avoid complacency and continuously improve.

In the course of a team's development, it is inevitable that change will occur. For example, new team members will be added and old team members may leave. In the course of continuously improving, the team may rethink its mission or set new goals. The team may also be affected by changes to the company, such as a reorganization, a merger, or an acquisition of some kind. When change occurs, it can affect the team's ability to maintain or advance its current stage of growth. The best teams accept and embrace change by taking a step back to the forming stage in an effort to clarify the team's purpose and team members' roles and responsibilities. They can then move quickly through the storming and norming stages back to peak performance. Figure 7-3 illustrates the way teams continually move through the developmental stages.

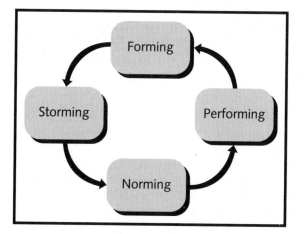

Figure 7-3 The ongoing nature of team development

Some teams never make it to the performing stage. For example, some teams avoid conflict during the storming stage and never develop the ability to deal with negative issues or achieve a consensus. A **consensus** is an opinion or position reached by all of a team's members or by a majority of its members. Conflict is inevitable in a team setting, and successful teams learn to work through it in a fair and constructive manner.

Reaching a consensus does not mean that team members agree with the majority just to avoid conflict. Typically, a consensus is reached when all team members can say that they agree with a decision or that they feel their point of view on a matter has been heard and understood, even if it has not been accepted. When a consensus is reached, some team members may still disagree with the decision but they are willing to work toward its success.

Managing Conflict in a Team Setting

Conflict is a normal part of human interaction that, when approached positively, can actually produce very creative and innovative results. In a team setting, conflict usually results from team members' varying perceptions and expectations. For example, a team member who stays late every night may resent the fact that a team member who is dedicated to his family leaves "early"—on time—one or two nights a week. In a technical setting, a team member may resent the fact that a co-worker has been selected to work on a choice project and as a result will be acquiring state-of-the-art skills. Another team member may feel that her technical skills are not being fully utilized and as a result are becoming stagnant. Or, a team member may feel that his accomplishments are not being acknowledged and appreciated. Conflict can even arise simply as a result of the stress that is inherent in a help desk setting. For example, a stressed team member may snap at co-workers, causing hurt feelings.

An issue is typically at the heart of a conflict. Because people often take the issue personally, they experience an emotional reaction, such as disappointment, hurt, and even anger. The best way to handle conflict is for team members to focus on the issue and not on the personalities of their teammates. Each team member must also be honest about his or her feelings, while striving to understand the feelings of his or her teammates. Engaging in a conflict is not a pleasant experience for most people. It is better, though, to resolve the issue rather than avoid it and allow it to turn into something even bigger.

Gossip is often a sign of unresolved conflict. It is best to avoid gossip by encouraging the parties who are gossiping—including yourself—to talk directly to the person or persons who are the subject of the gossip.

The following tips will enable you to resolve conflict in a team setting in a constructive manner. These tips will also enable you to maintain and perhaps even strengthen the relationship you have with the other party. When faced with a conflict, remember that:

➤ The person on the other side of the conflict has a point of view that is just as legitimate and reasonable to him or her as yours is to you. Listen actively to the other person's point of view and strive to understand his or her perspective.

➤ The other person may be as uncomfortable talking about the conflict or disagreement as you are. Suggest to your co-worker that you want to have a positive working relationship and that you would like to find a mutually agreeable way to resolve the conflict.

➤ It is safer and wiser to keep to the issues of a discussion. Avoid making comments that attack your teammate's personal character or question his or her motives.

➤ Saying the same thing over and over will not resolve the conflict. If you feel strongly about your point of view and your co-worker doesn't seem to be getting it, state your point of view in a different way, or try presenting your point of view from the other person's perspective.

➤ Little can be gained by discussing or debating the past. Rather than dwell on what or who caused the conflict, try to determine what can be done now and in the future to eliminate the source of conflict.

➤ The other person may be willing to accept a solution if you can make it sufficiently attractive. To achieve a compromise, both you and your teammate must be willing to make concessions. You must strive to identify a middle ground that you both find acceptable.

➤ It is okay to change your mind. Sometimes we form an opinion without having all of the facts. Should you discover through discussion that you were misinformed or that you were simply wrong, graciously acknowledge your co-worker's point of view and, when appropriate, apologize for causing or prolonging the conflict.

Although it is typically best to resolve a conflict rather than avoid it, there are times when it is appropriate to delay discussing a difficult situation. It is appropriate to avoid an issue if the timing is wrong and more harm than good will come from engaging someone in a discussion. For example, the person may be highly upset or angry and, as such, incapable of having a reasonable discussion, or you may be feeling highly emotional and unable to maintain an open mind. This does not mean you should avoid the issue altogether. Doing so may lead people to perceive you don't care about the outcome or that you are unwilling to be a team player. Instead, you should choose a time when both you and the person can calmly discuss the issue and seek a resolution. Being a team player requires that people work together in an effort to resolve not only their customers' problems, but problems within the team as well.

BEING A TEAM PLAYER

Being a team player requires personal commitment and a willingness to put the needs of your team ahead of your personal goals. As a team player, you contribute to the team's success by cooperating freely and communicating openly with your teammates. This does not mean that you must abandon your personal goals to be a team player. The most successful team players seek out a team setting that enables them to work toward their personal goals while contributing to the team's goals. People feel the greatest sense of job satisfaction when their skills are fully utilized and when their personal working style is acknowledged and accommodated. For example, some people like to continuously learn new skills and become bored when their work becomes routine. Other people enjoy routine and feel most comfortable when they have fully mastered the tasks they are expected to complete. A successful team is made up of a mix of people who contribute a variety of skills and personal working styles to the help desk and to the entire support organization.

BO WANDELL
SAFEHARBOR.COM CORPORATION
VICE PRESIDENT AND COMPANY DIRECTOR
SATSOP, WASHINGTON

SafeHarbor.com Corporation (SafeHarbor.com) is the pioneer in providing dynamic, loyalty-building Web-based customer relationship management and support. SafeHarbor.com was founded in 1998 to provide emerging technology companies with next generation support services. To do this, SafeHarbor.com incorporates the multimedia capabilities of the Web into a self-help environment that is enhanced by direct support analyst interaction. In other words, SafeHarbor.com delivers Web-based services (known as e-SupPort) that are enhanced by the telephone, rather than telephone-based services that are enhanced by the Web. Companies can outsource their support services to SafeHarbor.com for a flat monthly fee, or they can hire SafeHarbor.com to develop an e-SupPort application that they can then use to do support themselves.

From the point at which they apply to work at SafeHarbor.com, candidates and employees know that this company intends to do things differently. For example, the only way that candidates can submit their resume is via the Web. During an initial phone interview, candidates are given an appreciation of what it means to work for a start-up company--a state that Bo Wandell compares to being inside a tornado. Candidates are also told how they will be expected to contribute to the development of SafeHarbor.com's corporate strategy and growth. Candidates who are still interested go through an extensive interview process that ensures they have the skills that SafeHarbor.com requires, including the ability to work with the public, an understanding of the Web and its possibilities, and a burning desire to work in a start-up environment. Candidates take a computer literacy test during which they must demonstrate the ability to operate a computer. They also take a literacy test during which they must demonstrate the ability to read and write at a 12th grade level.

Once hired, employees are offered a wealth of opportunities that span the range of skills needed to support SafeHarbor.com's state-of-the-art technical infrastructure and deliver its innovative support services. Job positions include, support analysts, knowledge engineers, account managers, Web designers, database administrators, and IT staff. In keeping with SafeHarbor.com's nautical theme, staff members are organized into "crews." Each crew is dedicated to supporting a specific customer account and is responsible for that account's satisfaction. This includes capturing the knowledge needed to develop and deploy solutions to the account's customers.

SafeHarbor.com's knowledge engineers use sophisticated knowledge publishing tools to design, acquire, develop, and deliver a customized knowledge base that customers can access twenty-four hours a day, seven days a week. SafeHarbor.com's unique self-service environment offers customers multiple ways to access information, including free-form text queries, online browsing of frequently asked questions, and a powerful online tool called InfoPath. InfoPath allows customers to drill down to the right solution by specifying topics and responding to simple questions. When customers need additional help, they can use advanced online chat, e-mail, or the telephone to interact with support analysts.

Support analysts can use a myriad of tools to deliver solutions to customers. The most effective techniques use the Web's multimedia capabilities in conjunction with the telephone. For example, when describing a solution, analysts can use the Web to exchange documents, graphics, images, and even audio and video files with their customers. Analysts and customers can jump to other useful Web sites, or share an electronic whiteboard to illustrate a point and solve a problem. Support analysts can also use remote control tools to diagnose problems and deliver "how-to" demonstrations.

Because analysts are often encountering problems that are not found in the knowledge base, they are considered the first link in the chain of knowledge base development. When they encounter a new problem, they use workflow built into their call tracking system to document the solution. Knowledge engineers then refine the solutions--incorporating visual aids such as diagrams, screen shots, and schematics whenever possible to make the solution easier to use--and then post the solution in the knowledge base. Other customers can then use the new solution. Because customers are able to answer many questions on their own, analysts can focus on solution development. This disciplined and innovative approach enables SafeHarbor.com to deliver high quality services, at a lower cost.

SafeHarbor.com's mission is to provide unparalleled customer, technical, e-commerce, and sales support services. That means leveraging the Web. To do that, each and every employee is expected to work hard at revolutionizing the way support is delivered to customers. No complaining is allowed. If there is a problem to be solved, employees are given the resources they need to solve it. Time is the only constraint.

SafeHarbor.com is proud of the fact that it is doing today what many companies are talking about doing in the future—leveraging the Web—and it wants to maintain its competitive edge. To stay competitive, SafeHarbor.com looks for people who want a lifelong career, not just a job. It looks for people who understand not only how to support technology, but also how to use technology to deliver support. To keep good people, SafeHarbor.com offers competitive wages, a unique and comfortable working environment, ongoing training, and a lot of social activities. All it asks in return is that analysts serve their captain, respect their crewmates, and take their turn at the oars.

Understanding Your Role in the Help Desk

A common misconception is that being a team player means going along with the crowd. Some people believe they will have to give up their individuality and become just like everyone else on the team. This is not true. For a team to succeed, all team members must understand that they have a unique role to play. The role a person plays is a sum of his or her skills, knowledge, experience, and personal style.

In his book *Team Players and Teamwork*, Glenn M. Parker writes that research indicates that there are four types or styles of team players (*Team Players and Teamwork*, 1996, p. 63). Figure 7-4 lists the four types of team players.

- Challenger
- Collaborator
- Communicator
- Contributor

Figure 7-4 Team player styles

Each of these team player styles contributes to the team's goals in different ways. For example, a *challenger* serves as the team's "devil's advocate" and often questions the team's goals, methods, and procedures. A *collaborator* is goal-oriented and is willing to do what is needed to get the job done. A *communicator* is a good listener and encourages other team members to participate in team discussions and decisions. A *contributor* is task-oriented and does everything possible to provide the team with the skills, knowledge, and information needed to achieve its goals.

Each of these team player styles serves a purpose and each shines brightest at different times during the stages of a team's growth. For example, during the forming stage, a challenger will push the team to set high standards and may question the validity of the team's goals. During the storming stage, a communicator will facilitate discussion and encourage conflict resolution. During the norming stage, a contributor will help the team stay organized and will do the research needed for the team to succeed. During the performing stage, a collaborator will encourage the team to stay focused on its goals and, when needed, revisit its goals in an effort to continuously improve.

Each team player style can become ineffective if a team player overemphasizes his or her contribution or fails to acknowledge the contributions of others. Team players must be sensitive to the needs of the team and the needs of their teammates. For example, a collaborator who jumps in and takes over a task from a co-worker may believe that this is needed to get the job done. She may, however, be depriving her teammate of the opportunity to learn new skills. Furthermore, people can get "stuck in a rut," becoming a liability to the team. For example, there are times when it is no longer appropriate for a challenger to continuously question the team's goals and methods. Once a consensus has been achieved, the challenger must accept the goals and let the team move forward.

While most people have one style that predominates, each person is capable of exhibiting all of these team player styles. In fact, they may exhibit different styles in different situations. Your challenge as a team player is to determine your personal style and use the strengths of that style to contribute to your team. Knowing your personal style will also help you to identify and overcome your weaknesses. You can also strive to embrace the strengths of the other styles, thus increasing your ability to contribute to the team. People can change and they can exhibit incredible flexibility. If you want to develop a new style in an effort to increase your effectiveness, learn more about team player styles and team dynamics. The more you know about these concepts, the more effective you can be in a team setting.

Appendix A lists books, magazines, and organizations you can use to obtain self-study training materials and additional information about teams and team player styles.

Team players who embrace the diversity that a team setting offers are invariably happier and more successful. They continuously learn new skills from their co-workers. They become more open-minded and learn to accept, and even invite, new and challenging opportunities. They learn to respect the fact that people are entitled to their own viewpoints and they strive to understand other people's perspectives. They enjoy the camaraderie that comes from working with others and the feeling of satisfaction that comes when a common goal is achieved.

> *Diversity: the art of thinking independently together.*
> Malcolm Forbes

The most successful team players value the opportunity to work with others who are equally unique. They learn to rely on other people for their knowledge, experience, and support. They appreciate and respect their teammates and want their teammates to appreciate and respect them in return. These feelings of mutual appreciation and respect also extend beyond the help desk to the entire support organization.

Understanding Your Role in Your Company's Support Organization

Although each member of the help desk team plays a unique role, customers or other support groups tend to lump everyone together as "the help desk." This may not seem fair, but it is actually the essence of what makes a team a team. The help desk, as a team, has a role to play within the support organization. The help desk's mission and goals define what that role will be. The role of most help desks is to serve on the front-line between a company or department and its customers. This is a most important role. Customers form opinions of the entire company or department based on their interactions with the help desk. The help desk's performance also influences how efficiently and effectively other support resources, such as level two, level three, and external service providers, are utilized. Each and every member of the help desk team must embrace the help desk's mission and achieve his or her individual performance goals for the help desk team to achieve its goals.

Contributing to Team Goals

Each member of a team brings to the team a unique set of skills and a personal style. Those skills and that style are only of value if they enable the team to achieve its goals. Recall that help desk goals are measurable objectives that support the help desk's mission. Sample help desk goals include:

➤ Achieve an average 4 out of 5 rating on the annual overall satisfaction survey

➤ Provide each analyst 8 hours of training each month

➤ Resolve 80 percent of reported problems at level one

➤ Reduce calls to the help desk by 5 percent within 6 months

➤ Reduce support costs by 5 percent by year end

➤ Maintain a cost per contact at or below the industry average, which is $18 to $25

Cost per contact, historically called cost per call, is the total cost of operating a help desk for a given time period (including salaries, benefits, facilities, and equipment) divided by the total number of contacts (such as calls, e-mails, faxes, and Web requests) received during that period. Some companies also calculate **cost per unit**, the total cost of operating a help desk for a given time period (including salaries, benefits, facilities, and equipment) divided by the total number of units (such as devices and systems) supported during that period.

Team performance is only as good as the performance of the analysts on the team. Every analyst influences the team's ability to achieve its goals and expected service levels. If every analyst in the help desk achieves his or her individual performance goals, then the team will achieve its goals. Recall that individual performance goals are measurable objectives for people who support the help desk mission. Data is needed to measure and manage both team and individual performance. Help desk analysts often create the needed data by using tools. Some analysts mistakenly believe that management cannot measure their performance if the data is not available. The flaw in this line of thinking is that management will still measure performance; they'll simply do it without facts. In other words, management will measure performance based on what they *perceive* an analyst has accomplished. By capturing data and learning to use that data to create information, analysts can maximize their contribution to help desk goals and communicate that contribution to management.

Help desk tools that may be used to create performance measures, or **metrics,** for individuals include an automatic call distributor (ACD) and the call tracking and problem management system. Sample individual performance metrics captured with an ACD include:

➤ **Availability** — the length of time an analyst was signed on to the ACD compared to the length of time the analyst was scheduled to be signed on.

➤ **Average call duration** — the average length of time required to handle a call.

➤ **Time idle** — the average length of time an analyst was idle during a given period of time. An **idle state** means the analyst did not answer a call routed to his or her phone within the specified number of rings. When an idle state occurs, the ACD transfers the call to the next available analyst.

> ➤ **Wrap-up time** — the average length of time an analyst was in wrap-up mode during a given period of time. **Wrap-up mode** is an ACD feature that prevents the ACD from routing a new inbound call to an analyst's extension.

These metrics are combined with metrics produced using the help desk's call tracking and problem management system. Sample individual performance metrics captured with a call tracking and problem management system include:

> ➤ **Reopen %** — the percentage of incidents an analyst opens back up compared to the total number of incidents closed during a given time period.

> ➤ **Resolution %** — the percentage of incidents an analyst resolves compared to the total number of incidents that an analyst handled during a given time period.

> ➤ **Application of training investments** — a comparison of an analyst's resolution % and reopen % before and after attending training.

Customer satisfaction is another common individual performance metric. It is captured through the results of event-driven customer satisfaction surveys. Recall that event-driven surveys are a series of questions that ask customers to rate their level of satisfaction with a recent service event. Because event-driven surveys request customer feedback on a single service event, they are an excellent way to capture information about an individual analyst's performance.

Monitoring is yet another way that companies measure analysts' performances. Recall that monitoring is when a supervisor or team leader listens to a live or recorded call, or sits beside an analyst, to measure the quality of an analyst's performance during the call. The most effective monitoring programs provide analysts with a checklist that describes the specific criteria that supervisors or team leaders are using to measure the quality of a call.

Metrics are an excellent way for help desk management and staff to know whether they are achieving team and individual performance goals. It is important to note, however, that no single metric can be used to accurately measure team or individual performance. They all work together and can influence each other. The best help desks use metrics to monitor performance as well as to identify areas for improvement. For example, metrics can be used to identify the training needs of help desk analysts. They can be used to identify the need for new or improved tools or the need to refine the help desk's processes and procedures. Metrics can also be used to know when it is time to rethink the help desk's mission or revisit its goals.

Although management directs most of the performance metrics analysts must meet, you can suggest additional metrics and supply other information that further demonstrates your contribution to the team's goals. For example, you can prepare a brief report that shows how an FAQ you wrote has resulted in a reduction in the number of questions that customers have about a new product.

Remember to be specific. Indicate how many questions were asked for one or two months prior to your writing the FAQ, and how many questions were asked during the month or two after the FAQ was published. Many managers try to involve their staff when establishing performance measures, and you may be encouraged to suggest ways to measure and improve team and individual performance. You can also suggest possible solutions to a problem rather than finding fault or complaining. This positive, constructive approach will really raise your standing in management's eyes. By embracing performance metrics and, when appropriate, suggesting additional performance metrics, you can show management that you are a team player.

Communicating Effectively in a Team Setting

The way people communicate in a team setting influences their relationships with their teammates and the effectiveness of the entire team. In successful teams, team players communicate freely and in ways that encourage trust and respect. Communication is bi-directional and depends on active listening. Team members not only freely share information, thoughts, and opinions, they encourage their co-workers to share as well. For example, team players:

➤ Originate and propose new ideas and actively encourage others to contribute their ideas

➤ Articulate the team's goals and help to clarify the team's goals as needed

➤ Regard conflict as a normal part of team growth and strive to resolve conflict in a positive way

➤ Actively encourage teammates to participate in team activities and assert the right of each and every teammate to be heard

➤ Express their feelings about issues affecting the team in a positive way and seek to understand how teammates feel about issues

➤ Assume responsibility for guiding the team when their expertise or team player style is needed

➤ Encourage team growth by describing the benefits to be gained by making a change

> *Communication is the key that unlocks the door to teamwork.*
> Author Unknown

Another form of communication in a team setting is feedback. **Feedback** is communication from one team member to another about how the member's behavior is meeting the expectations of the team. Feedback is appropriate and necessary when:

➤ A person does something well

➤ A person's behavior does not appear to be aligned with the team's mission or goals

➤ A conflict needs to be resolved

To be effective, feedback must be delivered in a considerate, humane, and helping fashion. It must be specific and provide the recipient with a clear understanding of how his or her behavior affects the team. For example, sarcastically mumbling "It's about time you showed up" as a chronically late co-worker passes your desk does nothing to address the situation. A more appropriate form of feedback would be to let the co-worker know how it affects the team when he is late. For example, "When you are late, our work stacks up and we cannot respond to our customers in the timeframe they expect. It also affects our ability to take breaks and so things can get a little stressful. We really need for you to make it in on time."

> *He has the right to criticize who has the heart to help.*
> Abraham Lincoln

It is the responsibility of the person providing feedback to ensure the recipient received the correct message. It is the recipient's responsibility to receive the feedback in the spirit with which it was delivered. In other words, if a recipient becomes defensive or angry upon receiving feedback, it is the sender's responsibility to clarify the point he or she is trying to make and find a more positive way to communicate. In turn, the recipient must accept the fact that the person providing feedback is trying to be helpful and must try to glean from the feedback a positive message.

Interestingly enough, even positive feedback can be received negatively. For example, some people try to do their best day in and day out, and they may view a co-worker's seemingly arbitrary "good job" as frivolous and patronizing. For some people, basic courtesies, such as saying "please" and "thank you," are all they ask in return for a job well done. For example, if you praise a co-worker and she replies, "I'm just doing my job," you can surmise that she tends to be self-motivated. Remember, though, that people's needs can vary from one day to the next. Even a person who tends to scorn praise likes to get a pat on the back now and then. By listening actively to your co-workers you can get a feel for their feedback preference.

For a team to be successful, everyone must participate in the feedback process. For example:

➤ Employees must provide feedback to other employees.

➤ Employees must provide feedback to supervisors and team leaders.

➤ Supervisors and team leaders must provide feedback to employees.

➤ Supervisors and team leaders must provide feedback to other supervisors and team leaders.

This feedback process is particularly important in a help desk setting. Although diversity is a hallmark of a successful help desk team, unfortunately, it can quickly lead to division unless team members communicate by providing each other with feedback. Successful teams insist that all team members share their feelings, ideas, and knowledge with the rest of the team. It is unacceptable for team members to withhold information or ideas that could be useful to the team. This includes feedback that acknowledges the efforts of a team member or that will provide a team member with information needed to improve.

Communication in a team setting can occur formally or informally. For example, formal communication can occur during a team meeting or in the form of a publication, such as a newsletter or a procedure's guide. Informal communication can occur when two or more team members interact. Teams that communicate effectively strive to use the most appropriate method of communication for each situation. For example, announcing a new team goal or a team member's promotion is handled formally to ensure that everyone affected by the announcement is kept informed and involved. On the other hand, discussing a conflict with a co-worker is handled privately and informally with only the affected parties and perhaps a trusted facilitator. This enables the affected parties to feel more comfortable and thus more willing to communicate freely.

Effective communication enables teamwork. It ensures that everyone on the team knows what the team must do to succeed and what he or she must do to contribute to the team's success. Ineffective communication can cripple a team and damage the relationships that exist between team members beyond repair. It is the responsibility of each and every member of the help desk team to do all he or she can to enhance communication. Remember that a team player, by definition, contributes to the success of a team by communicating openly with teammates. Remember, too, that in an effective team setting, even conflict is viewed as a normal part of a team's functioning. Team members are encouraged to deal with conflict in a positive way by getting issues out on the table and seeking a viable solution.

What to Do When You Are New to a Team

Whether you are starting work at a new company, or simply joining a new team at the company where you work, there are a few steps you can take to quickly get oriented. Remember that when joining a new team you do have to earn your place by working hard and showing a willingness to work with others, even if you have been hired to serve as the resident expert on a particular subject. Respect and trust must be earned. You cannot assume you know what the team needs and you cannot decide what role you will play. The following steps can help you get settled into a new team as quickly as possible.

➤ **Meet and get to know your teammates.** As you are introduced to each of your teammates upon joining the team, make an effort to go beyond simple introductions and get to know your teammates. During your first week or two, make it a point to have a one-on-one conversation with all of your teammates. Shake their hand. Ask them what their role is, what their area of expertise is, what projects they are working on. Ask them to help you understand how the team operates. Let them know you are looking forward to working together. Even a brief conversation will build rapport and help each of you settle into a positive working relationship.

➤ **Try to gain an understanding of the "big picture."** Ask your co-workers and team leader or supervisor questions and ask for any documented policies and procedures. For example, make sure you receive a copy of the help desk's mission and its goals. Make sure you understand the factors that are critical to the team's success. In other words, make sure you understand why the team exists to begin with. You also want to gain an understanding of who your customers are and where the help desk fits into the overall support organization. Ask for copies of organization charts or ask someone to draw a diagram for you that shows how the help desk relates to other departments, such as level two support groups.

➤ **Learn the lingo.** Every company, and even teams within a company, have their own vocabulary. They may have unique naming standards for their systems and network components or use a lot of acronyms. If available, get a glossary of terms and use it to learn the language of your new team. If a glossary of terms is not available, you may want to start one. Every time you hear a new term, write it down. Fill in the definitions as you go along. The next new team member will greatly appreciate your efforts.

➤ **Determine exactly what is expected of you.** It doesn't matter how hard you are working if you are not working on the right things. Failing to do what's expected of you can also create a bad first impression that may be hard to overcome. Ask your supervisor or team leader for a detailed outline of what you should be doing during the first few months that you are with the team. It takes time to learn a team's culture and it takes time to learn all of the processes, procedures, and tools you will be using to do your work. You can't fully contribute until you understand how the team operates and the role you are expected to play. Let your supervisor or team leader know that you want to be a team player and that you want to make a contribution.

➤ **Volunteer.** While you want to resist the temptation to bite off more than you can chew, volunteering is an excellent way to get involved with a team. If you see an area where your expertise can be put to work, offer it, or you can offer to help out with a social or charity event that the team may be planning. Volunteering is an excellent way to let your personal interests and unique talents shine through.

Joining a team can be intimidating, especially when you are joining one that has been working together for a while. You may be tempted initially to keep your head down, do what you are told, and stay out of people's way. You'll never become a part of the team that way. A crucial element of teamwork is not only knowing what you are supposed to be doing, but also knowing what your teammates' roles and responsibilities are as well. When you first join a team it may feel as if you have blinders over your eyes. By asking questions and learning how your contributions fit into the bigger picture, you can remove the blinders and see clearly what needs to be done.

7

Developing Positive Working Relationships with Teammates

A help desk can be a hectic place to work. On the other hand, working in a help desk can be extremely rewarding. You have the opportunity to help other people. You can work with technology. You get to solve problems and continuously learn new skills and acquire new knowledge. Life really is good and you have the opportunity—the choice—every day of making it great. During tough times, remember that you are not alone. You are a member of a team. The following tips are designed to help you put your best foot forward in a team setting.

➤ **Get to know your teammates.** You should know your teammates well enough to know their strengths and weaknesses relative to the goals of your team. You should also know what your teammates view as the priorities in their lives. For example, if a teammate's children are very important to him, learn a little about his children and ask him how they are doing now and then. If a teammate is training for a marathon, ask her how the training is going and wish her well just before the big day. You do not have to be best friends. Simply acknowledge the fact that you work side-by-side with this fellow member of the human race day in and day out. Acknowledge and embrace each person's uniqueness.

➤ **Warmly acknowledge your co-workers each morning and at night.** Simply put, say "Good morning everyone" and "Have a good night everybody" when you walk in and out of the door each day. Some workers slink in and out of work each day in the hopes that no one will notice that they've come or gone. Unfortunately, this approach can quickly lead to animosity. Remember that a simple courtesy, such as greeting your teammates, will go a long way in creating a positive working relationship.

➤ **Listen with interest to your teammates.** In other words, listen to your teammates as actively as you do your customers. The nice thing about communicating with teammates is that you often can communicate face-to-face. Be considerate. Resist the temptation to work on your computer or perform some other task when speaking with a co-worker. Stop what you are doing. Make eye contact. Be attentive. If a conversation becomes too personal or lengthy, politely let your teammate know that you need to go back to work.

➤ **Inquire about and acknowledge your teammates' feelings.** If a normally upbeat co-worker seems to be having a down day, ask if there is anything that you can do. This doesn't mean you should become a busybody, just let your co-workers know that you care about their well-being and that if there is anything you can do to help, you are willing. You don't have to be soft on people, but give them your support.

➤ **Share your feelings openly and honestly.** No one feels comfortable around a person who has a scowl on his or her face and yet insists that nothing is wrong. Furthermore, no one likes to hear, after an extended time, that he or she has inadvertently offended a teammate but has not been given an opportunity to repair the relationship. By sharing your feelings openly and honestly with your teammates, you create a climate of trust. Your teammates will learn to view you as fair and reasonable and will respond by being open and honest with you in return.

➤ **Be willing to learn and teach.** Some people set out to learn "something new everyday," a philosophy that is easily quenched in a technical support setting. Some people, unfortunately, think they know it all. Others are content to get by knowing only the bare essentials, and defer to others when problems become complex. Still others are unwilling to ask questions. They fear they will look "stupid" or that they will lose their standing as an expert. A help desk setting is an excellent place to be a perpetual student. Technology is constantly changing. Customer needs and the needs of your business are constantly changing. You will never be bored working in a help desk setting if you have an inherent sense of curiosity and are willing to say "What's that?"

 Learning is the labor of the information age.

You must also be willing to share your knowledge and experience with your co-workers. It used to be considered "job security" if a person was the only one that possessed certain knowledge or experience. In this day and age, companies are looking for people that willingly share their knowledge and cross-train their co-workers. Keep in mind also that if you are spending all of your time answering questions and handling difficult problems in a given area of expertise, you may not have the time, or the energy, you need to pursue new skills. Spread your knowledge around.

➤ **Recognize your teammates' achievements.** We all want to be appreciated for the work that we do and for the things we accomplish. Sincerely congratulate your teammates when they successfully complete a project or solve an exceptionally complex problem. Encourage a co-worker who is studying for a certification test or who is gearing up for final exams. Teammates who are just getting started especially need to be encouraged. The first steps in any endeavor are often the hardest, and teammates who are trying to acquire new skills need your encouragement and support. A positive side effect of recognizing and acknowledging your teammates' achievements is that they will give you positive feedback in return.

➤ **Ask for help when you really need it.** A team cannot perform well unless each of its members is performing well. In a team setting, you cannot, and you should not, try to do everything on your own. Asking for help when you need it is not a sign of weakness. It says that you want to do things in the most efficient, effective way possible so that you contribute to the team's success. Keep in mind, though, that your teammates are just as busy as you are and may be struggling with new challenges as well. Don't be lazy. It is not okay to ask for help simply because you have let things slip through the cracks or because you want to get out of doing your homework. Effort in a team setting is as much about attitude as it is about skills and ability. Let your CAN DO attitude shine through. Remember, too, to help your teammates when they really need it.

7

> *Don't worry if you're feeling confused. Worry if you're not.* Tom Peters

If you want to work on a successful team that achieves its goals and reaps the associated rewards, you can't be an inactive or ordinary team player. You also can't leave it up to the team leader or to the other members of the team. Each and every member of a team has to contribute. This includes and begins with you. Know your role and know your strengths. Get clear on what is expected of you and do your best to give the team what it needs. Remember, there is no "I" in team.

CHAPTER SUMMARY

- Technical support lends itself to a team setting because no single person can know everything about all the products supported or provide all the support customers need. The demands are too great. A team is a group of people organized to work together toward the achievement of a goal. A team player is a person who contributes to the team's success by cooperating freely and communicating openly with his or her teammates.

- Assembling a group of team players does not make a successful team. To be successful, a team must share a clear sense of purpose, diversity, openness and trust, and positive relationships with other support groups. They must also have an open, pleasant working environment and a willingness to work through the stages of growth—forming, storming, norming, and performing—that all groups experience on their way to becoming a team. To reach the performing stage, teams must learn to work through conflict and achieve a consensus.

- Being a team player requires personal commitment and a willingness to put the needs of the team ahead of your own. This does not mean you have to give up your individuality. For a team to succeed, each team member must understand that he or she has a unique role to play. The role a person plays is a sum of his or her skills, knowledge, experience, and personal style. Team player styles include challenger, collaborator, communicator, and contributor. Each of these styles serves a purpose and each shines brightest at different times during the stages of a team's growth. Your challenge as a team player is to determine your personal style and use the strengths of that style to contribute to your team. You can also strive to embrace the strengths of the other styles, thus increasing your ability to contribute to the team.

- The help desk's mission and goals determine the role the help desk plays within the support organization. Each and every member of the help desk team must embrace the help desk's mission and achieve his or her individual performance goals for the help desk team to achieve its goals. Data is needed to measure and manage both team and individual performance. Help desk analysts often create needed data by using tools such as an automatic call distributor (ACD) and a call tracking and problem management system. Techniques such as customer satisfaction surveys and monitoring may also be used to capture information about an analyst's performance. In addition to measuring performance, help desk managers and staff can use the data these tools and techniques provide to identify ways they can improve.

- The ways people communicate in a team setting influence their relationships with their teammates and the effectiveness of the entire team. Team members must freely share information, thoughts, and opinions and they must encourage their co-workers to share as well. Another form of communication in a team setting is feedback. To be effective, feedback must be delivered in a considerate, humane, and helping fashion. Ineffective communication can cripple a team and damage the relationships that exist between team members beyond repair. Effective communication ensures that everyone on the team knows what the team must do to succeed and what he or she must do to contribute to the team's success.

- A help desk can be a hectic place to work. On the other hand, working in a help desk can be extremely rewarding. During tough times, remember that you are not alone. You are a member of a team. If you want to work on a successful team that achieves its goals and reaps the associated rewards, you cannot be an inactive or ordinary team player. You have to contribute. Remember, there is no "I" in team.

KEY TERMS

application of training investments — A comparison of an analyst's resolution % and reopen % before and after attending training.

availability — The length of time an analyst was signed on to the ACD compared to the length of time the analyst was scheduled to be signed on.

average call duration — The average length of time required to handle a call.

consensus — An opinion or position reached by all of a team's members or by a majority of its members.

cost per contact — The total cost of operating a help desk for a given time period (including salaries, benefits, facilities, and equipment) divided by the total number of contacts (such as calls, e-mails, faxes, and Web requests) received during that period; historically called cost per call.

cost per unit — The total cost of operating a help desk for a given time period (including salaries, benefits, facilities, and equipment) divided by the total number of units (such as devices and systems) supported during that period.

feedback — Communication from one team member to another about how the member's behavior is meeting the expectations of the team.

help desk goals — Measurable objectives that support the help desk's mission.

idle state — An ACD state that occurs when an analyst did not answer a call routed to his or her phone within the specified number of rings.

individual performance goals — Measurable objectives for people who support the help desk's mission.

metrics — Performance measures.

mission — A written statement of the customers the help desk serves, the types of services the help desk provides, and how the help desk delivers those services.

7

reopen % — The percentage of incidents an analyst opens back up compared to the total number of incidents closed during a given time period.

resolution % — The percentage of incidents an analyst resolves compared to the total number of incidents that the analyst handled during a given time period.

team — A group of people organized to work together toward the achievement of a goal.

team player — A person who contributes to the team's success by cooperating freely and communicating openly with his or her teammates.

time idle — The average length of time an analyst was idle during a given period of time.

wrap-up mode — An ACD feature that prevents the ACD from routing a new inbound call to an analyst's extension.

wrap-up time — The average length of time an analyst was in wrap-up mode during a given period of time.

REVIEW QUESTIONS

1. What is a team?

2. How does a team player contribute to a team's success?

3. What are the reasons technical support lends itself to a team setting?

4. What are the four characteristics of a successful team?

5. List the three components of a help desk mission.

6. Help desk goals are _____ objectives that support the help desk's mission.

7. Why is it important for a help desk to have a clearly defined mission and goals?

8. In business terms, what makes people with varying talents a team?

9. Why is it important for the help desk to have a positive working relationship with other support groups?

10. List the four stages of development reflected in the Tuckman Teamwork model.

11. How does the role of the team leader change as a team moves through these stages of growth?

12. Typically, when is a consensus reached?

13. Why does conflict usually occur in a team setting?

14. What should team members focus on when handling conflict in a team setting?

15. What is gossip often a sign of?

16. What must you remember about the other person's point of view when you are faced with a conflict?

17. How is a compromise achieved?

18. When is it appropriate to avoid a conflict?

19. Do you have to abandon your personal goals to be a team player?

20. What qualities influence the role a person plays on a team?

21. List the four types of team player styles.

22. When can a team player style become ineffective?

23. Why is it important to determine your personal team player style?

24. What two things determine the role a help desk will play in a support organization?

25. What influences team performance?

26. What are the four most common tools and techniques that companies use to measure individual performance?

27. What are four ways that help desk management and staff can use metrics?

28. Why is communication important in a team setting?

29. What is feedback?

30. How must feedback be delivered to be effective?

31. Whose responsibility is it to enhance communication in a team setting?

32. What are five things you can do to get settled into a new team?

33. What four basic courtesies, discussed in this chapter, will help you to have a positive working relationship with your teammates?

34. Why is it important to ask for help when you really need it?

HANDS-ON PROJECTS

Project 7-1

Evaluate a team's success. Interview a friend, family member, or classmate that works in a team setting. Describe for this person the characteristics discussed in this chapter of a successful team. Ask the following questions about the person's team:

- Does he or she work for a successful team? That is, is the team fulfilling its mission and achieving its goals?

- If yes, does the team exhibit all of the characteristics discussed in this chapter? How did the team develop these characteristics?

- If no, what characteristics could be improved to make the team more successful?

Prepare a brief report that presents any conclusions you can draw from this discussion.

Project 7-2

Determine a company's mission. Visit the Web site for a hardware or software company you do business with or are considering doing business with. For example, you could contact the company that manufactured your computer or published your favorite software package. From the Web site, determine the following:

- Do they have a help desk mission statement? If so, what is their mission?

- Do they describe the support services that they offer? If so, what services do they offer?

- How does the help desk say they deliver their services (for example, professionally, courteously, etc.)?

Write a one-page report that summarizes your findings.

Project 7-3

Discuss the stages of team development. Conduct a roundtable discussion within your class about the stages of team development. First, have each person in your class who is a member of a team of any kind assess the stage of development that his or her team has achieved. They may belong to a team at work, or they may be a member of a sports team or a study group. Next, ask all of your classmates who are in, for example, the forming stage to relate their current experience to the description of the forming stage discussed in this chapter. For example:

- What insight into the workings of their team have they gained while studying this chapter?

- Given what they have learned in this chapter, how do they feel they can help their team move forward or improve?

- What, if any, conclusions can you and your classmates draw from this discussion before moving on to the next stage of development?

Apply these questions to each of the four stages of team development. Briefly summarize the conclusions of your class. After you have finished this discussion, think of your class as a team. As a team, determine the stage of team development your class has achieved. Briefly outline the steps your team must take to achieve the next stage.

Project 7-4

Review your approach to managing conflict. Conflict is an inevitable part of human interaction. Think about a conflict that you have faced or are facing at home, school, or work. Review the tips discussed in this chapter concerning how to resolve conflict in a constructive manner. Use these tips to assess your ability to manage conflict in a positive way. Using your own words, make note of one or two of the tips you can use to improve your conflict resolution skills.

Project 7-5

Discuss team player styles. Assemble a team of three to five of your classmates. For each of the four team player styles described in this chapter, discuss the following:

- How does a team benefit by having a person or person who exhibits this team player style?

- How is a team impacted if a team player that exhibits this team player style becomes ineffective?

Compare the results of your discussion to the findings of other teams in the class.

Project 7-6

Learn how team and individual performance are measured. Interview a friend, family member, or classmate that works in a team setting. Ask this person the following questions:

- How is his or her team's performance measured?

- How is his or her individual performance measured?

- Does this person feel that his or her manager has clearly communicated what he or she must do to contribute to the team's goals?

- Does this person feel that his or her manager uses metrics to identify improvement opportunities as well as to monitor performance?

- What techniques does this person use to communicate his or her achievements to management?

- How does this person feel about the tools he or she is required to use and the amount of data that he or she is required to provide management with regard to his or her performance? If he or she feels it is a burden, determine why?

Prepare a brief report that presents any conclusions you can draw from this discussion.

Project 7-7

Assess your communication skills. Prepare a list of the effective ways to communicate in a team setting discussed in this chapter. For each skill listed, rate yourself on a scale of 1 to 5, where 1 is very weak and 5 is very strong. Then, further assess your communication skills by answering the following questions:

- In what areas are your communication skills strong?

- In what areas can you improve your communication skills?

- Given what you have learned in this chapter, how can you improve your communication skills?

Project 7-8

Provide feedback. The set of questions that follows is designed to enable constructive peer feedback (*Successful Team Building*, 1992, p. 92). It could also be used to perform a self-assessment or by a team leader to evaluate each member of a team. Use this peer feedback form to:

1. Assess your skills as a team member. You can apply these questions to your behavior at work, as a member of a sports team or study group, or as a member of your class.

2. Provide feedback to a co-worker. Again, this may be a co-worker at work, a member of a sports team or study group to which you belong, or a member of your class.

Peer Feedback Evaluation

In each category, circle the number that you believe best represents the usual behavior of [*name of team member*]:

Initiates ideas

10 9 8	7 6 5 4	3 2 1
Frequently offers ideas and solutions.	Initiates only moderately, but supports initiating by others.	Tends to let others take most of the initiative and often reserves support.

Facilitates the introduction of new ideas

10 9 8	7 6 5 4	3 2 1
Actively encourages others to contribute without worrying about agreement.	Provides support for ideas with which he or she agrees.	Often resists the introduction of new ideas; looks for flaws.

Is directed toward group goals

10 9 8	7 6 5 4	3 2 1
Often helps to identify and clarify goals for the group.	Sometimes helps the group define its goals; sometimes confuses it with side issues.	Tends to place priority on own goals at the expense of the group's.

Manages conflict

10 9 8	7 6 5 4	3 2 1
Regards conflict as helpful in promoting different perspectives and in sharpening the differences in views.	Generally disengages from conflict.	Tries to smooth over points of disagreement; plays a pacifying role.

Demonstrates support for others

10 9 8	7 6 5 4	3 2 1
Actively encourages the participation of others and asserts their right to be heard.	Encourages certain members part of the time, but does not encourage all members.	Does not offer support or encouragement for other members.

Reveals feelings

10 9 8	7 6 5 4	3 2 1
Openly expresses feelings about issues; ensures that feelings parallel views.	Sometimes disguises feelings or tries to keep them to self.	Denies both the existence of own feelings and the importance of expressing them in the group.

Displays openness

10 9 8	7 6 5 4	3 2 1
Freely and clearly expresses self on issues so that others know where he or she stands.	Sometimes employs tact and speaks circumspectly to camouflage real views.	Is vague about views on issues, even contradictory when pressed.

Confronts issues and behavior		
10 9 8	7 6 5 4	3 2 1
Freely expresses views on difficult issues and on team members' nonproductive behavior.	Is cautious about taking a visible position on issues and on others' actions without first ensuring widespread approval.	Actively avoids issues and any conflict by talking about "safe" issues that are irrelevant to current group work.
Shares leadership		
10 9 8	7 6 5 4	3 2 1
Assumes responsibility for guiding the group when own resources are needed or when problems lend themselves to his or her solving.	Competes with other members for visibility and influence.	Dominates group discussions and exerts disproportionate influence that subverts group progress.
Exhibits proper demeanor in decision-making process		
10 9 8	7 6 5 4	3 2 1
Actively seeks a full exploration of all feasible options.	Becomes impatient with a deliberate pace in generating and evaluating all options when he or she does not concur with them.	Moves strongly toward early closure of discussion to vote on a preferred option.

Case Projects

1. **Becoming an Effective Team Leader**

   You were just promoted to team leader of your help desk. Research the subject of leadership and what it takes to be an effective team leader. Go to the library, search the Web, or speak to people that you respect and think of as leaders. Develop a sign that you can hang in your office that lists the three leadership qualities that you think are most important and that you want to develop. If you like, include a quote about leadership that you consider meaningful.

2. **Recognizing Achievement**

   You are the manager of a small help desk that is starting to perform well as a team. You have a very small budget and it is difficult for you to give people monetary rewards when they accomplish good things. You also would like the members of the team to acknowledge each other's accomplishments and not always look to you to dole out rewards. Conduct a brainstorming session with your team (choose five classmates) and identify creative ways the team can celebrate individual and team accomplishments.

3. **Back to Basics**

   You recently began working as a help desk analyst. The help desk is very large and you are trying to become more conscious about using common courtesies, such as saying "please," "thank you," "good morning," and "good night," in an effort to build a positive working relationship with your new co-workers. You are also trying to make it a habit to use these basic courtesies whenever you interact with other people, whether they are friends, family members, co-workers, or even strangers you encounter during your day. For the next week, use these basic courtesies whenever you interact with others. Observe your feelings when people do not use these basic courtesies when interacting with you. Notice how you can influence others to use these basic courtesies by using them yourself. Discuss your observations with your classmates.

7

MINIMIZING STRESS AND AVOIDING BURNOUT

After reading this chapter and completing the exercises you will be able to:

➤ Reduce the negative effects of stress by determining the causes of stress in your life and by developing effective coping skills

➤ Manage your time wisely and achieve personal success by using proven techniques to get and stay organized, meet deadlines, and eliminate time robbers

In the United States, customer service is ranked as one of the top ten most stressful occupations. Because of this, help desk personnel need good self-management skills in addition to good business skills, soft skills, and technical skills. **Self-management skills** are the skills, such as stress and time management, that people need to complete their work efficiently and effectively, feel job satisfaction, and avoid frustration or burnout. Self-management skills also include the ability to get and stay organized and continuously and quickly learn new skills.

The support industry is particularly fast paced and things are never "normal." If you have good self-management skills, you will be able to enjoy the variety of responsibilities and challenging situations that a help desk offers. Self-management skills provide a solid foundation upon which you will always be able to draw regardless of how hectic the help desk becomes. Furthermore, skills such as stress management and time management are excellent life skills that will serve you well regardless of your chosen profession.

REDUCING THE NEGATIVE EFFECTS OF STRESS

Stress is a normal and unavoidable side effect of living. **Stress** is the adaptation of our bodies and minds to the demands of life. In other words, stress is the wear and tear our bodies and minds experience as a result of life's ups and downs. Properly managed, stress is an excellent source of motivation and can be a positive part of life. For example, have you ever experienced the enormous sense of satisfaction that comes when you avert a crisis or meet a deadline? Have you ever felt the adrenaline rush that accompanies the attainment of a long sought-after goal? Conversely, high levels of stress can sap your motivation and become a negative. For example, have you ever been so overwhelmed by a task that you simply gave up? Have you ever been so anxious about an upcoming event, such as a job interview, that you sabotaged yourself by staying out late the night before or leaving late for your appointment?

For stress to be a positive part of life, it must be managed. Too little stress can lead to complacency and boredom. On the other hand, too much stress can lead to anxiety and panic. Either extreme can lead to health problems. According to one estimate, 80 percent of medical complaints are stress-related (*Stress for Success*, 1991, p. xi). Health problems that can be related to or aggravated by too much or too little stress include:

➤ Alcoholism

➤ Back and muscle aches

➤ Depression

➤ Drug abuse

➤ Eating disorders, such as anorexia and bulimia

➤ Excessive illness, including heart disease, ulcers, chronic diarrhea, and cancer

➤ Fatigue

➤ Headaches, including migraine headaches

➤ Low energy and concentration levels

➤ Premature aging

To manage stress and minimize its effects, you must first determine the causes of stress in your life.

Determining the Causes of Stress

A help desk is a particularly stressful place to work because analysts are exposed to multiple sources of stress. Figure 8-1 lists the sources of stress analysts may experience.

- Institutional
- Situational
- Personal

Figure 8-1 Sources of stress

People respond to each of these sources of stress in different ways.

➤ **Institutional stressors** are the stressors that accompany the type of business you are in or the state of the company where you work. For example, nonprofit organizations often lack the financial resources of for-profit companies. Small companies often lack the redundancy in their workforce that is found in larger companies. Start-up companies often lack the infrastructure and discipline found in more mature companies. Institutional stressors exist anywhere you work. Your challenge is to figure out which institutional stressors you want to experience. For example, some people enjoy working for a start-up company. They relish being in on the ground floor and helping the company grow and flourish. They love the seat-of-the-pants approach that start-up companies tend to require. On the other hand, some people prefer a more stable environment and find the dynamic nature of a start-up company overwhelming. They may want to work for a company that has a proven track record or that offers a greater sense of job security. They may prefer the formality and discipline of a more mature company. You have very little ability to influence institutional stressors. They simply come with the territory. You can, however, choose where you work very carefully.

➤ **Situational stressors** are the stressors that accompany the type of work you do. For example, people who work in customer service must handle difficult customer situations. People who work in technical support are constantly exposed to new technologies and must continuously learn new skills. People who work in a help desk setting must be able to handle constant interruptions and must be able to juggle a number of outstanding issues at one time. Figure 8-2 lists some of the factors that cause situational stress in a help desk setting. Like institutional stressors, situational stressors exist anywhere you work. Ask yourself whether you have the attitude and the skills needed to handle these stressful situations. For example, some people enjoy handling difficult customer situations and view them as a personal challenge. They strive to do all they can to turn a dissatisfied customer into one who raves about the service he or she received from the help desk. They have also worked hard to develop the skills needed to handle these difficult situations. Some people would rather not interact directly with customers and lack the skills needed to do so. These people typically prefer

8

to be in more of a supporting role. You have a greater ability to influence situational stressors by developing a positive attitude and skills. For example, by striking negative phrases from your vocabulary or by using the techniques described in this book to become a better listener or to communicate more effectively, you can considerably reduce the amount of situational stress you experience.

Situational Stressors	
■ Conflict with co-workers	■ Insufficient knowledge resources, such as tools, procedures, and resident experts
■ Difficult customer situations	
■ Heavy workload	■ Interruptions
■ Inability to predict or control workload	■ Lack of career opportunity
	■ Lack of management commitment and direction
■ Insufficient training	
■ Insufficient time for training	■ Poor product quality in terms of the products that the help desk supports
■ Insufficient tools, such as call tracking and problem management systems, knowledge management systems, and remote control systems	
	■ Talk time restrictions
	■ Understaffing

Figure 8-2   Factors that cause situational stress in a help desk setting

➤ **Personal stressors** are the stressors that accompany your personal life experience. For example, you may be starting a new job or planning a wedding. You may drive through heavy traffic each day to get to work or school. You may have a boss who changes the direction of the team whenever he feels like it so you are never sure what you are supposed to be doing. Or, you may be fatigued from your physical fitness regimen. Figure 8-3 shows some of the many factors that can cause personal stress. It is important to note that even positive life experiences, such as getting promoted or having a child, can cause stress. The good news is that you have the greatest ability to influence your personal stressors. You can determine ways to either eliminate the stressor or minimize its effects on your life.

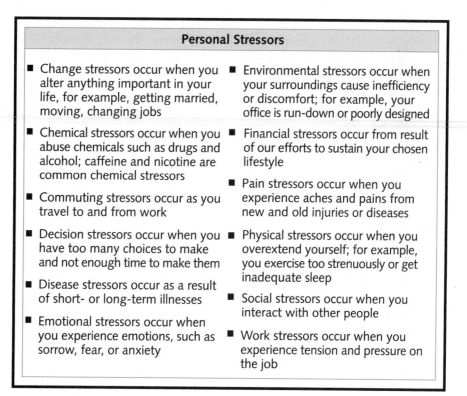

Personal Stressors

- Change stressors occur when you alter anything important in your life, for example, getting married, moving, changing jobs

- Chemical stressors occur when you abuse chemicals such as drugs and alcohol; caffeine and nicotine are common chemical stressors

- Commuting stressors occur as you travel to and from work

- Decision stressors occur when you have too many choices to make and not enough time to make them

- Disease stressors occur as a result of short- or long-term illnesses

- Emotional stressors occur when you experience emotions, such as sorrow, fear, or anxiety

- Environmental stressors occur when your surroundings cause inefficiency or discomfort; for example, your office is run-down or poorly designed

- Financial stressors occur from result of our efforts to sustain your chosen lifestyle

- Pain stressors occur when you experience aches and pains from new and old injuries or diseases

- Physical stressors occur when you overextend yourself; for example, you exercise too strenuously or get inadequate sleep

- Social stressors occur when you interact with other people

- Work stressors occur when you experience tension and pressure on the job

Figure 8-3 Factors that can cause personal stress

Working for a bad boss can be extremely stressful. A bad boss can squelch your motivation and undermine your efforts to advance your career. When working for a bad boss, use the opportunity to (1) focus on the goals of your company, (2) make yourself as marketable as possible, and (3) commit yourself to your personal goals and relaxation. If your boss fails to clearly communicate what you are expected to do, get clear on the goals of your company and ensure your actions contribute to those goals. If your boss is taking credit for your work or seems unwilling to help you advance, get to know people in other departments, or at other companies, and tell them about the good things that you and your team are doing. If your boss doesn't hesitate to point out your mistakes, but rarely acknowledges your accomplishments, put your accomplishments in writing and ask that they be incorporated into your personnel file and considered at review time. If your boss won't authorize training, seek out self-study opportunities. If your boss expects you to regularly work overtime, do your best to arrange your schedule in such a way that you can still participate in your exercise program or hobby. Simply put, figure out what you *can* do.

Having all of these layers of stressors piled on top of each other may cause you to feel completely overwhelmed. To deal effectively with the stress in your life, take the time to identify the real source or sources of your stress. For example, when you are feeling exceptionally stressed, ask yourself the following questions:

➤ Do you like the business you are in?

➤ Do you like the work that you do?

➤ Are you happy with your personal life?

There may be times when you answer "No" to one of these questions. That is normal. If you answer "No" to all of these questions, however, it is time to make a change. Otherwise, you may be risking your health. Identifying the sources of stress in your life will not make the stress go away, but it will enable you to develop a plan of action and a stress management program that works for you.

Developing Effective Coping Mechanisms

People's ability to influence the impact that a stressor has on their life depends on the source of the stress. Some stressors you can influence. Others stressors you must either learn to live with or find a way to minimize their effects. You can minimize the effects of stress by managing how you respond. Two key factors that affect how people respond to stress are:

1. How much control a person has over a stressor.

2. Whether or not a person chooses to be exposed to a stressor.

How much control a person has over a stressor — Some people want to control every aspect of their life and become stressed when they feel they cannot control the events that occur throughout the day. The reality is that there are times when matters *are* out of your control. For example, people working in a help desk cannot control the number of calls they will receive on any given day. They can be proactive and try to manage the number of calls they will receive, but they must also accept that a variable call volume is a help desk characteristic. However, help desk analysts can be as prepared as possible for that variable call volume by making it a habit to get focused. They can also strive to stay organized so that they can work effectively when busy times hit. Remember that you may not be able to control what happens around you or what other people do, but there is always something you can do. You can choose whether or not to expose yourself to a stressor.

Whether or not a person chooses to be exposed to a stressor — If you want to manage and minimize the stress in your life, you must understand this very important concept: *You choose the stress you experience each and every day.* When you cannot control a situation, you have two choices:

1. Change the situation.

2. Control the way you respond to the situation.

Let's say that your drive to and from work each day has become unbearable. You have two choices. You can *change the situation* by changing the hours that you work so that you arrive before the heaviest traffic begins, leaving for work after the heaviest traffic subsides, looking for a job that is closer to your home, or looking for housing that is closer to where you work. On the other hand, if you love where you work and live and you like the hours that you work, you can choose to accept the stressor and *control the way you respond to the situation.* For example, once you accept a stressor, you can stop complaining about it. Complaining simply makes you unhappy and may even magnify the stressor in your mind. Complaining may also annoy the people to whom you are complaining. Next, you can determine what you can do to minimize the effect that the stressor is having on your life. For example, you can buy soothing CDs and books on tape that you can listen to while driving to work. You can also leave a little earlier than necessary each day so that you do not become stressed if you encounter an accident on the way to work that causes a delay. Be positive. Continuously remind yourself that you are accepting this stressor for a reason.

8

Accepting responsibility for the stress you are experiencing is the most important step you can take in terms of coping with stress and avoiding burnout. **Burnout** is the physical and emotional exhaustion that is caused by long-term stress. People often experience burnout when they are not managing their stress day-in and day-out. To manage stress effectively, remember that you are not a victim. *There is always something that you can do.* You can determine the best course of action to take by staying calm and in control. If you feel yourself losing control and becoming incapable of making a good decision, use the calming techniques discussed in Chapter 5.

➤ Take a deep breath

➤ Take a sip of water

➤ Use positive imagery

➤ Use positive self-talk

These techniques help you to manage how you respond to stressors when they occur. Positive imagery and positive self-talk are particularly effective ways to handle ongoing stress and avoid burnout. For example, you may be going to school and holding down a full- or part-time job. Such a busy schedule may seem overwhelming at times. To minimize the stress, identify why you are choosing to expose yourself to such considerable stress. Do you want to get a better job? Do you want to change careers? Do you want to pay off your school loan by the end of the year? Whatever the reason, use positive imagery to stay focused on your goals. Imagine yourself working in the profession of your dreams. Imagine a gift that you will buy for yourself once your school loan is paid off. Periodically take a deep breath and use positive self-talk to remind yourself that you can do it. You can and you will achieve your goals.

These techniques will help you feel more in control and more able to handle the stress in your life.

Stress is a normal part of life and you cannot eliminate it altogether. You can learn to identify the causes of stress in your life and develop effective coping mechanisms. You can also learn to use stress as a positive, motivating force.

Learning to Master Change

Welcome to the Information Age. Brainpower is replacing brawn as people do more and more work with their heads and less with their hands. Advances in technology have dramatically changed when, where, and how people work and live. Computers are everywhere—at work, home, and school. As a result, today's business economy is shifting more and more toward technology-related services and knowledge work. The good news is that there has never been a time so laden with opportunity for people who want to pursue a technology-related career. However, the pace of change means that today's technology will be replaced in a few years, if not sooner. In fact, some jobs, and even professions, may not exist in the future. The rate of change keeps accelerating, and it is not likely to slow down anytime soon.

Success in today's business world belongs to the people who embrace change and who are ready and willing to reinvent themselves as needed to contribute to the company's goals. Companies want people who can quickly abandon outdated tools and methods and accept new and improved ways of working. The career opportunities go to people who can look to the future, anticipate coming changes, and quickly adapt.

> *"It is not the strongest of the species that survive, nor the most intelligent, but the most responsive to change."*
> Charles Darwin

The following tips will help you keep pace with the changing world of work. They will also enable you to take personal responsibility for your career. By accepting responsibility for your future, you can minimize much of the stress and fear that comes from putting your well being in the hands of someone else, such as an employer.

Recognize learning as the labor of the Information Age — Technology changes quickly and it doesn't take long for technical skills to become obsolete. The skills and experience that served you well in the past may, at any time, outlive their usefulness or relevance. Take the time to continuously update and improve your technical skills as well as your business, soft, and self-management skills. For example:

➤ Stay in school or go back to school

➤ Take advantage of training classes offered where you work

➤ Seek out self-study resources that you can use as time allows

➤ Keep up with industry trends and continuously evaluate how those trends affect your skills

➤ Join organizations and get to know the experts in your industry

➤ Ask people who have the skills you need to serve as your mentor

➤ Let your supervisor or team leader know what your interests are and ask to be assigned to projects that will enable you to learn new skills

Knowledge is power and working in a help desk offers you a tremendous opportunity to expand your knowledge and develop and enhance a broad base of skills. Do your homework and don't forget the extra credit—self-study—assignments. After all, it's your career.

8

Develop flexibility — Many of today's job descriptions contain a simple phrase — ". . . other duties as assigned." This means that you must expect on any given day to be asked to do something new, something you've never done before, perhaps even something you will never do again. People who need structure hate this phrase. However, everyone must learn to accept this phrase and the uncertainty that it implies. Don't push back and wait for your responsibilities to be described in perfect detail. Don't wait for the information you need to come to you. Develop the ability to quickly figure out what needs to be done and do it. It you need help, ask for it. If no help is available, do your best. Prove your worth by being willing to do what needs to be done for the company to achieve its goals.

Speed up — In today's business world, slow and steady no longer wins the race. Companies that fail to keep pace with their competition cannot survive. However, companies can't go fast if their employees go slow. Approach all of your work with a sense of urgency. The goal is to get it done, get it done right, and get it done quickly. Avoiding a task or approaching it half-heartedly will not make it go away. You must also try not to get bogged down in endless discussion and planning in an effort to ensure that the outcome of a task is perfect. Some people give a task 120 percent of their effort and energy and get it done late. In today's business world, a better approach is to give a task 99 percent and get it done early. The reality is that you are probably the only person that will see value in that extra 21 percent. High quality is important, but you don't need to be perfect. Strive for excellence and do it *fast*.

Develop project management skills — People often make the mistake of thinking that only people who work on large projects or develop new systems need project management skills. Furthermore, most help desks are too reactive to think about project management. In reality, anyone who has to juggle more than one task at a given time can use project management skills. Project management skills provide you with the ability to identify and attend to details while at the same time stay focused on the big picture. They provide you with the discipline to think before you jump in and do. In a help desk setting, project management skills enable you to define the tasks that need to be completed in order to solve a problem or handle a request. These skills also enable you to define the dependencies associated with those tasks (in other words, determining the tasks that must be completed before the next task can begin). Project management skills also provide you with the ability to proactively identify issues and communicate concerns that may affect the outcome of your efforts. To develop project management skills:

➤ Visit your local library or bookstore and pick up a book on project management

➤ Attend a seminar or buy a project management video

➤ Serve as an apprentice on a project team

➤ Ask someone who has a lot of experience to serve as your mentor

➤ Trust, empower, and rely on your team; don't try to do it all yourself

➤ Learn from your mistakes and thank everyone, even your critics, for their feedback

Good project management skills take time to develop and can improve only through experience. Project management skills are highly transferable and will serve you well now and in the future.

 If you've never managed a project before, *ask* for the opportunity. Start with a small project and then ask for and be willing to accept help and feedback. You can also start by simply getting in the habit of creating and completing a "To Do" list each day, or by thinking about and writing down the steps you need to perform before you begin a task.

Job security is a thing of the past. That doesn't mean you can't be highly employable. Learning to master change will open you up to greater opportunities and options. These skills will also give you the confidence to handle any challenges that come your way without wasting precious energy and enthusiasm.

You can't stop the world from changing and you can't expect the company where you work to accommodate your desire to stay put. Rather than feel stressed, you must accept the fact that change is constant and learn to adapt—*fast*.

Getting and Staying Mentally and Physically Fit

Coping with stress and mastering change takes energy—physical and emotional energy. Stressful and challenging situations can sap your energy and cause your enthusiasm to waver. Stressful situations, even pleasurable ones, such as a wedding or the birth of a child, cause a physical response that, left unchecked, can lead to illness.

Our bodies and minds are tightly connected, particularly when it comes to stress. Upon perceiving a stressful event, our mind triggers an alarm that mobilizes our body for action. These physiological changes are known as the **fight-or-flight reaction.** Our ancestors, surrounded by predatory animals, needed this ability to instantly mobilize to survive. Today, most people are not even aware of their bodies' minute-to-minute responses to stressful—perceived or otherwise—situations. They may not notice that their heart has begun to beat faster or that their breathing has become shallow. We often learn to ignore or accept short-term stress responses, such as butterflies in our stomach, a lump in our throat, tension in our muscles, and the feelings of anxiety. In time, however, this tension can accumulate and lead to serious health problems.

Research has shown that the immune system breaks down when we do not handle stress well. This breakdown of the immune system can lead to illnesses ranging from the common cold to cancer.

The following techniques can help you relieve the physical tension that accompanies stress. These techniques will also help you to rejuvenate your spirit and acquire the emotional strength needed to handle everyday stress.

➤ **Exercise** — Exercise provides a way of releasing a great deal of the muscle tension that can accumulate from stress. Exercise can also be used to clear your mind. People who exercise report that time away from working diligently on a problem gives them a chance to sort things out in a more relaxed way. Try to fit in exercise during the workday. For example, if your office has exercise facilities, use them at lunch or before or after work, or go for a brisk walk before or after you eat lunch.

➤ **Practice good nutrition** — Skipping meals can cause you to feel irritable. Eating too much can cause you to feel sluggish and tired. Eating the right amount of food at the right time helps you sustain your energy level and maintain an even temperament. Have fruit or bagels at your desk that you can eat when you feel hungry or when you need energy. Bring your lunch from home so you can eat healthy and have time to relax during your lunch break.

➤ **Avoid the use of stimulants** — Stimulants, such as the caffeine found in coffee, soda, and chocolate, will exaggerate all of the body's stress responses by causing a surge of adrenaline and other hormones. Excessive caffeine causes some people to feel nervous and jittery, and may even affect their ability to sleep at night. It is best to avoid stimulants altogether, but if you do choose to consume caffeine, limit your intake and time your consumption carefully. For example, having one cup of coffee in the morning is far better than drinking two cups of coffee after dinner. You may also want to keep a water bottle (sports bottles work great) at your desk for those times when you are unable to get to a water cooler.

➤ **Drink plenty of water** — Fatigue is one of the first signs of dehydration, so you should make sure you are drinking plenty of water. Drinking plenty of water increases your energy level and mental capacities. A side benefit of drinking plenty of water is that your body lets you know when it's time to take a break.

➤ **Ergonomically align your workspace** — A poorly designed workplace can cause physical symptoms such as headaches, wrist and shoulder pain, backaches, and swollen ankles. Ergonomics helps reduce these symptoms and prevent repetitive stress injuries. **Ergonomics** is the applied science of equipment design intended to maximize productivity by reducing operator fatigue and discomfort. **Repetitive stress injuries (RSIs)** are physical symptoms caused by excessive and repeated use of the hands, wrists, and arms; they occur when people perform tasks using force, repeated strenuous actions, awkward postures, and poorly designed equipment. RSIs include carpal tunnel syndrome, tendonitis, bursitis, and rotator cuff injuries. **Carpal tunnel syndrome** is a common repetitive stress injury that affects the hands and wrists and is linked to repetitious hand movements, such as typing on a computer keyboard. You are susceptible to RSIs when working in a help desk because you are required to do a considerable amount of typing. To improve the ergonomics of your workspace, align your chair with your monitor and keyboard so that when you sit up straight in the chair, the monitor is at or below eye level and your wrists are straight on the keyboard. Figure 8-4 illustrates the relationship between your chair, monitor, and keyboard.

➤ **Take breaks** — Working nonstop often leads to fatigue and burnout. Take time throughout the day to rejuvenate yourself. Stretch, spend a moment looking out the window, or simply close your eyes and take a few deep breaths to regain a sense of calm. You can take a short walk, even if it's only to the restroom or to get a drink of water.

Figure 8-4   Ergonomically aligned chair, monitor, and keyboard

> Periodically shake out your hands and perform shrugging exercises to relax your shoulders. Keep it loose!

➤ **Let your sense of humor shine through** — Laughter truly is the best medicine. It can cause you to relax when you are feeling tense and it can restore your sense of optimism and self-confidence. Surround yourself with positive people and seek them out when you need a good laugh. Seize opportunities to make others feel better by sharing a good laugh over the ups and downs of life. Have fun on the help desk. Some help desks have a funniest hat day or a mismatched clothes day. Some take breaks when the phones are slow and see who can make a paper airplane and fly it the farthest. Some help desks have a "toy box" that contains stress-relieving toys, such as stress balls and squeeze toys.

➤ **Commit yourself to relaxation** — A relaxing activity is one that leaves you free of tension and refreshed both physically and mentally. People relax in different ways. For example, some people enjoy hobbies such as gardening and astronomy. Some people like to read. Others enjoy activities, such as hiking, that enable them to commune with nature. For optimum stress-relieving benefits, a relaxing activity should consume you to the extent that you temporarily forget about your stressors and focus on your personal well-being.

➤ **Set realistic goals** — Many people cause the very stress they are experiencing by setting unrealistic goals. Realistic goals are attainable. That doesn't mean they are easy to achieve. Don't set yourself up to fail by choosing goals that are so unrealistic they are impossible to achieve. Also, avoid goals where you will have to sacrifice so much to achieve them that they become worthless. The most successful people establish short- and long-term goals as well as professional and personal goals. This balanced approach provides the ability to feel successful in all areas of your life and also provides you the impetus to continuously improve. At work, ask your supervisor or team leader to help you establish reasonable goals along with a timetable for reviewing your accomplishments. Make sure you also understand your team's goals and how your personal goals fit in with them.

> *Live a balanced life. Learn some and think some and draw and*
> *paint and sing and dance and play and work every day some.*
> Robert Fulghum

The bottom line is that in order to use stress as a positive, motivating force in your life, you must take care of yourself both physically and mentally. Take responsibility for how you experience each and every moment of your life. Take time, every day, to think about your physical and emotional needs, and devote time to fulfilling those needs. Remember that it is just as important to foster your mental health as it is to care for your physical well-being.

ERGONOMICALLY ALIGNING YOUR WORKSPACE

A majority of ergonomic problems can be eliminated by making simple, no-cost adjustments to your personal workspace. For example, you can easily adjust your chair, monitor, keyboard and mouse, telephone and headset, and lighting to create a workspace that fits your needs. Making these adjustments goes a long way to helping you stay healthy on the job.

Chair — The placement and use of your chair, monitor, keyboard, and mouse are related and must be aligned properly with each other and with you. How you adjust and sit in your chair are equally important. You should adjust your chair until your back is erect, slightly back, and firm against the backrest. If necessary, further support your back with a lumbar pillow, back support (as shown above) or a rolled up towel.

Thighs and legs should be relaxed and feet should be flat on the floor. You can also place a footrest, box, or stack of books under the desk to keep your feet from dangling.

Monitor — The chair height can affect and be affected by the placement of your monitor. The best position for a monitor is directly in front of you at, or just below, eye level. When you are sitting straight with your head erect, the monitor should be no more than 24 inches away from your eyes. If necessary, place a book under the monitor to raise it up to the right level. If the monitor is too high, remove anything under it to make it lower, adjust your chair, or replace the desk or table with a lower one as a last resort.

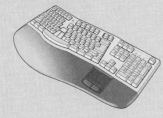

Keyboard and mouse — Correct placement and use of the keyboard and mouse can help you avoid repetitive stress injuries. The proper form for keyboarding and using the mouse is to keep your wrists straight and avoid resting them on hard surfaces. Keys should be pressed gently rather than pounded to prevent injury to both your hands and the keyboard. Also, the mouse should be gripped loosely. You can also consider using an ergonomic keyboard (as shown below) and a sloping keyboard tray to reduce the symptoms of carpal tunnel syndrome. A **wrist rest**, a firm cushion that lays parallel to the keyboard, can also help. Avoid soft wrist rests that wrists sink into because they put unnecessary pressure on your wrists.

Remember that all of these components—chair, monitor, keyboard and mouse—work together. Whenever you adjust your chair, you will most likely need to readjust your monitor, keyboard and mouse as well.

Telephone and headset — A telephone is one of the most basic pieces of equipment at help desks. The type or style of telephone you use is less important than making sure that the telephone is positioned correctly in relation to your computer. If you have to stretch or turn around to answer the telephone, you are at risk for a repetitive stress injury. A good rule of thumb is to place the telephone either directly in front of you or at less than a 25 degree angle and no more than 10 inches away.

A telephone headset rids you of a traditional handheld receiver. Headsets relieve stress and tension by freeing your hands for typing and prevent neck pain by eliminating the need for you to balance a receiver between your tilted head and shoulder. In fact, a study conducted at Santa Clara Valley Medical Center in San Jose, California, found that headsets reduce neck, shoulder, and upper back tension by as much as 41 percent. Headsets also enable you to speak normally while jotting notes or typing.

8

There are numerous styles of headsets, including over-the-ear headsets and headbands that fit over one ear or both ears. Wireless headsets provide you with the added ability to stand up an dmove about the help desk. If possible, you should try on several models before making a final selection. Although the style of headset you select is a matter of personal choice, there are a couple factors to consider. For example, you may prefer a headset that covers only one ear so you can still remain aware of what is going on around you, or you may prefer a headset that covers both ears so you can block out noise. Some headsets offer a noise-canceling microphone to help filter out noise from the help desk that the customer may hear. Regardless of the style, a headset should keep your head and neck in a neutral position and free your hands for activities such as keyboarding. Consider also that your head is the heaviest part of your body. While headsets are fairly light, do not use a headset that encourages you to tilt or hang your head. Leaving your head tilted for even a short period of time causes tension in your neck, shoulders, and back.

Lighting — The brightness of your workspace can greatly affect your well-being. Too much lighting can produce a glare on the monitor, which can cause eyestrain, headaches, and fatigue. You can reduce this glare by spraying an anti-glare coating on the glass surface or by installing an anti-glare filter. Too little lighting can cause you to squint and strain in order to see paperwork or the monitor. Adjustable task lighting on the desk provides directed lighting to supplement the overhead lighting. Natural light, or the lack of it, can also influence your mood. To experience a positive psychological lift, make a conscious effort to look out a window periodically throughout the day.

Any time you move into a new office or workstation, take the time to arrange the equipment to meet your requirements. If you need additional equipment, such as a task light or footrest, speak with your manager. After all, you're worth it!

MANAGING YOUR TIME

Help desks are high-activity places to work and some days can be very hectic. Analysts must handle incoming calls with grace, stay on top of outstanding problems, and assist their co-workers whenever possible. Along the way, they must take time out to relieve stress and take care of their physical and emotional well-being. Analysts who manage time wisely are able to feel in control during exceptionally busy times at the help desk and stay motivated during slow times. Good work habits, such as getting and staying organized, enable you to view work as a challenge to be enjoyed. Good work habits also enable you to maintain physical and mental fitness on the job and to achieve personal success.

Getting and Staying Organized

Strong organizational skills are the hallmark of an excellent service provider and enable analysts to stay on top of incoming and outstanding problems and requests. How you manage your workload will not only influence customer satisfaction and your relationship with other service providers, it will influence your personal stress level as well. The following techniques will help you get and stay organized.

Create a BOD — Successful analysts often develop routines that enable them to stay organized and remember things. A **beginning of day (BOD) check-list**, such as the one shown in Figure 8-5, is a list of tasks an analyst performs at the start of each workday.

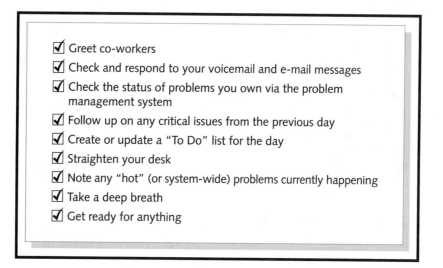

- ☑ Greet co-workers
- ☑ Check and respond to your voicemail and e-mail messages
- ☑ Check the status of problems you own via the problem management system
- ☑ Follow up on any critical issues from the previous day
- ☑ Create or update a "To Do" list for the day
- ☑ Straighten your desk
- ☑ Note any "hot" (or system-wide) problems currently happening
- ☑ Take a deep breath
- ☑ Get ready for anything

Figure 8-5   Beginning of day (BOD) checklist

Try to arrive at your help desk a few minutes early so that you can complete your BOD before you begin taking calls or greeting customers. A BOD is a habit that sets the tone for the rest of the day. Start the day off right.

In addition to a BOD checklist for each analyst, some help desks create a BOD for the entire help desk. An end of day (EOD) checklist is also a good idea. Help desks that work in shifts may also have a beginning and end of shift checklist. The policies of the help desk determine what tasks are included in these lists.

Create a "What I Need to Know" list — Lists of commonly used information are a great way for analysts to get and stay organized. Analysts should create a list of important telephone numbers, filenames, dates, and so on that they need on a fairly regular basis and place it in clear view. These items are not necessarily ones they use daily, which analysts tend to memorize. Rather, they are pieces of information they use regularly but not often enough to memorize, or during a short time period, such as the roll-out date of a new system.

Create a "What Co-workers Need to Know" list — Similar to the "What I Need to Know" list, the "What Co-workers Need to Know" list contains important information co-workers may need to know if an analyst is out of the office for a period of days or weeks. For example, the analyst could be at a training class, on vacation, or so forth. This list should include the status of any current and ongoing projects, the names of folders or the location of documents the analyst is responsible for maintaining, the dates during which the analyst will be gone, and the names of people who provide backup in their absence. During work-related travel, such as attending a training class or an offsite meeting, analysts may include a way for co-workers to reach them in the event of an emergency.

Some help desks have a quick meeting each morning, and analysts share information that other analysts need to know along with tips and tricks that they learned the previous day.

Keep up with your paperwork — All jobs come with a certain amount of paperwork. For example, you may be required to fill out a time sheet, prepare a status report, or maintain and close tickets in the call tracking and problem management system. When you complete your paperwork in a timely fashion, it takes less time because the information you need is fresh in your mind. Your co-workers and your supervisor or team leader also appreciate your maintaining up-to-date paperwork because then they have the information they need to do their work if you are not available.

A great way to reduce the stress associated with a large task is to occasionally switch to a smaller task. For example, if producing the month-end report is something you find stressful, take a break in the middle and fill out your expense report or time sheet, update your "To Do" list, or check for new e-mail messages. This way, you can relieve your stress and complete another task. Don't do this too often, though, or you will lose your focus.

Log all problems real time — Some analysts write customer and problem data on a piece of paper during the call and then log the information in the call tracking system once they have hung up the telephone. They may even log the problem later in the day. This is an unproductive practice because they are handling the problem twice. They may also find later that they have not collected all of the information needed to log the problem, making it necessary to contact the customer. This may prompt the customer to perceive that the help desk is disorganized or that no one has been working on his or her problem. Another reason to log problems in real time is that it is an excellent way for help desk managers to know and show when the help desk is short-handed. If you are logging problems in real time and calls are backing up, it is much easier to justify additional resources than if you work after hours or after your shift to do all of the logging. Logging calls real time is a habit and you may need practice to become proficient. If you don't feel you know how to use your team's call tracking and problem management system or any of the tools available to you efficiently and effectively, ask for help.

Check the status of your open tickets daily — Rather than keeping paper lists that can become out of date or disorganized, learn to use your company's call tracking and problem management system to manage your tickets. Learn to create online reports or run queries that list all of the tickets you own so that you can stay organized. If a high volume of tickets makes it difficult for you to check the status of each ticket every day, make a note in each ticket indicating when followup is needed.

You can never predict what will happen in a help desk on any given day. Regardless, your customers, co-workers, and supervisor or team leader are counting on you to manage your workload and take care of those tasks that are urgent. Getting and staying organized will enable you to assume your responsibilities and feel in control at all times.

Coping with Deadlines

Like stress, deadlines are a normal part of life and can be a positive, motivating force. If you have too much work or too little time, however, deadlines can become a considerable source of stress. The best way to cope with deadlines is to (1) clearly define the work to be done, and then (2) be realistic about what you can accomplish each day, week, and year. Overcommitting is a major cause of stress and can diminish your ability to do high-quality work. When facing deadlines, remember the following guidelines:

Avoid procrastination — Putting off a task until the last minute can cause analysts to miss a critical deadline or produce a low-quality product. The best way to avoid this is to break large tasks into smaller ones and try to complete the task a little bit at a time. Also, you can set a time limit and work on a task for at least that period of time. Even if it's only ten minutes, at least you will have started. Who knows, you may find that the project captures your interest and you will want to keep going. Also, by breaking large tasks into smaller ones, you will know a lot sooner whether you can meet your deadline and can then inform your supervisor or team leader.

Manage your priorities — Many analysts create a "To Do" list that shows all of the tasks they are required to complete. Once you create your "To Do" list, you can assign a priority to each task that indicates the order in which you will work on tasks that day. A simple priority scale rates each task on a scale from A to D, as shown in Table 8-1.

Table 8-1 Simple priority scale

Rating	Priority
A	Urgent: Must do today
B	Important: Should do this week
C	Do when time permits
D	Delegate

After each task has a priority rating, you should check for a balance of priorities. When faced with more "A" priority tasks than can be completed in one day, you can consider the following questions about each task:

1. Who asked me to complete this task?
   A task assigned by a customer or a manager may have a higher priority than a task assigned by a co-worker.

2. What is the risk if I don't complete this task? What is the value if I do complete this task?
   Failing to complete a task may cause you (or someone waiting on your input) to miss a critical deadline. Completing a task may make you eligible for a promotion.

3. When am I expected to have this task done? That is, what is my deadline for this task?
   If the task is due that day, it is a high priority. If it is not due for several weeks, you can assign it a lower priority and strive to simply start the task.

Based on your answers to these questions, you can refine the priorities of the tasks on your "To Do" list.

Utilize peak productivity times — Are you an early bird or a night owl? Most people have about four hours each day during which they are most productive and alert. Because this time varies from person to person, you should determine your personal peak productivity time. If possible, you should schedule your work to take advantage of the time during which you function best.

Eliminate time robbers — Time robbers are activities that take up time and do not add value to the work that you perform. In fact, time robbers usually decrease productivity and increase stress levels. You can use the following techniques to avoid time robbers:

➤ **Log calls as they come in.** This avoids the need to handle the call twice, eliminates the possibility that you forget critical information, and ensures that the time stamps, which indicate when the incident record was entered, correspond to the actual time when the customer reported the incident. Also, when a severe problem occurs that may affect many customers, such as a server down, logging calls as they come in ensures that other analysts are aware of the problem.

➤ **Avoid distractions.** Overall, you should stay focused on your work and resist the temptation to get involved in every conversation going on around you. It is, however, appropriate for you to get involved when it appears there is a system-wide problem and you need a status report or you need to participate in joint problem solving with a co-worker.

➤ **Avoid gossip and excessive socializing.** Some socializing is appropriate and is, in fact, an important element of teamwork. Excessive socializing, however, is unproductive and may cause your co-workers to resent the fact that you are not getting the job done. Sharing news about other people is a normal part of socializing when it is well-meaning and up front. For example, sharing the fact that a co-worker just became engaged is okay unless the person is trying to keep this fact a secret. It is best to steer clear of gossip that is mean spirited or that reveals secrets.

➤ **Ask for help when you really need it.** It's human nature to want to figure things out on your own, but sometimes we all need help. Try to distinguish between just "taking a little more time to figure things out" and really needing help and guidance to avoid aggravation and wasted time.

➤ **Keep your desk and files organized.** Organization is a key to success. You should devise a system that you can use to get and stay organized. Get in the habit of always putting away files after you use them and handling papers and folders only one time. A good guideline is: Do it, file it, or dump it (that is, throw away unneeded junk mail or other paper work).

➤ **Suggest constructive ways to make improvements.** Complaining just wastes time. If you see opportunities to make improvements, tell your team leader or send an e-mail message or memo that outlines the steps you think could help eliminate or minimize a problem situation.

➤ **Automate recurring tasks.** Every job contains tasks that must be done on a regular or frequent basis. Identify these tasks and then set up shortcuts and function keys that you can use, for example, to access frequently used Web sites or perform routine lookups in the call tracking system.

8

Companies are increasingly asking employees to do more work, often with fewer resources. People who manage their time well can meet this challenge because they prioritize their work and stay focused on producing the desired results. An added benefit is that people who manage their time well experience lower levels of stress and burnout.

 Your local library has numerous books on time and stress management. They contain many excellent tips about how to manage your time wisely and how to avoid and alleviate stress.

Understanding the Time / Stress Connection

Time management involves making an endless series of small and large decisions about what you will accomplish each day. Inappropriate decisions, such as those that result in wasted time, can lower self-esteem and increase stress levels. On the other hand, people who maintain a positive attitude, manage their priorities, and use time wisely, feel good at the end of each day because they know they have done their best.

Time and stress management skills are tightly linked. People who are highly stressed may be contributing to that stress by making poor decisions in terms of how they use their time. For example, some people believe that "If I want something done right, I have to do it myself." In reality, all that does is result in them having more work to do. A better approach is to teach and help others so that they can in turn help you. Some people also have a hard time saying no, particularly in the workplace. It is appropriate, however, to let your boss or co-workers know when you are feeling overwhelmed or can't know which of your tasks take priority. It is better to let people know that your plate is full than to miss a deadline or let them down because you run out of time. This doesn't mean you should whine. Calmly ask for clarification about what you should consider your priorities or state what you *can* do.

> "I was planning on finishing the month-end report this morning. Does this task take priority over that?"

> "I'm working on a deadline today. Can I get that information to you tomorrow?"

Highly stressed people often feel they don't have time for time management or for training in stress management. It is important to remember though that *you choose the stress you experience each and every day.* Practicing good time and stress management will help you take control of your life and achieve your full potential.

If you choose a career in the help desk industry, an exciting and rewarding profession awaits. It is a rapidly growing and ever-changing field that offers tremendous opportunities to people who like working with technology and enjoy helping customers. To seize these opportunities, you must hone your soft and self-management skills, along with your business and technical skills. In developing these skills, you lay the foundation for a successful career, regardless of your chosen profession. You also develop the "life" skills needed to handle even the most challenging situations—whether in your professional life or in your personal life—with confidence and enthusiasm. Be optimistic. With your skills, the future is bright.

CHAPTER SUMMARY

- Customer service is a very stressful occupation and help desk analysts need to develop good self-management skills, such as stress and time management. Stress is the adaptation of our bodies and minds to the demands of life. Properly managed, stress is an excellent source of motivation and can be a positive part of life. Too much stress or too little stress can lead to health problems. To deal effectively with the stress in your life, take the time to identify the real source or sources of your stress. Begin to develop a plan of action and a stress-management program that will work for you.

- Two key factors that affect how people respond to stress are (1) how much control they have over the stressor, and (2) whether or not they choose to be exposed to the stressor. Remember that even when you feel a situation is out of your control, there is always something you can do. You can change the situation or you can control the way you respond to the situation. Accepting responsibility for the stress you are experiencing is the most important step you can take in terms of coping with the stress and avoiding burnout.

- The rate of change in today's business world keeps accelerating, and it is not likely to slow down any time soon. To be successful, learn to embrace change and be willing to reinvent yourself as needed to contribute to your company's goals. Take personal responsibility for your career. Keep learning, develop flexibility, speed up, and develop project management skills. By accepting responsibility for your future, you can minimize much of the stress and fear that comes from putting your well-being in the hands of someone else, such as an employer.

- Coping with stress and mastering change takes energy—physical and emotional energy. Stressful and challenging situations can sap your energy and cause your enthusiasm to waver. To relieve the tension that accompanies stress, and to use stress as a positive, motivating force in your life, take care of yourself both physically and mentally. Take time, every day, to think about your physical and emotional needs, and devote time to fulfilling those needs.

8

- Companies are increasingly asking employees to do more work, often with fewer resources. People that manage their time well are able to meet this challenge because they prioritize their work and stay focused on producing the desired results. Good work habits, such as getting and staying organized, will enable you to feel in control and make good time management decisions. An added benefit is that when you manage your time well, you will experience lower levels of stress and burnout. Time and stress management are tightly linked, and practicing both will help you take control of your life and achieve your full potential.

KEY TERMS

beginning of day (BOD) — A list of tasks an analyst performs at the start of each workday.

burnout — The physical and emotional exhaustion that is caused by long-term stress.

carpal tunnel syndrome — A common repetitive stress injury that affects the hands and wrists and is linked to repetitious hand movements, such as typing on a computer keyboard.

ergonomics — The applied science of equipment design intended to maximize productivity by reducing operator fatigue and discomfort.

fight-or-flight reaction — A set of physiological changes that occur when the mind, upon perceiving a stressful event, triggers an alarm that mobilizes the body for action.

institutional stressors — The stressors that accompany the type of business you are in or the state of the company where you work.

personal stressors — The stressors that accompany your personal life experience.

repetitive stress injuries (RSIs) — Physical symptoms caused by excessive and repeated use of the hands, wrists, and arms; they occur when people perform tasks using force, repeated strenuous actions, awkward postures, and poorly designed equipment. RSIs include carpal tunnel syndrome, tendonitis, bursitis, and rotator cuff injuries.

self-management skills — The skills, such as stress and time management, that people need to complete their work efficiently and effectively, feel job satisfaction, and avoid frustration or burnout.

situational stressors — The stressors that accompany the type of work you do.

stress — The adaptation of our bodies and minds to the demands of life.

wrist rest — A firm cushion that lies parallel to the keyboard.

REVIEW QUESTIONS

1. How do self-management skills benefit people in a help desk setting?

2. What is stress?

3. What are the symptoms of too little stress?

4. What are the symptoms of too much stress?

5. List five of the health problems that can be related to or aggravated by too much or too little stress.

6. How can you influence institutional stressors?

7. How can you influence situational stressors?

8. How can you influence personal stressors?

9. What two factors affect how people respond to stress?

10. What are your choices when you are faced with a situation that you cannot control?

11. What is burnout?

12. When do people experience burnout?

13. Why is it important to stay calm and in control when facing a stressful situation?

14. What calming techniques can you use if you feel yourself losing control?

15. Why is it important to take personal responsibility for your career?

16. What techniques can you use to keep pace in the changing world of work?

17. How can help desk analysts use project management skills?

18. Describe six symptoms our bodies and minds experience as a result of the flight-or-fight reaction.

19. How does exercise help relieve stress?

20. How does good nutrition help relieve stress?

21. List three symptoms you may experience if your workspace is not arranged ergonomically.

22. What help desk activity puts you at risk for repetitive stress injuries?

23. How can you improve the ergonomics of your workspace?

24. What are the benefits of laughter?

25. What are realistic goals?

26. What are the benefits of good work habits?

27. Why is it important to log all problems real time?

28. What are two ways to avoid procrastination?

29. What should you do after you have assigned a priority to each task on your "To Do" list?

30. What are time robbers?

31. What does time management involve?

32. Describe the relationship that exists between time and stress management.

33. Why is it important to let people know when you are feeling overwhelmed?

34. You _____ the stress you experience each and every day.

35. What are the benefits of practicing good time and stress management?

HANDS-ON PROJECTS

Project 8-1

Visit a local help desk. Arrange a visit to the help desk where you work, at your school, or at a company in your community. Determine the following:

- How does the help desk measure customer satisfaction?

- What training do employees receive to improve their skills, such as listening, communication, and telephone skills?

- How is the help desk utilizing technologies, such as e-mail and Web technology?

- What training do employees receive to improve their writing skills?

- What difficult customer situations do analysts experience and how do they handle these situations?

- What techniques and training do analysts use to enhance and improve their problem-solving skills?

- What roles exist within their team and what techniques are used to build a solid team?

- How does the team, and how do analysts within the team, manage stress and burnout?

Given everything you have learned in this book, what conclusions can you draw from visiting this help desk? Write a report that summarizes your findings and conclusions.

Project 8-2

Interview a help desk employee. Arrange to interview a manager or analyst who works in a help desk either at your school or in the community about how that person, and his or her team, minimize stress and avoid burnout. Before the interview, prepare a list of questions you would like answered and send it to the person so that he or she can prepare. For example, you may ask the person to describe:

- What institutional stressors are inherent in his or her industry?

- What situational stressors does he or she encounter working in a help desk?

- What does his or her team do to minimize stress?

- What does he or she personally do to minimize stress?

Write a report that summarizes what you learned from this person.

Project 8-3

Identify the causes of stress in your life. Prepare a list of the causes of stress in your life and consider the effect those stressors have on your life by answering the following questions:

- What, if any, institutional stressors are you experiencing?

  - Do you like the business you are in?

- What, if any, situational stressors are you experiencing?

  - Do you like the work that you do? (Consider your answers to Project 1-8 when answering this question.)

- What, if any, personal stressors are you experiencing?

  - Are you happy with your personal life?

Given what you have learned in this chapter, what conclusions can you draw about the stress you are experiencing?

Project 8-4

Assess your stress management skills. Using the list of stressors you identified in Project 8-3, assess the effectiveness of your current efforts to manage
stress in your life by answering the following questions:

- Am I doing all that I can do to control the effect that this stressor has on
  my life?

- Am I choosing to be exposed to this stressor?

- What changes, if any, can I make to (1) the situation and (2) my response to
  the situation that will result in less stress?

- Can I reduce the stress I am experiencing by eliminating negative phrases
  and demonstrating a positive, CAN DO attitude? (Consider your answers to
  Project 1-6 when answering this question.)

Given what you have learned in this chapter, what conclusions can you draw
about your stress management skills?

Project 8-5

Learn about mastering change. Interview someone, such as an acquain-
tance, family member, or co-worker, who has a career that you believe is interesting or challenging. Write a short paper that answers the following questions:

- What changes have occurred in the business world since this person began
  working in his or her current profession?

- What changes does this person anticipate in the future?

- How does this person continuously improve his or her technical, business,
  soft, and self-management skills during and in anticipation of changing times?

- Does this person have project management skills? If so, how did he or she
  develop those skills?

- What advice, if any, can this person give you in terms of dealing with
  changing times?

Project 8-6

Learn to manage your fight-or-flight reactions. For one month, keep a
list of the physiological changes you experience when your mind perceives a
stressful event. For example, when facing a stressful situation, does your heart
begin to beat faster or does your breathing become shallow? For each physiological change you experience, identify a coping mechanism that you can use
to relieve the symptom of stress and then try to apply it. As the month goes
on, assess the effectiveness of your efforts to manage your fight-or-flight reactions. For example, have you found that by taking a deep breath you can
relieve the butterflies in your stomach?

Project 8-7

Create a BOD. Create a BOD for a typical day in your life. For ex.,
your typical day involves going to school and going to work, prepare a
tasks you must complete before leaving the house to ensure you are reac
both. While creating your BOD, think back over the last couple of weeks.
there days when you felt disorganized or when you forgot items you needed
Include tasks on your BOD that can prevent the frustration of this type of situation. Were there days when you really felt you had your act together?
Include tasks on your BOD that enable you to regularly feel that confident
and organized. Post your BOD in a place where you can view it each day in
an effort to make these tasks a habit.

Project 8-8

Evaluate your workspace. A properly arranged workspace increases productivity and reduces stress and fatigue. Look closely at the workspace where you
complete most of your writing, computer work, and reading or studying.
Then, briefly outline your answers to the following questions:

- Have you ever experienced any of the negative symptoms of a poorly
  designed workspace, such as headaches, wrist and shoulder pain, back pain,
  or swollen ankles? If so, given what you have learned in this chapter, were
  your symptoms the result of poor workspace design or poor work habits?

- In what ways can you improve the ergonomics of your workspace?

- In what ways can you improve your work habits?

Unless you share your workspace with other people, arrange your workspace
so that it meets your ergonomic requirements.

Project 8-9

Manage your priorities. Create a "To Do" list or ensure that your existing
"To Do" list is complete. Ensure that each task has a priority rating. Review
your "To Do" list. Do you have a balanced set of priorities? If not, use the
questions contained in this chapter to refine your priorities. Given what you
have learned in this chapter, what, if any, changes can you make in terms of
how you manage your "To Do" list to better manage your priorities?

Project 8-10

Identify time robbers. Assemble a team of at least three of your classmates.
Discuss the list of time robbers presented in this chapter. Add to the list other
time robbers that you and your classmates are exposed to in school or at work.
Select three time robbers that you and your classmates consider particularly
unproductive. Brainstorm and prepare a list of ways to eliminate these time
robbers. Share your ideas with the rest of the class.

8

Case Projects

Case Projects

1. **Lunch and Learn Training Session**

   Your boss asks you to prepare for and facilitate an informal training session and discussion on stress management to be presented during a luncheon meeting. This meeting is optional, and people who want to attend can bring their lunch and participate in the meeting. Prepare a ten- to fifteen-minute presentation on stress—what it is, what causes it, and ten ways it can be prevented or minimized. Submit an outline of your presentation to her for review.

2. **Preparing for Vacations and Holidays**

   Your team is facing a vacation and holiday season during which many team members will be out of the office. In an effort to minimize the stress associated with having people out of the office, your team has decided to put together a vacation checklist. This checklist will ensure that team members are consistent in their efforts to prepare for time out of the office and consistent in their efforts to get up to speed quickly when they return to the office. Conduct a brainstorming session with your teammates (choose three classmates) and (1) develop a checklist to be completed prior to going on vacation, and (2) develop a checklist to be completed upon returning from vacation. For example, the checklist to be completed before going on vacation would include activities such as changing your voicemail message to one that indicates that you are out of the office and when you will return, and transferring ownership of all your open problems. The checklist to be completed when you return would include activities such as changing your voicemail greeting back to the standard greeting, and reading and responding to e-mail messages.

3. **Preventing Carpal Tunnel Syndrome**

   You have been hired as a consultant to help a large help desk prevent carpal tunnel syndrome. Several members of the help desk have recently developed carpal tunnel syndrome and the manager wants you to help the staff understand what causes it, how it is treated, and how it can be prevented. Prepare an article for the help desk's monthly newsletter that answers the following questions:

   - What are the symptoms of carpal tunnel syndrome?

   - How is it caused?

   - How is it treated or how can its symptoms be controlled?

   - How long does it take to relieve the symptoms?

   - How can it be prevented?

ADDITIONAL SOURCES OF HELP

This appendix lists resources that can be used to develop a self-study program and to obtain additional information about the help desk (technical support services) industry in general. Resources include:

➤ Books

➤ Certification programs

➤ Self-study programs

➤ Magazines

➤ Membership organizations

BOOKS

Anderson, Kristin and Ron Zemke. *Delivering Knock Your Socks Off Service*. New York: AMACOM, 1997.

Anderson, Kristin and Ron Zemke. *Knock Your Socks Off Answers*. New York: AMACOM, 1996.

Bailey, Joseph V. *The Speed Trap: How to Avoid the Frenzy of the Fast Lane*. San Francisco: Harper, 1999.

Baker, Sunny and Kim Baker. *The Complete Idiot's Guide to Project Management*. New York: MacMillan General Reference, 1998.

Blake, Gary and Robert W. Bly. *The Elements of Technical Writing*. New York: Macmillan, 1993.

Bruton, Noel. *How to Manage the IT Helpdesk*. Oxford: Butterworth-Heinemann, 1997.

Carlson, Richard. *Don't Sweat the Small Stuff at Work: Simple Ways to Minimize Stress and Conflict While Bringing Out the Best in Yourself and Others*. New York: Hyperion, 1998.

————. *Slowing Down to the Speed of Life: How to Create a More Peaceful, Simpler Life from the Inside Out*. San Francisco: Harper, 1998.

————. *Don't Sweat the Small Stuff—and it's all small stuff*. New York: Hyperion, 1997.

Carnegie, Dale. *How to Enjoy Your Life and Your Job: Selections from How to Win Friends and Influence People and How to Stop Worrying and Start Living*. New York: Pocket Books, 1986.

Charlesworth, Edward A. and Ronald G. Nathan. *Stress Management (A Comprehensive Guide to Wellness)*. New York: Ballantine Books, 1984.

Cook, Ann. *American Accent Training: A Guide to Speaking and Pronouncing American English for Anyone Who Speaks English as a Second Language*. Hauppauge, N.Y.: Barrons Educational Audio, 1991.

Coscia, Stephen. *Tele-Stress—Relief for Call Center Stress Syndrome*. San Francisco: Telecom Books/Miller Freeman, 1998.

Covey, Stephen R., et al. *First Things First: To Live, to Love, to Learn, to Leave a Legacy*. New York: Fireside, 1996.

Culp, Stephanie. *Streamlining Your Life*. Cincinnati: Writer's Digest Books, 1991.

Czegel, Barbara. *Running an Effective Help Desk.* Wellesley: Mass.: Wiley-QED Publishing, 1994.

Davis, Martha, et al. *Relaxation & Stress Reduction Workbook.* Oakland, Calif.: New Harbinger Publications, 1998.

Dupré, Lyn. *Bugs in Writing: A Guide for Debugging Prose.* Boston: Addison-Wesley, 1998.

Fisher, Roger, et al. *Getting It Done: How to Lead When You're Not in Charge.* New York: Harperbusiness, 1998.

George, Mike. *Learn to Relax: A Practical Guide to Easing Tension and Conquering Stress.* San Francisco: Chronicle Books, 1998.

Gleeson, Kerry. *The Personal Efficiency Program: How to Get Organized to Do More Work in Less Time.* New York: John Wiley & Sons, 1997.

Hanson, Peter G. *Stress For Success.* New York: Ballantine Books, 1989.

Houp, Kenneth W. and M. Provenzo. *Reporting Technical Information,* 9th ed. New York: John Wiley & Sons, 1998

Jones, Morgan D. *The Thinker's Toolkit: Fourteen Skills for Making Smarter Decisions in Business and in Life.* New York: Random House, 1995.

Karten, Naomi. *Managing Expectations: Working with People Who Want More, Better, Faster, Sooner, NOW!* New York: Dorset House Publishing, 1994.

Kessler, Lauren and Duncan McDonald. *When Words Collide: A Media Writer's Guide to Grammar and Style,* 5th ed. Belmont, Calif.: Wadsworth Publishing, 1999.

Khandpur, Navtej (Kay) and Lori Laub. *Delivering World-Class Technical Support.* New York: John Wiley & Sons, 1997.

Knapp, Donna. *A Guide to Help Desk Concepts.* Cambridge, Mass.: Course Technology, Inc., 1998.

Koch, Richard. *The 80/20 Principle: The Secret of Achieving More with Less.* New York: Bantam Doubleday Dell, 1998.

Leland, Karen D. and Keith M. Bailey. *Customer Service for Dummies.* San Mateo, Calif.: IDG Books Worldwide, 1995.

Leviton, Richard. *Brain Builders! A Lifelong Guide to Sharper Thinking, Better Memory, and an Age-Proof Mind.* Upper Saddle River, N.J.: Prentice Hall, 1995.

Luhrs, Janet. *The Simple Living Guide: A Sourcebook for Less Stressful, More Joyful Living.* Broadway Books, 1997.

Lusk, Julie T. *Desktop Yoga: The Anytime, Anywhere Relaxation Program for Office Slaves, Internet Addicts, and Stressed-Out Students.* Perigee, 1998.

MacKenzie, R. Alec. *The Time Trap.* New York: AMACOM, 1997.

Microsoft Corporation, *Microsoft Sourcebook for the Help Desk: Techniques and Tools for Support Organization Design and Management,* 2d ed. Redmond, Wash.: Microsoft Press, 1997.

Morgan, Rebecca L. and Tony Hicks, eds. *Calming Upset Customers (50-Minute Series).* Menlo Park, Calif.: Crisp Publications, 1996.

O'Conner, Patricia T. *Woe Is I: The Grammarphobe's Guide to Better English in Plain English.* New York: Riverside Books, 1998.

Parker, Glenn M. *Team Players and Teamwork.* San Francisco: Jossey-Bass Publishers, 1996.

Rye, David E. *1,001 Ways to Inspire: Your Organization, Your Team and Yourself.* New York: Penguin Audiobooks, 1999.

Smith, Hyrum W. *The 10 Natural Laws of Successful Time and Life Management: Proven Strategies for Increased Productivity and Inner Peace.* New York: Warner Books, 1995.

Snead, G. Lynne and Joyce Wycoff. *To Do Doing Done!: A Creative Approach to Managing Projects and Effectively Finishing What Matters Most.* New York: Fireside, 1997.

Stunk, Jr., William and White, E. B. *The Elements of Style,* 3d ed. New York: Macmillan, 1972.

Williams, Paul B. *Getting a Project Done on Time: Managing People, Time, and Results.* New York: AMACOM, 1996.

Wilson, Paul F., et al. *Root Cause Analysis: A Tool for Total Quality Management.* American Society for Quality, 1993.

Zemke, Ron and John A. Woods. *Best Practices in Customer Service.* New York: AMACOM, 1999.

CERTIFICATION PROGRAMS

Call Center University

(615) 221-6850

www.callcenteru.com

The purpose of CCU's certification program is to provide comprehensive, job-specific call center education and training resulting in improved individual and call center performance and to equip call center professionals with the knowledge and skills necessary to meet industry-defined competency standards for professional certification. Certification can be achieved in one or more of the following tracks:

➤ Manager

➤ Supervisor

➤ Technical Manager/Specialist

Help Desk 2000

(800) 350-5781 or (770) 280-2640

www.helpdesk2000.org

Help Desk 2000's certification programs involve a stringent testing process, which includes a three-hour written exam along with an oral exam or a specific help desk project. Certification levels include:

➤ Certified Help Desk Professional

➤ Certified Help Desk Manager

➤ Certified Help Desk Director

Support Center Practices (SCP) Certification

(674) 674-4864

www.supportgate.com

The Support Center Practices (SCP) Certification program establishes the service quality benchmark for all IT services support centers and help desks. The program consists of eleven major criteria required to operate a successful support center or help desk. These criteria are then broken down into detailed elements with specific measurable results. The outcome is approximately one hundred points of major service factors that are used to determine the overall effectiveness of a support center.

Support Services Career Certification (S²C²)

(800) 248-5667 or (719) 268-0174

www.s2c2.org

The Support Services Career Certification (S²C²) program is striving to establish standardized levels of knowledge and expertise for the staffs of customer support centers or help desks. Certification levels that the S²C² program will offer, in addition to technical and managerial certifications, include:

➤ Certified Support Services Representative (CSSR)

➤ Certified Support Services Associate (CSSA)

➤ Certified Support Services Specialist (CSSS)

SELF-STUDY PROGRAMS (AUDIO CASSETTES, VIDEO TAPES, ETC.)

CareerTrack, Inc.

(800) 488-0928

www.careertrack.com

Titles include: *How to Give Exceptional Customer Service; Professional Telephone Skills;* and *Pleasing Your Hard-to-Please Customers.*

Crisp Publications, Inc.

(800) 442-7477

www.crisp-pub.com

Titles include: *Calming Upset Customers; Measuring Customer Satisfaction;* and *Telephone Courtesy and Customer Service.*

The Economics Press, Inc.

(800) 526-2554 or (973) 227-1224

www.epinc.com

Titles include: *Achieving Telephone Excellence; Blue Ribbon Service;* and *Practical Telephone Techniques.*

The Economics Press also offers a biweekly booklet called *Your Telephone Personality.* Each booklet deals with one topic vital to the skillful handling of telephone calls.

JWA Video

(800) 327–5110 or (312) 829–5100

www.jwavideo.com

Titles include: *50 Ways to Keep Your Customers; How to Develop Effective Communication Skills;* and *Listen and Win.*

The Telephone Doctor

(314) 291–1012

www.telephoneskills.com

Titles include: *Six Cardinal Rules of Customer Service; How to Handle the Irate Caller;* and *Telephone Skills from A to Z.*

MAGAZINES

Call Center Magazine
(888) 824–9793
www.callcentermagazine.com

LifeRaft
(800) 248–5667 or (719) 268–0174
www.helpdeskinst.com

IT Support News
(215) 788–7112
www.itsupportnews.com

Support Management
(203) 857–5656 x155
www.supportmanagement.com

MEMBERSHIP ORGANIZATIONS

Association of Support Professionals

(617) 924–3944 x14

www.asponline.com

The Association of Support Professionals (ASP) is an international organization dedicated to the advancement of the technical support professional. It is also a community where individual members can share ideas, insight, and experiences with their colleagues.

Help Desk Institute

(800) 248-5667 or (719) 268-0174

www.helpdeskinst.com

The Help Desk Institute (HDI) provides targeted information about the technologies, tools, and trends of the help desk and customer support industry. HDI offers a variety of services to meet the evolving needs of the customer support professional.

Help Desk Professionals Association

(425) 398-9292

www.hdpa.org

The Help Desk Professionals Association (HDPA) is a nonprofit organization with the goal of providing technical support professionals a means to network and share information. This organization also provides these professionals a source for invaluable state-of-the-industry information.

Software Support Professionals Association

(877) ASK-SSPA or (619) 674-5491

www.supportgate.com

The Software Support Professionals Association (SSPA) provides a value-added forum where service and support professionals in the software industry can share ideas, discuss developing trends, and network with their peers—skilled professionals who work with every conceivable platform, application, and operating system in the industry.

GLOSSARY

24×7 support
Help desk services that are provided twenty-four hours a day, seven days a week.

a caring attitude
A help desk's ability to communicate the fact that it wants to satisfy its customer's needs.

acronym
A word formed from the initials of a name.

active listening
Listening that involves participating in a conversation and giving the speaker a sense of confidence that he or she is being heard.

application of training investments
A comparison of an analyst's resolution % and reopen % before and after attending training.

automatic call distributor (ACD)
A technology that answers a call and routes, or distributes, it to the next available analyst.

automatic number identification (ANI)
A service provided by your long distance service provider that tells you the telephone number of the person calling.

availability
The length of time an analyst was signed on to the ACD compared to the length of time the analyst was scheduled to be signed on.

average call duration
The average length of time required to handle a call.

beginning of day (BOD)
A list of tasks an analyst performs at the start of each workday.

best effort
A policy that states analysts do their best to assist a customer within a predefined set of boundaries, such as a time limit.

best practice
The current best knowledge about how to deliver a service.

burnout
The physical and emotional exhaustion that is caused by long-term stress.

business skills
The skills people need that are unique to the profession they support, such as accounting skills or banking skills. Business skills also include skills that are unique to the service industry, such as understanding the importance of meeting customer's needs and managing their expectations.

caller identification (caller ID)
A service provided by your local telephone company that tells you the telephone number of the person calling.

CAN DO attitude
Telling a customer what you can do rather than what you cannot do.

capture
To collect.

carpal tunnel syndrome (CTS)
A common repetitive stress injury that affects the hands and wrists and is linked to repetitious hand movements, such as typing on a computer keyboard.

case-base reasoning (CBR)
A searching technique that uses everyday language to ask users questions and interpret their answers.

client-server
A computing model where some computers, known as clients, request services and other computers, known as servers, respond to those requests.

closed-ended questions
Questions that prompt short answers, such as "yes" and "no."

cold transfer
A way of transferring a telephone call that occurs when you stay on the line only long enough to ensure that the call has been transferred successfully.

communication
The exchange of thoughts, messages, and information.

computer telephony integration (CTI)
An interface that links telephone technology with computing technology to exchange information and increase productivity.

consensus
An opinion or position reached by all of a team's members or by a majority of its members.

cost per contact
The total cost of operating a help desk for a given time period (including salaries, benefits, facilities, and equipment) divided by the total number of contacts (such as calls, e-mails, faxes, and Web requests) received during that period; historically called cost per call.

cost per unit
The total cost of operating a help desk for a given time period (including salaries, benefits, facilities, and equipment) divided by the total number of units (such as devices and systems) supported during that period.

customer data
Identifying details about a customer, including the customer's name, telephone number, department or company name, address or location, customer number, and employee number or user ID.

customer record
All of the data and text fields that describe a single customer.

customer satisfaction
The difference between how a customer perceives he or she was treated and how the customer expects to be treated.

customer satisfaction surveys
a series of questions that ask customers to provide their perception of the support services being offered.

customer support
Services that help a customer understand and benefit from a product's capabilities by answering questions, solving problems, and providing training.

customer
A person who buys products or services.

data
Raw facts that are not organized in a meaningful way.

data field
An element of a database record in which one piece of data is stored.

decision tree
A branching structure of questions and possible answers designed to lead an analyst to a solution.

detailed problem description
A comprehensive accounting of the problem and circumstances surrounding the problem's occurrence.

emoticons
Symbols used to convey feelings.

empathy
Identifying with and understanding another person's situation, feelings, and motives.

ergonomics
The applied science of equipment design intended to maximize productivity by reducing operator fatigue and discomfort.

event-driven surveys
Customer satisfaction surveys that ask customers for feedback on a single recent service event.

expectations
Results that customers consider reasonable or due to them.

expert system
A computer program that stores human knowledge in a knowledge base and has the ability to reason about that knowledge.

external customers
A person or company that buys another company's products and services.

external help desk
A help desk that supports customers who buy their company's products and services.

fax
technology that sends or receives printed matter or computer images electronically.

fax-on-demand
Technology that enables customers to use their touch-tone telephone to request that answers to FAQs, procedures, forms, or sales literature be delivered to the fax machine at the number provided by the customer.

fee-based support
Customers pay for support of certain services on a per-use basis.

feedback
Communication from one team member to another about how the member's behavior is meeting the expectations of the team.

fight-or-flight reaction
A set of physiological changes that occur when the mind, upon perceiving a stressful event, triggers an alarm that mobilizes the body for action.

flow chart
A diagram that shows the sequence of tasks that occur in a process.

follow-through
The act of keeping your promises, including calling the customer back when you said you would—even if you don't have a resolution to the problem.

follow-up
The act of having a help desk or company representative verify that the customer's problem has been resolved to the customer's satisfaction and that the problem has not recurred.

form
A predefined document that contains text or graphics users cannot change and areas in which users enter information being collected.

frequently asked questions (FAQs)
Well-written answers to the most common customer queries.

front-line service providers
People who work in a help desk who interact directly with customers and help desk management personnel.

fuzzy logic
A searching technique that presents all possible solutions that are similar to the search criteria, even when conflicting information exists or no exact match is present.

help desk
A single point of contact within a company for managing customer problems and requests and for providing solution-oriented support services.

help desk goals
Measurable objectives that support the help desk's mission.

hot transfer
A way of transferring a telephone call that occurs when you stay on the line with the customer and the service provider whom you are engaging in the call; also known as a conference call.

hyperlinks
See links.

idle state
An ACD state that occurs when an analyst did not answer a call routed to his or her phone within the specified number of rings.

incident management
See problem management.

individual performance goals
Measurable objectives for people who support the help desk's mission.

information
Data that are organized in a meaningful way.

inquiries
Customer requests for information, such as "When will my equipment arrive?"

institutional stressors
The stressors that accompany the type of business you are in or the state of the company where you work.

internal customer
A person who works at a company and at times relies on other employees at that company in some way to perform his or her job.

internal help desk
A help desk that responds to questions, distributes information, and handles problems and service requests for its company's employees.

Internet
A global collection of computer networks that are linked together to provide worldwide access to information.

intranet
An internal collection of linked computers that provide a company's employees and other authorized people, such as customers, access to secured information.

jargon
The specialized or technical language used by a trade or profession.

job shadowing
Working side-by-side with another person in an effort to understand and potentially learn that person's job.

keyboarding
Typing.

keyword searching
The technique of finding indexed information by specifying a descriptive word or phrase, called a keyword.

knowledge base
A collection of information sources, such as customer information, documents, policies and procedures, and problem solutions.

knowledge engineer
A person who develops and oversees the knowledge management process and ensures the information contained in the help desk's knowledge base is accurate, complete, and current.

knowledge management system
A system that combines the reasoning capability of an expert system with other information sources, such as databases, documents, and policies and procedures.

links
Colored and underlined text or graphics, which when clicked might open a pop-up window with a definition, instructions, a still picture, or an animated picture; run video clips; or jump to Web pages; also called hyperlinks.

listening
To pay attention; make an effort to hear something.

metrics
Performance measures.

mission
A written statement of the customers the help desk serves, the types of services the help desk provides, and how the help desk delivers those services.

monitoring
when a supervisor or team leader listens to a live or recorded call in order to measure the quality of an analyst's performance during the call.

multi-level support model
A common structure of help desks, where the help desk refers problems it cannot resolve to the appropriate internal group, external vendor, or subject matter expert.

network and system administration
Activities such as setting up and maintaining user accounts, ensuring the data that the company collects is secure, and performing e-mail and database management.

network monitoring
the use of tools to observe and control network performance in an effort to prevent and minimize the impact of problems.

nonverbal communication
The exchange of information in a form other than words.

notification
An activity that informs all of the stakeholders in the problem management process (including management, the customer, and help desk analysts) about the status of outstanding problems.

off-the-shelf products
Personal computer software products that are developed and distributed commercially.

one-to-many relationship
One solution solves many trouble tickets.

open-ended questions
Questions that cannot be answered with a "yes" or "no" response.

outsourcing
When companies have help desk services provided by an outside supplier (service agency or outsourcer), instead of providing them in-house.

overall satisfaction surveys
Customer satisfaction surveys that ask customers for feedback about all calls they made to the help desk during a certain time period.

paraphrase
Restating the information given by a customer using slightly different words in an effort to verify you understand.

passive listening
Listening that involves simply taking in information and shows little regard for the speaker.

peer-to-peer support
A practice where users bypass the formal support structure and seek assistance from their co-workers or someone in another department whom they believe can help.

people
The component of a help desk that consists of the staff and structure put in place within a company or department to support its customers by performing business processes.

personal stressors
The stressors that accompany your personal life experience.

pitch
The highness or lowness of vocal tone.

positive imagery
The act of using mental pictures or images to influence your thinking in a positive way.

positive self-talk
The act of using words to influence your thinking in a positive way.

post-sales support
Helping people who have purchased a company's product or service.

pre-sales support
Answering questions for people who have not yet purchased the company's products or service.

probable source
The system, network, or product that is most likely causing a problem.

problem
An event that disrupts service or prevents access to products.

problem data
The details of a single problem, including the problem category (such as hardware or software), affected component or system (such as a printer or monitor), symptom, date and time problem occurred, date and time problem was logged, analyst who logged problem, problem owner, description, and severity.

problem management
The process of tracking and resolving problems; also called incident management.

problem owner
An employee of the support organization who acts as a customer advocate and ensures a problem is resolved to the customer's

problem priority
Identifies the order for working on problems with the same severity.

problem record
All of the fields that describe a single problem.

problem statement
See short problem description.

procedure
A step-by-step, detailed set of instructions that describes how to perform the tasks in a process.

process
A collection of interrelated work activities—or tasks—that take a set of specific inputs and produce a set of specific outputs that are of value to the customer.

query by example (QBE)
A searching technique that uses queries, or questions, to find records that match the specified search criteria.

questions
Customer requests for instructions on how to use a product, such as "How do I…?"

queue
A line.

record
A collection of related fields.

remote control system
A technology that enables an analyst to take over a customer's keyboard, screen, mouse, or other connected device in order to troubleshoot problems, transfer files, provide informal training, and even collaborate on documents.

reopen %
The percentage of incidents an analyst opens back up compared to the total number of incidents closed during a given time period.

repetitive stress injuries (RSIs)
Physical symptoms caused by excessive and repeated use of the hands, wrists, and arms; they occur when people perform tasks using force, repeated strenuous actions, awkward postures, and poorly designed equipment. RSIs include carpal tunnel syndrome, tendonitis, bursitis, and rotator cuff injuries.

request
A customer order to obtain a new product or service, or an enhancement to an existing product or service.

requirement
Something that is required—a necessity.

resolution %
The percentage of incidents an analyst resolves compared to the total number of incidents that the analyst handled during a given time period.

responsiveness
The help desk's ability to (1) be available when customers need help and (2) make it easy for customers to contact the help desk.

root cause
The most basic reason for an undesirable condition or problem, which, if eliminated or corrected, would prevent the problem from existing or occurring.

root cause analysis
A methodical way of determining the root cause of problems.

screen pop
A CTI function that enables information about the caller to appear, or "pop" up, on an analyst's monitor based on caller information captured by the telephone system and passed to a computer system.

script
A standard set of text and behaviors.

search criteria
The question or problem symptom entered by a user.

search operators
Connecting words such as AND, OR, and NOT.

self-management skills
The skills, such as stress and time management, that people need to complete their work effectively, feel job satisfaction, and avoid frustration or burnout. Self-management skills also include the ability to get and stay organized and to continuously and quickly learn new skills.

self-services
Services that enable customers to help themselves.

Service Level Agreement (SLA)
A written document that spells out the services the help desk will provide the customer, the customer's responsibilities, and how service performance is measured.

severity
The category that defines how critical a problem is based on the nature of the failure and the available alternatives or workarounds.

short problem description
A succinct description of the actual results a customer is experiencing; also called problem statement.

situational stressors
The stressors that accompany the type of work you do.

skill
The help desk's ability to quickly and correctly resolve customer problems and requests.

soft skills
The skills and personality traits that people need to deliver great service, such as listening skills, verbal communication skills, customer service skills, problem-solving skills, writing skills, and the ability to be a team player.

solution
A definitive, permanent resolution to a problem, or a proven workaround.

speakerphone
A telephone that contains both a loudspeaker and a microphone.

stress
The adaptation of our bodies and minds to the demands of life.

subject matter expert (SME)
A person who has a high level of experience or knowledge about a particular subject.

support center
A help desk with a broader scope of responsibility and with the goals of providing faster service and improving customer satisfaction.

symptom
A sign or indication that a problem has occurred.

synonym
A word with the same or very similar meaning to another word.

target escalation time
A time constraint placed on each level that ensures problem resolution activities are proceeding at an appropriate pace.

target resolution time
The timeframe within which the support organization is expected to resolve the problem.

team
A group of people organized to work together toward the achievement of a goal.

team player
A person who contributes to the team's success by cooperating freely and communicating openly with his or her teammates.

technical skills
The skills people need to use and support the specific products and technologies the help desk supports.

technical support
A wide range of services that enable people and companies to continuously use the computing technology they acquired or developed.

technology
The tools and technologies people use to do their work.

template
A predefined item that can be used to quickly create a standard document or e-mail message.

text field
A field that accepts free-form information.

time idle
The average length of time an analyst was idle during a given period of time.

trend analysis
A methodical way of determining and, when possible, forecasting service trends.

value
The perceived worth, usefulness, or importance of a product or service to the customer.

verbal communication
The exchange of information using words.

voice response unit (VRU)
A technology that integrates with another technology, such as a database or a network management system, to obtain information or to perform a function; also called interactive voice response unit (IVRU).

voicemail
An automated form of taking messages from callers when no one is available to take their calls.

warm transfer
A way of transferring a telephone call that occurs when you introduce the customer and the service provider to whom you are going to transfer the call but you do not stay on the line.

weight
a rating scale of importance.

world class
A company that has achieved, and is able to sustain, high levels of customer satisfaction.

wrap-up mode
An ACD feature that prevents the ACD from routing a new inbound call to an analyst's extension.

wrap-up time
The average length of time an analyst was in wrap-up mode during a given period of time.

INDEX

A

accuracy of technical writing, 112
ACDs (automatic call distributors), 66
    metrics, 217–218
acknowledging customer's emotional state, 141
acronyms, 56
    e-mail communication, 107
    technical writing, 111
active listening, 32–42
    avoiding distractions, 38–41
    benefits, 37–38
    knowing what to listen for, 41–42
    passive listening versus, 32
    winning over difficult customers, 140–141
active problem solving, winning over difficult
    customers, 142
active voice, technical writing, 109–110
aggressive people, 54
agreement, gaining from difficult customers,
    141–142
American Accent Training, 46–50
angry customers, calming, 142–143
ANI (automatic number identification), 68
answering telephones, 69–72
application of training investments, 218
Association of Support Professionals, 273
attitude
    caring, 13, 88–89
    positive, 15–18
audience, knowing for technical writing, 109
Audio cassettes, 272–273
automatic call distributors (ACDs), 66
    metrics, 217–218
automatic number identification (ANI), 68
automating recurring tasks, 257
availability, 217
average call duration, 217

B

beginning of day (BOD) checklist, 253
best-effort policies, 73
best practices for technical writing, 109–113
BOD (beginning of day) checklist, 253

books, 268–270
breaks for stress management, 249
burnout, 243
business skills, help desk requirement, 20

C

call(s). *See also* telephone
    average duration, 217
Call Center University, 271
caller identification (caller ID), 67
call tracking system, reviewing information, 185
calming irate customers, 142–143
calmness, under pressure, 147–150
CAN DO attitude, 15–18
capital letters in e-mail communication, 107
capturing data, 99
caring attitude, 13, 88–89
carpal tunnel syndrome, 248
case-base reasoning (CBR), 124
certification programs, 271–272
change, learning to master, 244–247
chatterers, 54–55
choice, about exposure to stressors, 242–243
client-server, 167
closed-ended questions, 54–55
closing telephone calls, 75
cold transfers, 83–85
communicating with customers, 42–57
    communication styles, 53–56
    e-mail, 102–108
    forbidden phrases, 44
    rapport. *See* rapport
    speaking the listener's language, 56–57
communication
    building relationships with other support
      groups, 187–188
    with customers. *See* communicating with cus-
      tomers
    within teams, 219–221
complainers, 55
completeness of technical writing, 112
computer telephony integration (CTI), 68
conciseness of technical writing, 110
conference calls, 81–82

283